PANZERGRENADIER DIVISIONS
1939–45

THE SPELLMOUNT
VEHICLE IDENTIFICATION GUIDE

PANZERGRENADIER
DIVISIONS
1939–45

CHRIS BISHOP

SPELLMOUNT

British Library Cataloguing in Publication Data:
A catalogue record for this book is available
from the British Library

ISBN-13: 978-1-86227-384-9
ISBN-10: 1-86227-384-7

First published in the UK in 2007 by
SPELLMOUNT LTD
The Mill
Brimscombe Port
Stroud
Gloucestershire GL5 3QG

Tel: 01453 883300
Fax: 01453 883233
e-mail: enquiries@spellmount.com
Website: www.spellmount.com

Editorial and design by
Amber Books Ltd
Bradley's Close
74-77 White Lion Street
London N1 9PF
www.amberbooks.co.uk

Project Editor: Michael Spilling
Design: Hawes Design
Picture Research: Terry Foreshaw
Illustrations: Alcaniz Freson's S.A (www.quironediciones.com)

Printed in Dubai

PICTURE CREDITS
Art-Tech/Aerospace: 6, 8, 9, 10, 12, 28, 32, 41, 42, 44, 84, 91, 103, 104, 112,
114, 123, 139, 155, 156, 161, 173
Art-Tech/MARS: 21, 48, 89, 106
Cody Images: 18, 50, 62, 127, 130, 132, 136, 140, 147, 151, 152, 177
U. S. Department of Defense: 73, 179

Unless listed below all illustrations were supplied by Alcaniz Freson's S.A.
Art-Tech/Aerospace: 17, 25(t), 34(b), 99(t), 105(b), 108, 128(c), 142, 153(t,c),
158, 161(c), 178(t)
Jorge Rosado: 168(b), 171(t)

Contents

Introduction

**Through most of history, the pace of warfare
was dictated by the speed of a marching infantryman.
The development of the internal combustion engine brought
about a revolution in tactics, a revolution that saw its first
expression in the use of *Blitzkrieg* tactics.**

A S LATE AS 1942, the US Army analysis of German offensive doctrine was that its primary aim was to encircle the enemy and destroy him. 'The objective of the combined arms in attack', a staff paper concluded, 'is to bring the armored forces and the infantry into decisive action against the enemy with sufficient firepower and shock. Superiority in force and firepower, the employment of armored forces, as well as the surprise element, play a great part in the offensive.'

The truth was very different. German tactics did everything they could to avoid a decisive engagement, relying on speed and flexibility to wreak havoc in enemy rear areas. The fact that the Germans were inevitably the aggressors in the early stages of the conflict allowed them to pick the point of attack, and they were helped by the fact that their opponents in the first three years of war were much less organized than the *Wehrmacht*. The Germans substituted mobility for power, which meant that all the

supporting arms had to move at the same speed as the tanks. Although the bulk of the German Army was still largely horse-drawn, the Panzer divisions that raced through France in 1940 were entirely motorized, with infantry and support units being carried on trucks.

Motorizing infantry is the first stage towards the mechanization of an army. Civilian trucks and lorries are readily adaptable to a variety of military uses, including transporting soldiers, towing guns, and carrying equipment and supplies. Motorization greatly increases the strategic mobility of the infantry, which would otherwise rely on railways or on marching into battle.

Motorization provides no direct tactical advantage in combat, because trucks and cars are vulnerable to artillery and smallarms fire. But it does increase the infantry's flexibility, because motorized elements can get to the fighting much more quickly than 'leg' infantry. They also travel with their own integral

◀ **Mobile warfare**

Germany's panzer and motorized infantry divisions were known as *Schnell*, or 'fast', troops. Carried in and supported by a multitude of vehicles, the *Wehrmacht* used the speed offered by such transport to outmanoeuvre and overwhelm its enemies.

support weapons such as heavy machine guns, mortars, anti-tank weapons and artillery. The disadvantage of motorization is that the formation becomes dependent on supplies of fuel.

Guderian and *Blitzkrieg*

The creation of the German motorized infantry and Panzergrenadier arms came as a direct consequence of General Heinz Guderian's revolutionary concept of mobile warfare. Known as *Blitzkrieg*, this required that mobile infantry units should accompany the Panzers into action, supporting the tanks against enemy infantry.

Guderian had learned from British experiments with fully mechanized formations, which had taken place in the 1920s. The first experimental Panzer formations were created in 1934. In addition to two regiments of tanks, the new Panzer divisions would include a *Schützen-Brigade* (rifle brigade) with one *leichte Schützen-Regiment* (light rifle regiment) and one *Kradschützen-Bataillon* (motorcycle rifle battalion). Motorcycles were used in large numbers primarily because the German Army did not have enough wheeled transport to carry the infantry, though the motorcycle battalions also served an important reconnaissance function. Infantry in Panzer divisions were classed as *Panzertruppen*: they wore the same rose pink *Waffenfarbe*, or uniform piping, as the tank crews.

The first independent motorized infantry units were established in 1937. Four standard infantry divisions became known as *Infanterie-Divisionen (mot)*, *mot* standing for *motorisierte*. Motorized units wore the standard white piping of the infantry. Additional motorized infantry units were raised for the four *leichte Divisionen*, which were created in 1938 as a sop to the influential cavalry faction within the German high command. The motorized infantry units within a *leichte Division* were known as *Kavallerieschützen*.

In 1938 Hitler appointed Guderian, now a *General der Panzertruppen*, as Chief of *Schnelle Truppen* (mobile troops), with authority over the development and training of Germany's mechanized forces. These included troops in *Panzer*, *Schützen*, *Kavallerieschützen*, *Panzerabwehr* (anti-tank), *Motorisierte Infanterie* and *Kavallerie* units.

Guderian put his theories to the test during the German occupations of Austria in 1938 and of Czechoslovakia in 1939. There was no fighting, but valuable lessons were learned on how to move large formations of motorized troops in a short time, lessons that were to be put into practice in Poland in 1939 and in the West in 1940.

▼ **Panzer general**
General Heinz Guderian (centre), the architect of *Blitzkrieg*, observes from his command half-track during the campaign in France and the Low Countries, May 1940.

The final retreat

Panzergrenadiers from Army Group Vistula man an SdKfz 250/10 in East Prussia, February 1945.

The motorized infantry units proved to be a key component in the success of *Blitzkrieg*, and their numbers were expanded in the autumn of 1940. Other motorized units included the first *Waffen*-SS divisions, and the outsize *Grossdeutschland* Regiment.

Motorized infantry units were assigned to the four *Panzergruppen* assembled for Operation *Barbarossa* in June 1941. Armoured armies in all but name, these spearheaded the German drive into the Soviet Union, and their mobility was tested to the full across the vast expanses of the Steppes. They continued to fight through Russia in 1942, when the shortcomings of German vehicle manufacturing capacity started to become apparent.

Panzergrenadiers

After the defeats in Africa and at Stalingrad, many of the German Army's motorized divisions had been destroyed. During their reconstruction, in June 1943, a major reorganization of the German Army saw most of the motorized infantry formations redesignated as Panzergrenadier, or armoured infantry, formations. The term Panzergrenadier had been introduced in 1942, and was applied to the infantry component of Panzer divisions as well as to the new divisions. In theory, the infantry component of the Panzergrenadier division was to be carried in half-track armoured personnel carriers. In practice,

German industry could never provide enough of these vehicles, and as many as 90 per cent of the infantry battalions remained truck-borne. Equally most of the artillery, anti-tank, and anti-aircraft elements were equipped with towed rather than self-propelled weapons.

The Panzergrenadier divisions were organized as combined-arms formations, usually with six battalions of infantry, one with half-tracks and the remainder with trucks. These were organized into either two or three regiments. The division also had a battalion of tanks, along with artillery, reconnaissance assets, combat engineers, anti-tank, anti-aircraft and divisional support units. On paper, a Panzergrenadier division had one fewer tank battalion than a Panzer division, but two more infantry battalions, and thus was almost as strong as a Panzer division, especially on the defensive. As the war progressed, the armoured battalions in Panzergrenadier divisions were often equipped with heavy assault guns rather than tanks. Tanks were expensive and complex to produce, while *Sturmgeschütze* (StuG) could be manufactured much more quickly.

In 1943 and 1944, several Panzergrenadier divisions were raised by the *Waffen*-SS. Late in 1944, a number of Panzer brigades were raised in an attempt to hold the collapsing Eastern Front. These formations were a combination of both Panzer and Panzergrenadier arms under the same command, and they became the nuclei of the late-war 'Type 45' reduced-size Panzer divisions.

KEY TO TACTICAL SYMBOLS USED IN ORGANIZATION CHARTS

Tactische Fernzeiche, or map symbol, for division

Map symbol, for regiment or larger-sized formation

Map symbol for battalion or *Abteilung*

St   *Stab*, or HQ, companies of Panzer regiments

m   *Mittlerer*, or medium, as applied to a Panzer company

l   *Leichte*, or light, as applied to a Panzer company

Chapter 1

Early Motorized Divisions

The re-formed German Army announced
in 1935 was based on the *Reichswehr* formations permitted
under the Treaty of Versailles. Most infantry units were just
that – infantry, expected to march into battle. However,
the mobile warfare theories inspired by forward-looking
officers like Heinz Guderian meant that infantrymen on foot
would not be able to keep up with the new, fast-moving
Panzer divisions then being created. At the very least,
some infantry divisions would have to be motorized, to make
possible the all-arms means of waging war which would
come to be known as *Blitzkrieg*.

◀ **Soviet Russia, July 1941**
From the start, German *Blitzkrieg* theorists had envisaged that the mobile infantry accompanying the new
Panzer divisions would be mounted in armoured cross-country vehicles like these SdKfz 251 half-tracks.
For much of the war, however, most such infantrymen, known as grenadiers, were carried in trucks.

2nd Infantry Division (motorized)

One of the first of the *Wehrmacht*'s infantry units to be motorized, the 2nd Infantry Division was formed at Stettin during Germany's secret rearmament in October 1934.

THE DIVISION INCORPORATED the 4th and 5th (Prussian) Infantry Regiments of the *Reichswehr*'s 2nd Infantry Division, though it took nothing of the previous division's command structure. Originally known as the *Wehrgauleitung Stettin*, it recruited its personnel mainly from Pomerania and East Prussia, and was known unofficially as the *Pommerische* or Pomeranian Division.

Soon after its creation it was given the cover name of *Artillerieführer II* to disguise its real function. Once Hermann Göring formally announced the establishment of the *Wehrmacht* in October 1935, the formation officially became known as the 2nd Infantry Division.

Motorized division

In 1937, the division was reorganized to become one of the *Wehrmacht*'s first motorized divisions, becoming known as the 2.*Infanterie-Division (mot)* in

▼ **France, May 1940**

German industry was never able to provide enough motor transport for the army. From the beginning of World War II, German motorized formations like the 2nd Infantry Division were equipped with a quartermaster's nightmare of vehicles.

INSIGNIA

Early divisional insignia carried by units of the re-forming German armed forces tended to be heraldic in nature.

The outbreak of war saw a series of simpler insignia introduced. They were quicker and much more easy to apply in the field.

Commanders

Gen.Lt Hubert Gercke
  October 1934 – March 1937

Gen.Maj Josef Harpe
  October 1940 - January 1941

Gen.Lt Paul Bader
  April 1937 – September 1940

Divisional History	Formed
Wehrgauleitung Stettin	1934
Artillerieführer II	1934
2.Infanterie-Division	1935
2.Infanterie-Division (mot)	1937
12.Panzer Division	1941

October 1937. Although not fully mobilized, the division took part in the occupation of Czechoslovakia in March 1939. It formed part of the XIV *Armeekorps* under General Gustav von Wietersheim, and served alongside the 13th Motorized Infantry Division and the 17th Infantry Division.

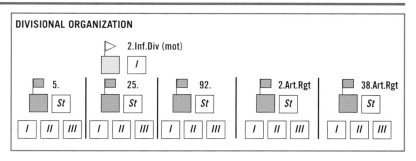

DIVISIONAL ORGANIZATION

2.Inf.Div (mot) / I

5. St | 25. St | 92. St | 2.Art.Rgt St | 38.Art.Rgt St

War in Poland

In August 1939, the 2nd Motorized Infantry Division was brought up to full strength ready for the attack on Poland. Based in Pomerania, it was assigned with the 20th Motorized Division to Guderian's XIX Corps in von Kluge's Fourth Army. Guderian had first call on the motorized infantry divisions, as only they had the mobility to support the 3rd Panzer Division, which was the corps' spearhead.

It took part in the action that cut the Polish Corridor, driving out of Pomerania into East Prussia. From there, it supported Guderian's Panzers as they pushed on to Brest-Litovsk.

After the end of the Polish campaign, the division was transferred to the West to recuperate and refit, and by May 1940 it was ready for Germany's attack on France.

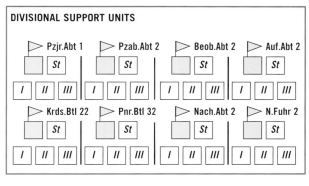

DIVISIONAL SUPPORT UNITS

Pzjr.Abt 1 St | Pzab.Abt 2 St | Beob.Abt 2 St | Auf.Abt 2 St

Krds.Btl 22 St | Pnr.Btl 32 St | Nach.Abt 2 St | N.Fuhr 2 St

▼ Morris Umbauwagen Kfz 11
5.Inf.Regt (mot)

Germany's victory in France brought a windfall of captured British and French equipment. In German service, this Morris Commercial PU was fitted with an *Einheits* (*Wehrmacht* military standard) Kfz 11 body.

Specifications

Crew: 1	Engine: four-cylinder, 3.5 litre (213ci)
Weight: 0.99 tonnes (0.9 tons)	petrol engine
Length: 4.80m (15ft 9in)	Speed: 75km/h (47mph)
Width: 1.80m (5ft 11in)	Range: 225km (136 miles)
Height: 1.85m (6ft 1in)	Radio: None

▶ Mittlerer Zugkraftwagen 8t SdKfz 7
2.Artillerie-Regiment (mot) / IV Battalion

Designed by Krauss-Maffei, the 8-tonne SdKfz 7 medium half-track entered service in 1933. The definitive variant, the KM m 11, entered service in 1937 and remained in production to the end of the war in 1945.

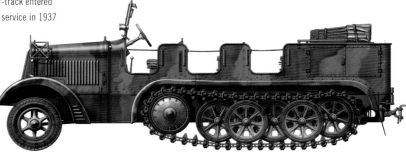

Specifications

Crew: 2	Engine: Maybach HL 62
Weight: 1.16 tonnes (1.06 tons)	6-cylinder engine (140hp)
Length: 6.85m (20ft 3in)	Speed: 50km/h (31mph)
Width: 2.40m (7ft 10.5in)	Range: 250km (156 miles)
Height: 2.62m (8ft 7.1in)	Radio: None

Battle of France
MAY–JUNE 1940

As an experienced, battle-tested motorized formation, the 2nd Infantry Division (mot) might have been expected to remain with Guderian's XIX Corps in the invasion of France.

ALTHOUGH NOMINALLY assigned to the corps while Germany built up its forces in the Eifel Mountains, it was placed in reserve in the initial stages of the campaign in the West, coming under the orders of Sixteenth Army, which was supporting the Panzer spearheads. The division played a minor part in the Ardennes breakthrough and in the drive to the Channel, which isolated the Maginot Line and stranded the Allied field armies in Belgium. It fought in the battle to seize Stonne, near Sedan, and units also took part in the capture of Bouvellement.

In June, the division was returned to the front. It was attached to *Panzergruppe* Kleist in von Kluge's Fourth Army, part of von Bock's Army Group B. After Dunkirk fell, the German divisions hastily regrouped ready to drive further into France. Kleist's Panzers and their associated infantry were tasked with attacking across the Somme. By 5 June, 10 Panzer divisions had been redeployed into five armoured corps, three under Bock, two under Rundstedt, and that morning at dawn, preceded as usual by clouds of dive-bombers, two of them burst out of bridgeheads west of Amiens and drove for the Seine.

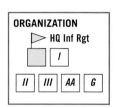

ORGANIZATION

Heavy fighting
French resistance had stiffened, and the division found itself in serious combat before the defences were penetrated. After reaching the Seine, the division fought with Rommel's 7th Panzer and Hartlieb's 5th Panzer Divisions as they pressed forwards towards Dieppe. The British 51st Highland Division, which had fought a successful delaying action to allow British and French troops to escape at Dunkirk, was brought to bay at Valéry-en-Caux and along with elements of the French IX Army Corps was forced to surrender. The 2nd Division continued on through Brittany to occupy Brest. With the signing of the Armistice, divisional troops were used to provide security along the demarcation line between occupied and non-occupied France.

The success of the *Wehrmacht*'s armoured formations in Poland and France prompted the high command to form a number of new Panzer divisions. It was decided to use the 2nd Infantry Division (mot) as the foundation of one of the new divisions, and in October 1940 the unit was moved to Poland where conversion would begin.

On 10 January 1941, the division was redesignated 12.*Panzer-Division*. It joined the war in Russia a month after Operation *Barbarossa* was launched, and would fight on the Eastern Front for the remainder of the war, eventually surrendering to the Soviets in May 1945 after being isolated in the Courland.

Infantry Company	Strength
HQ:	
motorcycles	5
field cars	1
Anti-tank section:	
light trucks	1
light anti-tank guns	1
1 platoon:	
motorcycles	1
medium trucks	4
2 platoon:	
motorcycles	1
medium trucks	4
3 platoon:	
motorcycles	1
medium trucks	4
Maintenance and support:	
motorcycles	1
field cars	2
light trucks	1
medium trucks	2

▶ Mittlerer geländegängig Lkw Henschel 33D1

25.Inf.Regt (mot)

The standard German medium truck was built by a variety of manufacturers, including Büssing-NAG, Henschel, Mercedes and Krupp. Henschel manufactured the Model 33 between 1934 and 1943.

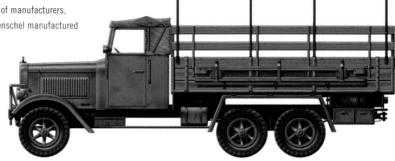

Specifications

Crew: 1	Engine: 10.7 litre (650ci),
Weight: 6.1 tonnes (6 tons)	six-cylinder petrol (100hp)
Length: 7.4m (24ft)	Speed: 60km/h (37mph)
Width: 2.25m (7ft 4in)	Payload: 3 tonnes (2.95 tons)
Height: 3.2m (10ft 6in)	or 18 troops

▼ 15-cm schwere Infanteriegeschütz 33

92.Inf.Regt (mot) / 12.Infanteriegeschütz-Kompanie (mot)

German infantry battalions were equipped with their own artillery support. The 15cm (5.9in) sIG 33 was a powerful and versatile weapon, but as a towed gun it was heavy and awkward in the field. Many were mounted onto light-tank chassis to provide increased mobility.

Specifications

Crew: 5	Muzzle Velocity: 241m/s (783 fps)
Weight: 1.75 tonnes (1.71 tons)	Range: 5504m (6000 yards)
Length: 1.64m (64.57in)	Ammunition: High explosive or smoke
Calibre: 149.1mm (5.9in)	

▶ Protz Kw Krupp L2H143 (Kfz 69)

25.Inf.Regt (mot)

Krupp's 6 x 4 L2H43 and L2H143 light truck was designed primarily as a light artillery tractor, but the vehicle was used for a wide variety of transport roles in motorized units.

Specifications

Crew: 2	Engine: Krupp 3.3L 4-cylinder (60hp)
Weight: 2.45 tonnes (2.23 tons)	Speed: 70km/h (43mph)
Length: 5.10m (16ft 8in)	Range: 450km (280 miles)
Width: 1.93m (6ft 4in)	Radio: None
Height: 1.96m (6ft 5in)	

▼ 3.7-cm Panzerabwehrkanone 35/36

2.Panzer-Abwehr-Bataillon / 1.Kompanie

The Pak 35/36 was developed by Rheinmetall in the late 1920s. At the time, it was highly influential, but the rapid development of armoured vehicles during World War II meant that by the time of the invasion of Russia in 1941 it could not penetrate the thickly armoured Soviet T-34 and KV-1 tanks.

Specifications

Crew: 3	Muzzle Velocity: 762m/s (2500 fps)
Weight: 0.43 tonnes (0.39 tons)	Range: 600m (656 yards)
Length: 1.67m (5ft 5in)	Ammunition: Armour-piercing
Calibre: 37mm (1.49in)	

3rd Infantry Division (motorized)

Like the 2nd Infantry Division, the 3rd Infantry Division was established in secrecy in 1934, before Germany announced its repudiation of the Versailles Treaty in 1935.

THE DIVISION WAS FORMED in October 1934 at Frankfurt on the Oder, as the German armed forces expanded from the seven divisions allowed the *Reichswehr* under the Treaty of Versailles to a total of 21 divisions. As the expansion was secret, all new divisions were given cover names. The infantry and artillery commanders of each of the seven divisions of the *Reichswehr* took command of 14 of the newly formed divisions. The other seven divisions were taken over by newly appointed commanders and given cover names such as *Kommandant von Ulm* and *Kommandant von Regensburg*.

Known initially as *Wehrgauleitung Frankfurt*, the new 3rd Infantry Division was given the cover name of *Kommandant von Frankfurt*. The core of the new division was provided by 8.*(Preussisches) Infanterie-Regiment* and 9.*(Preussisches) Infanterie-Regiment* of the 3rd Division of the *Reichswehr*. Manpower for the expansion of these units came mainly from Prussia. On 15 October 1935, it became officially known as the 3.*Infanterie-Division*.

Divisional History	Formed
Wehrgauleitung Frankfurt	1934
Kommandant von Frankfurt	1934
3.Infanterie-Division	1935
3.Infanterie-Division (mot)	1940
3.Panzergrenadier-Division	1943

Commanders

Oberst Curt Haase
April 1934 – July 1936

Gen.Maj Walter Petzel
July 1936 – October 1938

Gen.Lt Walther Lichel
October 1938 – May 1940

General der Artillerie Paul Bader
October 1940 – May 1941

General der Artillerie Curt Jahn
May 1941 – March 1942

Gen.Lt Helmuth Schlomer
April 1942 – February 1943

General der Panzertruppen Fritz-Hubert Graser
March 1943 – March 1944

Gen.Maj Hans Hecker
March 1944 – May 1944

Gen.Lt Hans-Günther von Rost
June 1944

Gen.Lt Walter Denkert
July 1944 – April 1945

The Rhineland and Czechoslovakia

While only three battalions marched into the demilitarized Rhineland on 7 March 1936, units were transferred from Prussia to the Rhine as a counter to a possible French attack. In the interests of

INSIGNIA

Unit insignia for vehicles of motorized infantry divisions were introduced in May 1939. Painted yellow, they were no larger than a 10cm (4in) square.

By 1943, German military vehicles were painted yellow, so units modified their symbols by changing the colours so they could be seen.

Many of the the symbols referred to the geographic origin of the divisions, but some, like the 3rd Division used ancient Runic symbols – in this case, the letter 'A'.

▶ **Leichte Panzerspähwagen (MG) (SdKfz 221)**

3.Kradschützen-Bataillon / Spähpanzerwagen-Kompanie / leichte Zug

Based on the chassis of the Horch 801 heavy passenger car, the SdKfz 221 was a light reconnaissance vehicle which was issued to the reconnaissance detachments of Panzer, light and motorized divisions early in the war.

Specifications

Crew: 2	Engine: Horch 3.5 litre petrol (75hp)
Weight: 4 tonnes (3.61 tons)	Speed: 90km/h (56mph)
Length: 4.80m (15ft 8in)	Range: 320km (199 miles)
Width: 1.95m (6ft 5in)	Radio: None
Height: 1.70m (5ft 7in)	Armament: 1 x 7.92mm (0.3in) MG

secrecy, none had been mobilized to a wartime footing, and it was fortunate that the French did not react to Hitler's gamble.

The 3rd Division was not involved in the *Anschluss* with Austria in 1938, but in March 1939 it formed part of the large invasion force which occupied Czechoslovakia. The division was assigned to General Johannes Blaskowitz' II Army Corps, serving alongside the 12th and 32nd Infantry Divisions and the 3rd Panzer Division.

The lack of any concrete reaction to the seizure by Britain and France encouraged Hitler to plan further conquests in central Europe, and on 1 August 1939 the 3rd Infantry Division was mobilized, being brought up to full wartime strength from its peacetime establishment, ready to attack Poland.

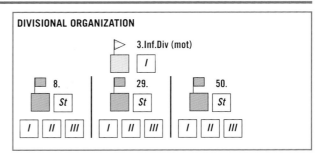

DIVISIONAL ORGANIZATION

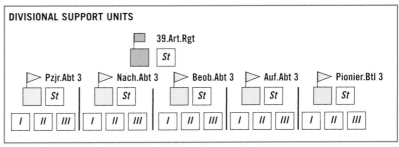

DIVISIONAL SUPPORT UNITS

▶ **Schwere Panzerspähwagen 6-Rad (SdKfz 231)**

3.Kradschützen-Bataillon / Spähpanzerwagen-Kompanie / schwere Zug

The six-wheeled SdKfz 231 was only a stopgap, truck-based design that served until the eight-wheeled SdKfz 231 entered service. Originally ordered in 1934, the eight-wheeler had much-improved cross-country ability.

Specifications

Crew: 4	or Magirus petrol (60–80hp)
Weight: 5.9 tonnes (5.35 tons)	Speed: 70km/h (43mph)
Length: 5.57m (18 ft 7in)	Range: 300km (186 miles)
Width: 1.82m (5ft 11.5in)	Radio: FuG Spr Ger 'a'
Height: 2.25m (7ft 4.5in)	Armament: 1 x 20mm (0.7in) cannon,
Engine: Daimler-Benz, Büssing-NAG	1 x coaxial 7.62mm (0.3in) MG

✝ Poland and France
SEPTEMBER 1939 – JUNE 1940

When the attack on Poland was launched on 1 September 1939, the 3rd Infantry Division was under the command of II Army Corps, Fourth Army, which was part of Army Group North.

LED BY GUDERIAN'S XIX CORPS, the Fourth Army was tasked with driving across the Polish Corridor between Pomerania and East Prussia, isolating the Polish forces around Danzig and cutting the rest of the Polish forces from any link to the Baltic. The 3rd Infantry Division was at the head of the Fourth Army attack, engaging the Polish 9th Infantry Division and Pomorska Cavalry Brigade in the Tuchola Forest. Breaking through the Polish defences at Seenkette, it crossed the Braha River west of Crone and reached the Vistula River at Topolno-Grabowko. The division pursued the retreating Polish forces towards Modlin.

▲ France, May 1940

Most German motorized infantry units employed large numbers of cars in their orders of battle.

It then took part in security operations against the Bzura Pocket between Woclawek and Wyscogrod, before fighting near Plock and advancing in the direction of Gostynin, ending its campaign in Poland near Lowicz. In October 1939, the division was transferred westwards, and was attached to III Corps, Sixth Army, as part of Army Group B in the Eifel Mountains along the German–Luxembourg border. The corps was later transferred to Twelfth Army in preparation for the invasion of the West.

In May 1940, the 3rd Division advanced though Luxembourg and Belgium to the Maas River at Nouzonville, where it made a combat crossing. After securing the area between Evergnicourt and Balham, the division advanced over the Aisne to Asfeld, moving further on to the Canal du Centre near Chalons. In July, it was transferred to the Second Army for security duries along the demarcation line between occupied and Vichy France.

In October 1940, the division was moved back into Germany, where it was reorganized and upgraded as a motorized division, being redesignated as the 3.*Infanterie-Division (mot)*.

German units engaged in the invasion of Poland were marked with high-visibility white crosses rather than the standard national markings to make recognition easier from the air or from a distance.

▶ Panzerfunkwagen 8-Rad (SdKfz 263)

3.Inf.Div (mot) / Stab

Developed alongside the related SdKfz 231 armoured car, the SdKfz 263 was a heavy communications armoured car issued to divisional *Nachrichten* detachments as well as at corps and army headquarters level.

Specifications	
Crew: 5	petrol (150hp)
Weight: 8.9 tonnes (8.1 tons)	Speed: 100km/h (62mph)
Length: 5.85m (19ft 2in)	Range: 300km (186 miles)
Width: 2.20m (7ft 2.5in)	Radio: Satz Funkgerat fur Pz
Height: 2.90m (9ft 6in)	Funktruppe
Engine: Büssing-NAG 8-cylinder	Armament: 1 x 7.92mm (0.3in) MG

▶ Schwere Panzerspähwagen 8-Rad (SdKfz 231)

53.Kradschützen-Bataillon / Spähpanzerwagen-Kompanie / schwere Zug

With origins dating back to the late 1920s, the six-wheel SdKfz 231 was basically a minimally modified truck chassis fitted with an armoured car body. Most were withdrawn from service after 1940.

Specifications	
Crew: 4	petrol (150hp)
Weight: 9.1 tonnes (8.3 tons)	Speed: 85km/h (52.8mph)
Length: 5.85m (19ft 2in)	Range: 300km (186 miles)
Width: 2.20m (7ft 2.5in)	Radio: FuG Ger 'a'
Height: 2.35m (7ft 8in)	Armament: 1 x 20mm (0.7in)
Engine: Büssing-NAG 8-cylinder	cannon

▶ Leichte Personenkraftwagen (Kfz 1)

8.Inf.Regt (mot)

Known as the *Kubel* ('Bucket') or *Kubelwagen*, the Kfz 1 was the standard light car bodywork of the German armed forces. Many different chassis carried similar bodies, but the most numerous during the war were based on the Volkswagen.

Specifications

Crew: 1	Engine: Volkswagen 998cc petrol (24hp). Later
Weight: 0.64 tonnes (0.58 tons)	Volkswagen 1131cc petrol (25hp)
Length: 3.73m (12ft 3in)	Speed: 100km/h (62mph)
Width: 1.60m (5ft 3in)	Range: 600km (375 miles)
Height: 1.35m (4ft 5in)	Radio: None

✝ Leningrad and Moscow
June 1941 – February 1942

After motorization, the 3rd Infantry Division (mot) was assigned to Hoth's 3.*Panzergruppe*, but was transferred to Höppner's 4.*Panzergruppe* before Operation *Barbarossa*.

THE GERMAN INVASION OF THE SOVIET UNION, Operation *Barbarossa*, took place along a broad front. Army Group North, under Field Marshal Ritter von Leeb, advanced through the Baltic States from East Prussia, with the ultimate aim of taking Leningrad. Commanded by General Erich Höppner, 4.*Panzergruppe* led the way for Army Group North. Advancing rapidly, the group's three Panzer divisions and three motorized divisions had reached and crossed the Dvina River by the end of June 1941.

On 2 July, the *Panzergruppe* set out on the 250km (156-mile) race to the Ostrov/Pskov area. The Panzer divisions smashed through the Stalin Line on 4 July, while the three motorized divisions crossed the old Latvian-Russian border opposite Opochka and were also driving up towards Pskov. However, progress slowed: the terrain encountered on the Soviet side of the border was so marshy and impenetrable that even the motorized infantry was reduced to the pace of the marching columns following some 100km (62 miles)

behind. In August, a German attack west of Lake Ilmen met severe Soviet resistance, but by 11 August the Germans were again advancing towards Leningrad, which had been encircled by September.

ORGANIZATION

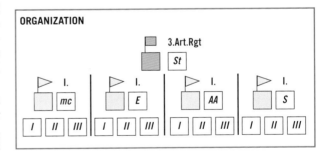

▼ Schwere Kraftrad 750cc mit Seitenwagen BMW R75

53.Kradschützen-Bataillon / 1.Kradschützen-Kompanie

The German Army made extensive use of motorcycles, classed as light (under 350cc), medium (350cc to 500cc) and heavy (over 500cc). Manufacturers of heavy machines included BMW, NSU and Zundapp.

Specifications

Crew: 2	Engine: BMW 750cc petrol (26hp)
Weight: 0.67 tonnes (0.61 tons)	Speed: 92km/h (57mph)
Length: 2.4m (7ft 10in)	Range: 340km (211 miles)
Width: 1.73m (5ft 8in)	Radio: None
Height: 1m (3ft 3in)	Armament: 1 x 7.92mm (0.3in) MG (if fitted)

Specifications

Crew: 1

Weight: 3.29 tonnes (3 tons)

Length: 6.02m (19ft 9in)

Width: 2.27m (7ft 5in)

Height: 2.18m (7ft 2in)

Engine: Opel 1920cc 6-cylinder petrol (36hp)

Speed: 80km/h (50mph)

Range: 410km (255 miles)

Radio: None

▲ Leichte Lkw Opel Blitz 2.0-12 (1t)

29.Inf.Regt (mot)

Most of the huge variety of light 4x2 trucks used by the *Wehrmacht* were commercial types. The two-litre, one-tonne (0.98-ton) variant of the Opel Blitz was one of the more successful designs, and was used as a foundation for a more rational system of standard truck production.

▶ Mittlerer Schützenpanzerwagen Ausf C (SdKfz 251/1)

103.Pz.Aufkl.Bn / schwere Schützenpanzerwagen-Aufklärungs-Kompanie

Development of the SdKfz 251 began in 1937. The chassis was designed by Hanomag, with the armoured body being the responsibility of Büssing-NAG. Production began in June 1939.

Specifications

Crew: 2 plus 12 troops

Weight: 9.9 tonnes (9 tons)

Length: 5.98m (19ft 7in)

Width: 2.1m (6ft 11in)

Height: 1.75m (5ft 8in) or 2.16m

(7ft) including MG shield if fitted

Engine: Maybach HL42TUKRM

Speed: 53km/h (33mph)

Range: 300km (186 miles)

Radio: FuG Spr Ger 1

Armament: 1/2 x 7.62mm

(0.3in) MG

Armoured Car Company	Strength
HQ:	
motorcycles	2
sidecar combinations	5
field cars	1
Heavy platoon:	
8-wheel armoured cars	6
Light platoons:	3
light armoured cars	4
light radio cars	2
Maintenance and support:	
sidecars	1
field cars	2
light trucks	5
medium trucks	2

Operation *Typhoon*

The 3rd Infantry Division was to play no part in the subsequent siege of Leningrad. After reaching Demyansk in September, the division was transferred to Army Group Centre for Operation *Taifun* (Typhoon), the delayed attack on Moscow, launched on 2 October. Assigned to LVII Corps of the Fourth Army, it advanced towards the Soviet capital through Roslavl and Juchnov that month. In spite of the onset of the fearsome Russian winter in November, the division had almost reached Moscow by the beginning of December.

The launch of a massive Soviet counteroffensive came as an unpleasant surprise to the Germans, and for the next four months the 3rd Infantry Division fought a series of bitter defensive battles around Gshatsk and Vyasma as the *Wehrmacht* strained to hold the resurgent Red Army in check.

☦ *Fall Blau* and Stalingrad

JULY 1942 – JANUARY 1943

In May 1942, the 3rd Motorized Infantry Division was withdrawn from the front, moving to Orscha in the rear of Army Group Centre where it was refitted and brought up to strength.

AFTER BEING DRIVEN from the gates of Moscow, most of the generals who had made *Blitzkrieg* possible had been fired by the *Führer*. Moscow was no longer the key; the massed Panzer and infantry formations were to drive southwestwards. In an operation known as *Fall Blau*, they would seize the city of Stalingrad on the Volga. From there, they would be within striking distance of the real prize: the vital oilfields in the Caucasus.

The 3rd Infantry Division was shifted to the Southern Front to take part in the battles across the Ukraine and Don regions. The division had been strengthened by the addition of the 103rd Panzer *Abteilung*. This reflected a new type of German divisional structure, in which fast-moving motorized troops would be accompanied by their own tank support instead of having tank support from Panzer divisions. As part of the Sixth Army, the division advanced into the Stalingrad region in September 1942. After repeated assaults, the city seemed ready to fall in November, when Sixth Army was encircled by a massive Soviet counterattack. In the ensuing battle of attrition, the division was destroyed.

Panzer Battalion	Strength
Panzer II	10
Panzer III (long barrel)	35
Panzer IV (long barrel)	8
Pz III command tank	1

▲ **Panzer infantry**

In a classic image of tank and infantry cooperation, Panzergrenadiers hunch close to a Panzer III tank amongst corn fields and mountains in southern Russia.

ORGANIZATION

3.Inf.Rgt (mot)
St

I. mc — I II III
I. E — I II III
I. AA — I II III
I. S — I II III

▶ **Mittlerer Lkw A-Typ Opel Blitz 4x4 3t (Kfz 305)**

3.Nachrichten-Abteilung / Funk-Kompanie

Most German trucks were produced in a variety of body styles. The multi-purpose van body could be used as an ambulance, as a communications vehicle, as a mobile workshop and in many other roles.

Specifications

Crew: 1
Weight: 3.29 tonnes (3 tons)
Length: 6.02m (19ft 9in)
Width: 2.27m (7ft 5in)
Height: 2.18m (7ft 2in)

Engine: Opel 6-cylinder petrol
(73.5hp)
Speed: 80km/h (50mph)
Range: 410km (255 miles)
Radio: None

Specifications

Crew: 2 plus 12 troops	Engine: Maybach HL42TUKRM
Weight: 9.9 tonnes (9 tons)	Speed: 53km/h (33mph)
Length: 5.98m (19ft 7in)	Range: 300km (186 miles)
Width: 2.1m (6ft 11in)	Radio: FuG Spr Ger 1
Height: 1.75m (5ft 8in) or 2.16m (7ft)	Armament: 1/2 x 7.62mm (0.3in) MG
including MG shield if fitted	

▲ **Mittlerer Schützenpanzerwagen Ausf C (SdKfz 251/1)**

103.Pz.Aufkl.Bn / schwere Schützenpanzerwagen-Aufklärungs-Kompanie

The Ausf B variant of the SdKfz 251 could be identified by the single vision port on each side; the original design had three ports. The Ausf C, which entered production in 1940, had an armoured cowling over the engine air intake behind the front wheel and featured an armoured shield for the MG 34 machine gun.

▶ **7.5-cm Pak 40/3 auf PzKpfw 38(t) Ausf H (SdKfz 138)**

103.Pz.Aufkl.Bn. / schwere Kompanie / Panzerjäger-Zug

Issued to Panzerjäger units from late 1942, this self-propelled anti-tank gun mounted the powerful 7.5cm (3in) Pak 40 on the Czech-built PzKpfw 38 chassis.

Specifications

Crew: 4	Speed: 35km/h (22mph)
Weight: 10.8 tonnes (9.8 tons)	Range: 240km (150 miles)
Length: 5.77m (19ft 11in)	Radio: FuG Spr Ger 1
Width: 2.16m (7ft 1in)	Armament: 1 x 75mm (3in) Pak 40/3 L/46
Height: 2.51m (8ft 3in)	anti-tank gun; 1 x 7.92mm (0.3in) MG
Engine: Praga EPA 6-cylinder (140hp)	

▶ **Leichter Funkpanzerwagen (SdKfz 250/3)**

103.Pz.Aufkl.Bn. / leichte Schützenpanzerwagen-Aufklärungs-Kompanie

Designed to complement the troop-carrying SdKfz 251, the SdKfz 250 was intended to carry a *Halbgruppe* (half-section) of four reconnaissance troops and a crew of two. Like the larger half-track, the SdKfz 250 was produced in a number of variants, including this communications model.

Specifications

Crew: 2 plus 4 troops	6-cylinder (100hp)
Weight: 5.35 tonnes (4.87 tons)	Speed: 60km/h (37mph)
Length: 4.56m (14ft 11.5in)	Range: 320km (199 miles)
Width: 1.95m (6ft 5in)	Radio: FuG Spr Ger 1
Height: 1.66m (5ft 5in)	Armament: 1 x 7.92mm (0.3in) MG
Engine: Maybach HL42TRKM	

☩ 3rd Panzergrenadier Division
1943 – ITALY AND THE WEST

In March 1943, it was decided to reform the 3rd Infantry Division after its destruction at Stalingrad, and units began to assemble at Lyon in France that spring.

THE REBORN DIVISION was based on the few surviving elements of the original *3.Infanterie-Division (mot)*, and it also absorbed the *386.Infanterie-Division (mot)*, which had also originally been formed at Frankfurt on the Oder. Late in 1942, the *Schützen*, or motorized infantry regiments, in *Wehrmacht* divisions were given the historically significant name of grenadiers, partly as a step to boost the morale of the troops. In summer 1943, it was decided to rename and re-equip motorized infantry divisions as *Panzergrenadier*, or armoured infantry, divisions. In June 1943, the 3rd Infantry Division, then almost at operational standard, became *3.Panzergrenadier-Division*.

```
DIVISIONAL ORGANIZATION

                  ▷   3.PzGren.Div
                 ▢    I

   ▢   8.          ▢   29.          ▢   103.
       St              St                St

   I  II  III     I  II  III      I  II  III
```

After completing its formation and refit, the new Panzergrenadier division was sent to Italy in June 1943. Initially assigned to *Oberbefehlshaber Süd* and located in north Italy, it was transferred to XIV Corps

▼ 3rd Artillery Regiment, 1st Battalion

As a motorized formation, the 3rd Infantry Division had been equipped with towed artillery. The 1st Battalion had two 15cm (5.9in) infantry support guns with the Staff Battery and three batteries of four towed 10.5cm (4.1in) *leichte FeldHaubitze* 18s (leFH 18). The 2nd Battalion also had LeFH 18s, but its Staff Battery was equipped with a pair of 15cm (5.9in) sFH 18 heavy howitzers. The 3rd Battalion operated a battery of 10cm (3.9in) long-range guns and a battery of 15cm (5.9in)

sFH 18s. A fourth battalion was equipped with light and heavy Flak batteries. Destroyed at Stalingrad, the division was rebuilt in 1943 as a Panzergrenadier division. In September 1943, the 2nd and 3rd Battalions remained towed artillery units, but the 1st Battalion of the 3rd Artillery Regiment was issued with a dozen 10.5cm (4.1in) Wespe self-propelled howitzers (see below), which were organized into three batteries each of four guns.

1st Battery

2nd Battery

3rd Battery

of the Tenth Army in the south later in the year. In September, the division was thrown against the Allied landings at Salerno in a powerful German counterattack that very nearly threw the British and American armies back into the sea. The Allied forces held out, and by 10 September the German Tenth Army was in retreat towards the Volturno.

At Christmas, the 3rd Panzergrenadier Division was held in reserve behind the defences at Monte Cassino. In January, following the Allied landings at Anzio, it was thrown into action in Aprilla and Cisterna. The division fought well, helping to stall the Allied advance and breakout until the general German retreat to Rome in May and June of 1944.

Defeat in France

After nearly a year of hard combat, the remnants of the division were transferred to Florence for refitting in June and July 1944. Once it had been brought up to strength, the division was transferred to France,

joining First Army near Paris in August. By this time, the Allies had broken out of the Normandy beachhead and were racing through the French heartland. After a vain attempt to stem the Allied tide, the division joined the general German withdrawal across France, eventually taking up positions in and around Nancy.

In September, the division was one of several units deployed towards Metz in an attack on General George S. Patton's fast-moving Third US Army. Defending doggedly, the German divisions managed to slow the American advance as the Allies tried to breach the German border defences of the *Westwall*.

On German soil

For the first time, the steady progress enjoyed by the Allied forces had been checked: by the defeat at Arnhem, the bloody fighting in the Hurtgenwald and now the defence of Metz. Soon, the division would be moved to the Hurtgenwald to reinforce the defence of Aachen, as part of a forward German defensive line west of the Rhine.

▶ **Panzerkampfwagen III Ausf G (SdKfz 141)**

103.Pz.Bn / I Batterie

Although nominally a motorized infantry formation, the 3rd Division was strengthened by the addition of the 103rd Panzer Battalion over the winter of 1941/2. The bulk of the unit's tank strength was provided by Panzer IIIs with 5cm (2in) guns.

Specifications

Crew: 4	Speed: 40km/h (24.9mph)
Weight: 22.4 tonnes (20.3 tons)	Range: 165km (102.5 miles)
Length: 5.41m (17ft 8in)	Radio: FuG5
Width: 2.95m (9ft 9in)	Armament: 1 x 37mm (1.5in) KwK L/46
Height: 2.44m (8ft)	or 50mm (2in) KwK L/38 gun; 2 x
Engine: Maybach HL120TRM petrol	7.92mm (0.3in) MG (one coaxial,
(300hp)	one hull-mounted)

▶ **Sturmgeschütz 7.5-cm Sturmkanone 40 Ausf F8 (SdKfz 142/1)**

103.Pz.Bn / II Batterie

The 103rd Panzer Battalion was equipped with StuGs when the division was rebuilt in 1943. The StuG had been upgunned with the powerful 7.5cm (3in) StuK 40, which could destroy any current Allied tank.

Specifications

Crew: 4	(300hp)
Weight: 25.6 tonnes (23.3 tons)	Speed: 40km/h (24.9mph)
Length: 6.77m (22ft 2in)	Range: 210km (87 miles)
Width: 2.92m (9ft 7in)	Radio: FuG15 or FuG16
Height: 2.15m (7ft)	Armament: 1 x 75mm (3in) StuK 40
Engine: Maybach HL120TRM petrol	L/48 gun

▶ **Panzerjäger IV mit 7.5-cm Pak 39 L/48 (SdKfz 162)**

10.Pz.Gren.Div Kampfgruppe / 7.Pz.Bn / 3.Kompanie

In June 1944, the division received two companies of Panzerjäger IVs.

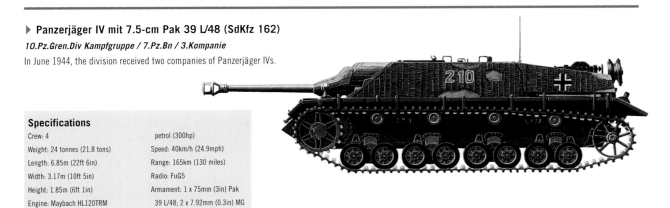

Specifications

Crew: 4	petrol (300hp)
Weight: 24 tonnes (21.8 tons)	Speed: 40km/h (24.9mph)
Length: 6.85m (22ft 6in)	Range: 165km (130 miles)
Width: 3.17m (10ft 5in)	Radio: FuG5
Height: 1.85m (6ft 1in)	Armament: 1 x 75mm (3in) Pak
Engine: Maybach HL120TRM	39 L/48; 2 x 7.92mm (0.3in) MG

▶ **Mittlerer Lkw S-Typ Opel Blitz 3.6-36S**

3.Panzergrenadier-Division

Under the *Wehrmacht*'s standardization system introduced in 1938, commercial standard 4x2 trucks were classed as 'S-Type' vehicles, while military standard 4x4 variants were designated 'A-Type'.

Specifications

Crew: 1	Engine: Opel 6-cylinder petrol
Weight: 3.29 tonnes (3 tons)	(73.5hp)
Length: 6.02m (19ft 9in)	Speed: 80km/h (50mph)
Width: 2.27m (7ft 5in)	Range: 410km (255 miles)
Height: 2.18m (7ft 2in)	Radio: None

☩ Ardennes and Remagen
DECEMBER 1944 – MARCH 1945

Aachen was known as the 'Gateway to the Rhine', and the 3rd Panzergrenadier Division saw intense action in November 1944 as German forces defended the city.

IT WAS HERE THAT THE DIVISION'S 8th Grenadier Regiment, vastly outnumbered, managed to fight off attacks by two American divisions, one of which was the 1st US Infantry Division, the famous 'Big Red One'. One grenadier company, commanded by *Leutnant* Zillies, held a line of three bunkers for five days. In close and brutal hand-to-hand fighting, one of the bunkers changed hands 16 times.

Despite everything the defenders could do, the city was lost and the division withdrew. Although Aachen was a tactical victory for the Americans, the German defence of the city cost the US Army valuable time and delayed a planned attack towards the Rhine.

Additionally, the fighting gave the German high command time to plan a daring offensive in the Ardennes, and to begin to assemble forces for the operation. Codenamed *Wacht am Rhein*, it was to become better known as the Battle of the Bulge.

The 3rd Panzergrenadier Division was assigned to *General der Panzertruppen* Hasso von Manteuffel's 5.*Panzerarmee*. After resting and recuperating behind the lines, the division took up a position around Monschau. The offensive was launched on 16 December. While Manteuffel's Panzer units sped westwards towards Bastogne and Dinant, the division provided flank protection and, along with left flank units of the Sixth SS Panzer Army, saw some heavy fighting around the villages of Krinkelt and Rocherath. Although the US 395th Infantry Regiment was driven back, it made a stand at Elsenborn, stopping any further German advances.

Once the Allies halted the offensive and began to flatten out the bulge, the division withdrew into the Eifel Mountains in January 1945, fighting a series of delaying actions. The division suffered heavy losses in the defence of Cologne and Remagen, and in March 1945 the remnants withdrew across the Rhine into the Ruhr. In April 1945, the 3rd Panzergrenadier Division was among the 300,000 German troops trapped by the Allies in the Ruhr Pocket. The division surrendered in April 1945, one month before the end of the war in Europe.

▶ Krankenkraftwagen I Phänomen Granit 25H (Kfz 31)

3.Sanitäts-Kompanie / 3.Krankenkraftwagen-Zug

German military ambulances all carried the designation Kfz 31, whatever their size or number of wheels. One of the most common types was the Phänomen Granit 25H, which could accommodate four stretchers or eight seated patients.

Specifications	
Crew: 1	Engine: Horch 3.5L or 3.8L V8 petrol
Weight: 1.89 tonnes (1.72 tons)	(82 or 92hp)
Length: 5.05m (16ft 7in)	Speed: 120km/h (74mph)
Width: 1.79m (5ft 10in)	Range: 400km (248 miles)
Height: 1.69m (5ft 6.5in)	Radio: None

▶ Mittlerer Schützenpanzerwagen Ausf C 2-cm Flak (SdKfz 251/17)

3.Flak-Bataillon / leichte Flak-Batterie

Armed with a 2cm (0.7in) Flak 38, the SdKfz 251/17 was issued to *Luftwaffe* and army Flak battalions.

Specifications	
Crew: 4 or 6	Speed: 50km/h (31mph)
Weight: 8.8 tonnes (8 tons)	Range: 300km (186 miles)
Length: 5.98m (19ft 7in)	Radio: None
Width: 2.1m (6ft 11in)	Armament: Flak 38 twin 20mm
Height: 2.25m (7ft 4.5in)	(0.7in) L/55 cannon; 1 x 7.92mm
Engine: Maybach HL42TUKRM	(0.3in) MG
6-cylinder petrol (100hp)	

▶ Skoda Type 952 (Kfz 21)

3.Panzergrenadier-Division

Germany's occupation of Czechoslovakia gave the *Wehrmacht* access to the products of the giant Skoda works. Based on the Skoda Superb saloon, the Kfz 21 was a field staff car used by senior officers. The same chassis was used as a communications vehicle, under the designation of Kfz 15.

Specifications	
Crew: 1	Engine: Skoda 3.1L 6-cylinder petrol (80hp)
Length: 4.8m (15ft 9in)	Speed: 100km/h (62mph)
Width: 1.72m (5ft 7in)	Radio: None
Height: 1.8m (5ft 11in)	

▼ 103rd Panzer Battalion

On 10 December 1944, as the 3rd Panzergrenadier Division prepared to take part in the Ardennes offensive, the 103rd Panzer Battalion had one Panzer III and two Panzer IVs on strength, acting as command tanks for its three *Sturmgeschütz* companies. Each company had 13 or 14 StuGs

Command tanks

Sturmgeschütz company

▶ Leichte Feldhaubitze 18/2 auf fahrgestell PzKpfw II (Sf) Wespe (SdKfz 124)

3.Artillerie-Regiment / I Bataillon / 1.Batterie

Intended as an interim self-propelled howitzer until purpose-designed equipment could be built, the Wespe, based on a modified Panzer II chassis, proved to be an effective weapon. Its first major action was at Kursk in 1943, and it was in service to the end of the war.

Specifications

Crew: 5

Weight: 12.1 tonnes (11 tons)

Length: 4.81m (15ft 10in)

Width: 2.28m (7ft 6in)

Height: 2.25m (7ft 4.5in)

Engine: Maybach HL62TR

Speed: 40km/h (24.9mph)

Range: 220km (136.7 miles)

Radio: FuG Spr 1

Armament: 1 x LeFH 18M L/28 105mm (4.1in) howitzer

10th Infantry Division (motorized)

Originally formed in October 1934 at Regensburg with troops drawn from northern Bavaria, the 10th Infantry Division incorporated units from the old 7th Division of the *Reichswehr*.

IN 1934, AS THE *REICHSWEHR* was secretly expanded to become the *Wehrmacht*, the seven original *Wehrkreiskommandos* became the nuclei of new corps formations. The original seven divisions ceased to exist, while their units were used as the basis for the formation of a series of 21 totally new divisions. The 10th Infantry Division was established at Regensburg around the 20.(*Bayerisches*) *Infanterie-Regiment*. Originally known as *Wehrgauleitung Regensburg*, the new division was given the cover name of *Kommandant von Regensburg*.

With the formal announcement of the creation of the *Wehrmacht* on 15 October 1935 – although it had in fact been in existence for more than a year – the cover name was dropped and the formation was offically designated as the 10.*Infanterie-Division*.

Austrian *Anschluss*

In 1936, the 10th Infantry Division was under the command of VII Army Corps in Munich. Late in 1937 Hitler, pursuing his aim of *Anschluss*, the political union of Germany and Austria, began to put pressure on the Austrian Government to effect this. Austrian Chancellor Kurt Schuschnigg opposed Hitler's demands but was forced to call for a plebiscite. However, Hitler continued to mobilize

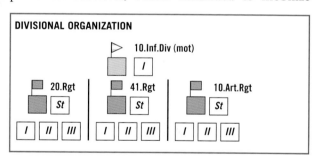

▲ Light anti-tank weapon
A Kfz 12 medium car from a motorized anti-tank company tows a 3.7cm (1.5in) Pak 36, the standard German anti-tank weapon in the early years of World War II.

Divisional History	Formed
Wehrgauleitung Regensburg/ Kommandant von Regensburg	1934
10.Infanterie-Division	1935
10.Infanterie-Division (mot)	1940
10.Panzergrenadier-Division	1943

Commanders

Generalleutnant Conrad von Cochenhausen
1 Sep 1939 – Oct 1940

Generalleutnant Friedrich-Wilhelm von Löper
Oct 1940 – Apr 1942

Generalleutnant August Schmidt
Apr 1942 – Oct 1943

Generalleutnant Hans Mikosch
Oct 1943 – Dec 1943

Generalleutnant August Schmidt
Dec 1943 – Sep 1944

Generalmajor Walter Herold
Sep 1944 – Nov 1944

Oberst Alexander Vial
Nov 1944 – Jan 1945

Generalmajor Karl-Richard Kossmann
Jan 1945 – 8 May 1945

DIVISIONAL ORGANIZATION

10.Inf.Div (mot)
I

20.Rgt — St — I II III
41.Rgt — St — I II III
10.Art.Rgt — St — I II III

INSIGNIA

The coat of arms of the city of Regensburg, where the division was formed, consists of crossed keys. The division used a key as its pre-war symbol. It was reintroduced with the 10th Panzergrenadier Division.

German divisional insignia were changed soon after the outbreak of war, with simple, easy-to-recognize shapes being introduced.

Variants of the basic divisional symbols were often used by formations in the field.

German troops on the Austrian border, and the plebiscite was never held. In this period, the division was transferred to XII Corps. Schuschnigg resigned on 11 March 1936 and was replaced by the pro-Nazi Interior Minister Arthur Seyss-Inquart.

On the morning of 12 March, the German Eighth Army crossed the German-Austrian border to be greeted by cheering Austrians. Badly organized and poorly coordinated, the occupation encountered no resistance, but provided valuable lessons for future large-scale operations.

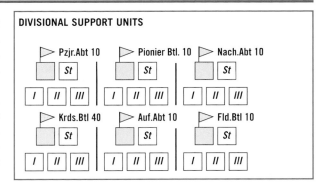

DIVISIONAL SUPPORT UNITS

Pzjr.Abt 10 — St — I | II | III
Pionier Btl. 10 — St — I | II | III
Nach.Abt 10 — St — I | II | III
Krds.Btl 40 — St — I | II | III
Auf.Abt 10 — St — I | II | III
Fld.Btl 10 — St — I | II | III

 # Poland and France

SEPTEMBER 1939 – JUNE 1940

In August 1939, the 10th Infantry Division was mobilized from its peacetime establishment to its full wartime strength, ready for Germany's invasion of Poland.

THE DIVISION JOINED XIII Corps of General Blaskowitz' Eighth Army, part of von Rundstedt's Army Group South. The corps was deployed near Breslau in Silesia. Rundstedt's army group comprised three armies. Eighth Army on the left drove for Lodz, while Fourteenth Army on the right aimed for Krakow. In the centre, von Reichenau's Tenth Army had the bulk of the group's armour.

War in Poland

The German invasion was launched on 1 September 1939, and after just three days of fighting, leading elements of the German Army had pushed 80km (50 miles) into Poland. Eighth Army smashed through Lodz. Army Groups North and South met at Wlodawa on 17 September, completing the outer ring of

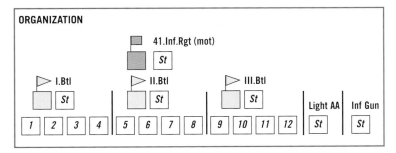

ORGANIZATION

41.Inf.Rgt (mot) — St

I.Btl — St — 1 | 2 | 3 | 4
II.Btl — St — 5 | 6 | 7 | 8
III.Btl — St — 9 | 10 | 11 | 12
Light AA — St
Inf Gun — St

▶ **Schwere Panzerspähwagen 6-Rad (SdKfz 231)**

40.Kradschützen-Bataillon / Spähpanzerwagen-Kompanie / schwere Zug

The SdKfz 231 was a standard body mounted on a 6x4 truck chassis built by Büssing-NAG, Mercedes and Magirus. It equipped motorized and Panzer reconnaissance units in Austria, Czechoslovakia, Poland and France.

Specifications

Crew: 4	(60-80hp)
Weight: 5.9 tonnes (5.35 tons)	Speed: 70km/h (43mph)
Length: 5.57m (18ft 7in)	Range: 300km (186 miles)
Width: 1.82m (5ft 11.5in)	Radio: FuG Spr Ger 'a'
Height: 2.25m (7ft 4.5in)	Armament: 1 x 20mm (0.7in)
Engine: Daimler-Benz, Büssing-	cannon, 1 x coaxial 7.62mm
NAG or Magirus petrol	(0.3in) MG

a massive German double pincer. Only a small fraction of the Polish Army could hope to escape. Surrounded and besieged, the final blow to the Poles came when Soviet forces entered the war on the German side. The final assault on Warsaw came on 26 September, and on the 28th Poland surrendered.

▼ Schwere Kraftrad 750-cc mit Seitenwagen

40.Kradschützen-Bataillon

The BMW sidecar combination, with both rear wheels driven, was introduced in 1938 and was used in combat and reconnaissance on all fronts. Strong enough to mount a machine gun, it could also be used to carry a mortar. Later in the war, many were replaced by the Volkswagen Kubel.

After a period in reserve at Marburg, the division was transferred to Army Group A for the Battle of France. Its mission was to follow the rapidly advancing Panzers of von Rundstedt's army group. In June 1940, the division saw action on the Aisne, advancing through Champagne to the Swiss border and pursuing the defeated French Army through Burgundy and the Côte d'Or.

With the Armistice, the division performed occupation and security duties before being sent back to *Wehrkreis* XIII in northern Bavaria for conversion to a motorized infantry division, which began in November 1940.

Specifications

Crew: 2	Engine: BMW 750cc petrol (26hp)
Weight: 0.67 tonnes (0.61 tons)	Speed: 92km/h (57mph)
Length: 2.4m (7ft 10in)	Range: 340km (211 miles)
Width: 1.73m (5ft 8in)	Radio: None
Height: 1m (3ft 3in)	Armament: 1 x 7.92mm (0.3in) MG (if fitted)

▶ Leichte Panzerspähwagen (MG) (SdKfz 221)

40.Kradschützen-Bataillon / Spähpanzerwagen-Kompanie / leichte Zug

Based on the Horch 801 4x4 heavy field car, the SdKfz 221 was manufactured from 1935 to 1940. The MG-armed variant almost invariably served alongside models armed with 2cm (0.7in) cannon and with Funk or radio-equipped cars.

Specifications

Crew: 2	Engine: Horch 3.5L petrol (75hp)
Weight: 4 tonnes (3.61 tons)	Speed: 90km/h (56mph)
Length: 4.80m (15ft 8in)	Range: 320km (199 miles)
Width: 1.95m (6ft 5in)	Radio: None
Height: 1.70m (5ft 7in)	Armament: 1 x 7.92mm (0.3in) MG

▶ Schwere Panzerspähwagen (Fu) 8-Rad (SdKfz 232)

40.Kradschützen-Bataillon / Spähpanzerwagen-Kompanie / schwere Zug

The communications variant of the SdKfz 231, the SdKfz 232 was issued to the heavy platoons of the *Aufklärungs*, or reconnaissance, detachments assigned to motorized and Panzer divisions.

Specifications

Crew: 4	Speed: 85km/h (52.8mph)
Weight: 9.1 tonnes (8.3 tons)	Range: 300km (186 miles)
Length: 4.67m (15ft 4in)	Radio: FuG12 plus FuG Spr Ger 'a'
Width: 2.2m (7ft 2in)	Armament: 1 x 20mm (0.7in) KwK
Height: 2.35m (7ft 8in)	30/38 L/55 cannon; 1 x 7.92mm
Engine: Büssing-NAG L8V	(0.3in) MG (coaxial)

F Operation *Barbarossa*

JUNE–DECEMBER 1941

Motorization of the 10th Infantry Division had been completed by the beginning of April 1941, and the formation was held in reserve for the German invasion of the Balkans.

THE DIVISION SAW NO ACTION, however, and in May it was transferred to Heinz Guderian's 2.*Panzergruppe* for Operation *Barbarossa*. Guderian's force, an armoured army in all but name, was the spearhead formation of Field Marshal Fedor von Bock's Army Group Centre.

Guderian's first task was to throw his *Panzergruppe* across the River Bug on each side of the fortress of Brest-Litovsk, capture the fortress and then race with his armoured spearheads towards the city of Minsk. He would curve up to it from the south to meet Hoth's spearheads coming down from the north. In this way, the Soviet frontline forces would be isolated. Once their supplies had run out, they would have little alternative but to surrender.

By 24 June, only 60 hours after the launch of the attack, 17th Panzer Division was driving into Slonim, over 140km (86 miles) from the frontier and halfway to the Germans' first objective. Three days later, on the afternoon of 27 June, the leading tanks of the 17th Panzer Division drove into Minsk to meet the spearheads of Hoth's 3.*Panzergruppe*, which had covered 350km (217 miles) in five days.

Into action

The 10th Division was held back as part of Guderian's reserve, but by the beginning of August it had been thrown into action as the Panzers fought to widen the German hold on the land east of Smolensk, turning it into a solid bridgehead for what everybody expected would be the final thrust towards the Soviet capital.

Everybody but Hitler. Plans for such an attack had to be delayed when on 24 August, in a personal interview, the *Führer* ordered Guderian to lead his

Panzerjäger-Abteilung	Strength
HQ:	
motorcycles	2
sidecar combinations	5
field cars	1
Motorized anti-tank company:	
trucks	5
37mm (1.5in) AT guns	4
SdKfz	5
half-tracks towing 50mm (2in) AT guns	10
SP anti-tank companies:	2
SP anti-tank guns	3
SP light AA company:	
SdKfz 10/4 with 2cm (0.7in) AA	4
SdKfz 10 without guns	2
Krupp Protze towing 2cm (0.7in) AA	4
Krupp Protze towing trailers	2

▶ **Leichte Panzerspähwagen (2-cm) (SdKfz 222)**

110.Pz.Aufkl.Bn / leichte Spähpanzerwagen-Kompanie

An upgunned version of the SdKfz 221 with an enlarged turret housing a 2cm (0.7in) cannon, the SdKfz 222 was designed to provide fire support for reconnaissance vehicles equipped with long-range radio sets.

Specifications

Crew: 3

Weight: 5.3 tonnes (4.8 tons)

Length: 4.8m (15ft 8in)

Width: 1.95m (6ft 5in)

Height: 2.00m (6ft 7in)

Engine: Horch 3.5L or 3.8L petrol

Speed: 85km/h (52.8mph)

Range: 300km (186 miles)

Radio: FuG Spr Ger 'a'

Armament: 1 x 20mm (0.7in) KwK 30 L/55 cannon; 1 x 7.92mm (0.3in) MG (coaxial)

▲ Flak gun

A 3.7cm (1.5in) flak gun mounted on board a Sd Kfz 10 ploughs through the snow of northern Russia, early 1943.

entire *Panzergruppe* down to assist in the occupation of the Ukraine. The ensuing campaign around Kiev was the largest battle of encirclement in history, but in spite of capturing huge numbers of prisoners, the Germans had lost one vital commodity – time.

Assigned the codename *Taifun*, the German drive on Moscow began on 2 October. The Russians had concentrated huge forces to bar the road to their capital, but these were smashed yet again. In two more great battles of encirclement, another 650,000 Russians were captured.

The attack on Moscow had been delayed too long. First the autumn rains turned the landscape into seemingly bottomless mud, and then the harsh Russian winter presented new challenges to the *Wehrmacht*, which had little winter gear.

Battle for Moscow

Despite the cold, Guderian's divisions took Tula and pressed on towards Moscow, but they were not ready for the huge Soviet counteroffensive which erupted on 5 December. Unable to dig in properly, the undermanned German units were torn apart; the few serviceable German tanks were unable to manoeuvre in the conditions and their fuel was stuck way back behind the front. For the first time, the myth of the invincibility of the German Army had been broken.

▶ Leichte Personenkraftwagen (Kfz 1)

10.Panzergrenadier-Division

Reliable and simple to maintain, the Volkswagen Kubel proved to be an effective vehicle from the North African desert to the snow and ice of Arctic Russia. Around 55,000 were built from 1940 to 1945 – a large number by German World War II standards, but insignificant compared to the more than 600,000 Jeeps built for the Allies in the same period.

Specifications	
Crew: 1	Engine: Volkswagen 998cc petrol (24hp). Later
Weight: 0.64 tonnes (0.58 tons)	Volkswagen 1131cc petrol (25hp)
Length: 3.73m (12ft 3in)	Speed: 100km/h (62mph)
Width: 1.60m (5ft 3in)	Range: 600km (375 miles)
Height: 1.35m (4ft 5in)	Radio: None

▶ 3.7-cm Panzerabwehrkanone 35/36

10.Panzerjäger-Abteilung

First seeing action during the Spanish Civil War, the Pak 35/36 was an effective weapon for its time. By 1940, however, it lacked the ability to penetrate heavy Allied tanks like the British Matilda and the French Char-B, and it was so ineffective against Soviet armour that it was derisively known as the 'Door-Knocker'.

Specifications	
Crew: 3	Muzzle Velocity: 762m/s (2500fps)
Weight: 0.43 tonnes (0.39 tons)	Range: 600m (656 yards)
Length: 1.67m (5ft 5.5in)	Ammunition: Armour-piercing
Calibre: 37mm (1.5in)	

▶ **Schwere Kraftrad Zundapp KS750**

40.Kradschützen-Bataillon / Stab

Most of the motorcycles operated by *Kradschützen* units were sidecar combinations, but solo machines were used by battalion and company headquarters for messenger duties. The BMW R75 and the Zundapp KS750 were built as heavy sidecar machines, but they were also used for solo work.

Specifications

Crew: 2	Engine: 750cc petrol (26hp)
Weight: 0.40 tonnes (0.36 tons)	Speed: 95km/h (59mph)
Length: 2.38m (7ft 10in)	Range: 330km (205 miles)
Width: 1.65m (5ft 5in) (with sidecar)	Radio: None
Height: 1.01m (3ft 4in)	

F With Army Group Centre

JANUARY 1942 – JULY 1943

The fresh Siberian divisions thrown into the battle for Moscow by the Red Army forced the understrength survivors of the *Wehrmacht*'s Army Group Centre back in confusion.

IN JANUARY 1942, 12 German armies were locked in combat with 22 Soviet armies. On a front stretching from the Crimea to the Gulf of Finland, 141 divisions, including 11 from Axis allies, faced more than 300 Russian formations.

The very size of the war zone was in the *Wehrmacht*'s favour. Stalin was trying not only to relieve Moscow and Leningrad but also to destroy Army Group Centre. His generals knew what happened to commanders who failed, and Red Army offensives were launched all along the line.

It was too much. Despite tattered uniforms stuffed with straw and newspaper in lieu of proper winter clothing, weapons that jammed in the arctic temperatures and a grave lack of tanks or aircraft, the German Army defended itself with extraordinary professionalism and courage.

The fighting conditions were appalling and favoured the Soviets, used as they were to the rigours of the Russian winter. As the petrol froze in their fuel tanks, the Germans came to place greater reliance on horse-drawn transport. But as the winter drew on, they succeeded in blunting the massed Russian attacks. The stubborn German defence exposed the Red Army's lack of experience, its problems exacerbated by shortages of all kinds. By March, even Stalin had to admit that his great offensive was over.

The 10th Infantry Division (mot) was forced to retreat from Moscow and Tula, eventually coming to a halt when the front line stabilized around Moshaisk and Juchnow. The division had been transferred from 2.*Panzergruppe* to the Fourth Army, under whose control it would remain for much of the next year.

Holding in the centre

In his *Führer* Directive No. 41, dated 5 April 1942, Hitler stated: 'The enemy has suffered enormous losses of men and material. In attempting to exploit their apparent initial successes, they have exhausted during this winter the mass of their reserves, which were intended for later operations.'

In this mistaken belief, Hitler set out his objectives for the coming summer offensive, codenamed *Fall*

Reconnaissance battalion, mot inf div (1942)	Strength
Battalion HQ:	1
Light armoured car company:	1
Motorcycle companies:	3
Heavy company:	1
Pioneer platoon	1
Panzerjäger platoon	2
Light infantry gun section	1

10th Signals Battalion	Strength
Battalion HQ:	1
Telephone company (mot):	1
platoons	4
maintenance section	1
Radio company (mot):	1
platoons	3
maintenance section	1
Signals light transport column:	1

Blau (Plan Blue). He set his revitalized armies, now numbering some 215 divisions, the task of destroying the last remaining enemy formations, and as far as possible capturing the main sources of raw materials on which the enemy's war economy depended.

The *Wehrmacht* spent the first months of 1942 rebuilding its strength. Hitler's plan called for all available forces to be concentrated on the southern

sector. Their mission was firstly to annihilate the enemy on the Don. Then they were to swing north and take Stalingrad, followed by a combined assault to conquer the oil-producing areas of the Caucasus. Without that oil, German Panzers would go nowhere. Lastly, they were to capture the passes through the Caucasus Mountains, giving access to the Middle East. Initially successful, the campaign was to end in disaster after Hitler divided his forces.

While this massive operation got under way in the south, those units remaining with Army Group Centre were committed to holding actions. In April 1942, the 10th Division was placed in Fourth Army reserve, before being returned to the front at Demyansk in June.

After almost a year of duties holding the line, the division was withdrawn in April 1943 to refit in reserve in the Orel sector. On 23 June, the division was upgraded and redesignated, becoming the 10.*Panzergrenadier-Division*.

▶ **Mittlerer Kommandopanzerwagen (SdKfz 251/6)**

20.Panzergrenadier-Regiment / Stab-Kompanie

Built to enable German divisional and higher commanders to keep up with their fast-moving Panzer spearheads, the SdKfz 251/6 was a fully equipped command post that enabled senior officers to control a battle while on the move.

Specifications

Crew: 8	6-cylinder petrol (100hp)
Weight: 9.4 tonnes (8.5 tons)	Speed: 53km/h (32.9mph)
Length: 5.98m (19ft 7in)	Range: 300km (186 miles)
Width: 2.1m (6ft 11in)	Radio: FuG11 plus FuG T2 100W,
Height: 1.75m (5ft 8in)	later FuG19 plus FuG12
Engine: Maybach HL42TUKRM	Armament: 1/2 x 7.92mm (0.3in) MG

▶ **15-cm Panzerwerfer 42 auf Selbsfahrlafette (SdKfz 4/1)**

10.Panzergrenadier-Division / Nebelwerfer-Regiment

The 10th Panzergrenadier Division's artillery assets were considerably beefed up in July 1943 for the Kursk offensive. Among the units attached was a Nebelwerfer regiment, which from April 1943 would have one self-propelled battery with eight armoured launchers.

Specifications

Crew: 3	Speed: 40km/h (24.9mph)
Weight: 7.8 tonnes (7.1 tons)	Range: 130km (80.8 miles)
Length: 6.0m (19ft 8in)	Radio: FuG Spr Ger 'f'
Width: 2.2m (7ft 3in)	Armament: 1 x 10-tube 150mm (5.9in)
Height: 2.5m (8ft 2in)	rocket launcher
Engine: Opel 3.6L 6-cylinder petrol	

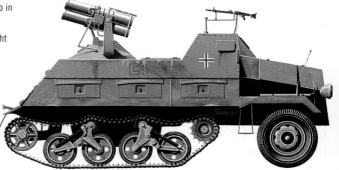

▶ **Leichter Schützenpanzerwagen (SdKfz 250/1)**

10.Panzer-Aufklärungs-Abteilung

Based on the chassis of the Demag D7 1-tonne (0.98-ton) half-track (SdKfz 10), the SdKfz 250 entered production in 1941. Most of these vehicles were used by the Aufklärungs, or reconnaissance, units of Panzer and Panzergrenadier divisions.

Specifications

Crew: 2 plus 4 troops	Engine: Maybach HL42TRKM 6-cylinder (100hp)
Weight: 5.9 tonnes (5.38 tons)	Speed: 60km/h (37mph)
Length: 4.61m (15ft 1in)	Range: 300km (186 miles)
Width: 1.95m (6ft 5in)	Radio: FuG Spr Ger 'f'
Height: 1.66m (5ft 5in)	Armament: 1 x 7.92mm (0.3in) MG

▶ **Mittlerer Schützenpanzerwagen (7.5-cm) (SdKfz 251/9 Ausf C)**

41.Panzergrenadier-Regiment

Designed to provide fire support for armoured infantry companies, the SdKfz 251/9 mounted the short-barrelled 7.5cm (3in) tank weapon made available by the large-scale upgunning of the Panzer IV in 1942 and 1943.

Specifications

Crew: 3	Speed: 53km/h (33mph)
Weight: 9.4 tonnes (8.53 tons)	Range: 300km (186 miles)
Length: 5.98m (19ft 7in)	Radio: FuG Spr Ger 'f'
Width: 2.83m (9ft 4in)	Armament: 1 x 75mm (3in) KwK L/24
Height: 2.07m (6ft 10in)	gun
Engine: Maybach HL42TUKRM	

10th Panzergrenadier Division

JUNE 1943 – AUGUST 1944

In the autumn of 1943, the renamed 10th Panzergrenadier Division had been assigned to Army Group South, serving with the Fourth and Eighth Armies at Poltava and Kremenchug.

OVER THE WINTER, THE DIVISION suffered heavily in the fighting around Kiev and in the retreat across the Dnieper. At the beginning of 1944, the *Wehrmacht* was pressed back along its entire front line in the East. In April 1944, the division was assigned to *Heeresgruppe Südukraine* in Bessarabia.

By May 1944, the army group had been pushed back to the pre-war Romanian frontier. A hastily formed defensive line on the Dniester was penetrated in two places by Soviet bridgeheads, but in June the fighting eased, allowing both sides to regroup.

During this period, Army Group South Ukraine lost much of its armour, transferred to the northern central fronts in response to numerous Red Army advances. The only armoured formations left to the army group were the 13th Panzer Division and 10th Panzergrenadier Division as well as the 1st Romanian Armoured Division.

As part of the series of Soviet summer offensives, the 2nd and 3rd Ukrainian Fronts mounted a major

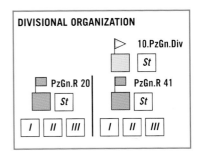

DIVISIONAL ORGANIZATION

10.PzGn.Div — St

PzGn.R 20 — St — I | II | III

PzGn.R 41 — St — I | II | III

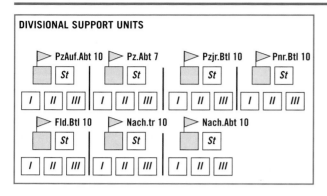

DIVISIONAL SUPPORT UNITS

offensive in August, aimed at encircling the German Sixth Army and parts of the Eighth, which included the 10th Panzergrenadier Division. The initial Soviet breakthrough was 40km (24.9 miles) deep by the evening of 21 August. By the 23rd, 13th Panzer Division had been destroyed and Sixth Army had been encircled to a depth of 100km (62 miles). The Red Army prevented any sort of coherent German retreat into Hungary. Most units, including 10th Panzergrenadier Division, were destroyed, only small remnants managing to escape the encirclement.

▶ m.E.Pkw Kommandeurwagen (Kfz 21)

10.Panzergrenadier-Division / Stab

Based on a standard medium car chassis, the Kfz 21 was used by senior commanders in the field.

Specifications

Crew: 6 including staff	Engine: Steyr 3.5L 8-cylinder petrol
Weight: 2.5 tonnes (2.28 tons)	(85hp)
Length: 5.8m (19ft)	Speed: 90km/h (56mph)
Width: 2.03m (6ft 8in)	Range: 400km (248 miles)
Height: 2.32m (7ft 9in)	Radio: None

▶ le.Zgkw U(f) Type P107

10.Panzergrenadier-Division

Following the fall of France in 1940, the *Wehrmacht* pressed large numbers of French halftracks into service. The P107 series was manufactured by Citroen-Kergresse and by Unic.

Specifications

Crew: 2	Engine: four-cylinder petrol (55/60bhp)
Weight: 4 tonnes (3.9 tons)	Speed: 45km/h (28mph)
Length: 4.85m (15ft 10in)	Range: 400km (248miles)
Width: 1.8m (5ft 10in)	Payload: 1000kg (2204lbs)
Height: 2.28m (7ft 6in)	

▶ Krankenkraftwagen Opel Blitz Typ A (Kfz 31)

10.Sanitäts-Kompanie (mot)

The 4x4 variant of the Opel Blitz was known as the *Allrad* (all-wheel drive). The Opel plant at Brandenburg/Havel completed as many as 25,000 vehicles, which were fitted with a wide range of bodies, including the ambulance variant seen here.

Specifications

Crew: 1	Engine: Opel 6-cylinder petrol
Weight: 3.29 tonnes (3 tons)	(73.5hp)
Length: 6.02m (19ft 9in)	Speed: 80km/h (50mph)
Width: 2.27m (7ft 5in)	Range: 410km (255 miles)
Height: 2.18m (7ft 2in)	

▶ **Gross Nachrichten-Kraftwagen Krupp L3H 163 (Kfz 63)**

10.Panzergrenadier-Division / attached to 17.Armee

The Kfz 63 was a large, six-wheel communications van used at divisional level and above by headquarters troops.

Specifications

Crew: 8	Engine: Hwa526D 6.2L diesel
Weight: 5.5 tonnes (5 tons)	Speed: 70km/h (43.4mph)
Length: 6.00m (19ft 8in)	Range: 330km (205 miles)
Width: 2.00m (6ft 6in)	Radio: Various, depending on
Height: 2.76m (9ft 1in)	deployment

Final destruction

JANUARY–MAY 1945

Late in 1944, the remnants of the 10th Panzergrenadier Division were re-formed into a *Kampfgruppe*, losing *Panzer-Bataillon* 110 and *Panzergrenadier-Regiment* 41 in the process.

IN JANUARY 1945, the 10th Panzergrenadier Division *Kampfgruppe* returned to the front, joining Seventeenth Army at Radom in Poland, where it was assigned to XXXXVIII Corps.

The unit was almost immediately thrown into the vicious fighting around Kielce along with elements of XXIV Panzer Corps from Fourth Panzer Army – the 16th and 17th Panzer Divisions and the 20th Panzergrenadier Division. The corps was pulling out to the northwest along the Kielce-Mniów road. The 10th Panzergrenadier Division *Kampfgruppe* was positioned at Skarzysko Kamienna to cover the withdrawal, before being moved to new positions at Ruski Bród.

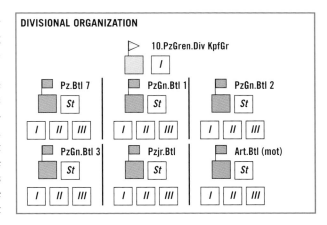

DIVISIONAL ORGANIZATION

10.PzGren.Div KpfGr

I

Pz.Btl 7 — St — I II III

PzGn.Btl 1 — St — I II III

PzGn.Btl 2 — St — I II III

PzGn.Btl 3 — St — I II III

Pzjr.Btl — St — I II III

Art.Btl (mot) — St — I II III

War in Poland

By late-war standards, this was a major concentration of German forces, with about 60,000 troops. Four infantry divisions, the 10th Division *Kampfgruppe*, together with the remnants of around a dozen independent regiments and battalions had fomed defensive positions by 18 January, awaiting the inevitable Soviet attack.

Marshal Konev ordered the Soviet Third Guards Army to reduce the pocket. On the 19th, a heavy artillery barrage preceded the attack by Soviet tanks. Over the next two days, the Soviets pressed inexorably forward. As the German defences collapsed, the survivors broke up into battalion or regimental groups that began to retreat towards Gowarczów. Losses, mainly to artillery, were exceptionally heavy. Among the 10th *Kampfgruppe's* casualties was its commander, *Oberst* Alexander Vial.

Once again, the 10th Panzergrenadier Division had been destroyed. Survivors were sent to Silesia in February, where the division was again partially reconstituted. In April, it was sent to join First Panzer Army in Bohemia, finally surrendering to the Soviets in Czechoslovakia early in May 1945, at the end of the war.

▼ 7th Panzer Battalion

As rebuilt in February 1945. The 7th Panzer Battalion had been assigned to the 10th Panzergrenadier Division after it was re-formed in October 1944.

Battalion *Stab*

1st *Kompanie*

2nd *Kompanie*

3rd *Kompanie*

4th *Kompanie*

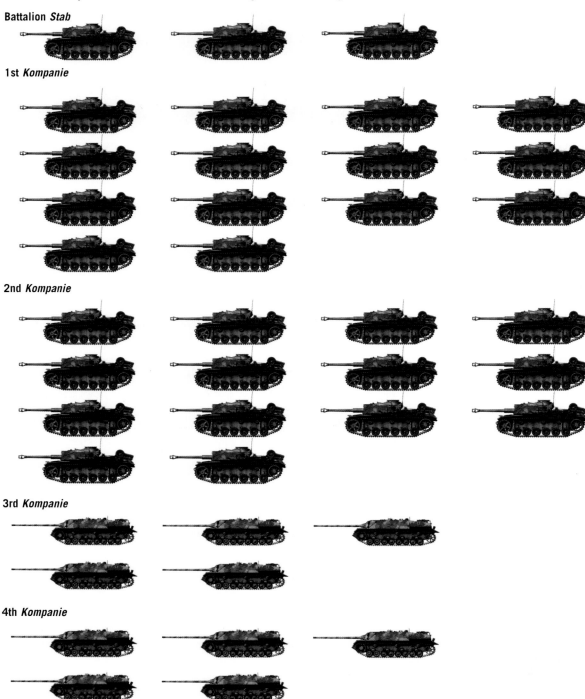

▲ Panzer IV/70 (V) (SdKfz 162/1)

10.Pz.Gren.Div Kampfgruppe / 7.Pz.Bn / 3.Kompanie

The 10th Panzergrenadier Division received 10 of these powerful tank-destroyers in February 1945.

Specifications

Crew: 4	Speed: 38km/h (23.6mph)
Weight: 27.6 tonnes (25 tons)	Range: 210km (130.5 miles)
Length: 6.7m (22ft 0in)	Radio: FuG 15 and FuG 160
Width: 2.27m (7ft 5in)	Armament: 1 x 75mm (3in) PaK L/48
Height: 1.85m (6ft 0in)	anti-tank gun
Engine: Maybach HI120TRM	

▶ 7.5-cm Sturmgeschütz 40 Ausf G (SdKfz 142/1)

10.Pz.Gren.Div Kampfgruppe / 7.Pz.Bn / 1.Kompanie

Late-model StuGs with long guns and side-armour were often used in place of tanks, being cheaper and quicker to build.

Specifications

Crew: 4	Speed: 40km/h (24.9mph)
Weight: 26.3 tonnes (23.9 tons)	Range: 155km (96.3 miles)
Length: 6.77m (22ft 2in)	Radio: FuG 15 and FuG 16
Width: 2.95m (9ft 8in)	Armament: 1 x 75mm (3in)
Height: 2.16m (7ft 0in)	StuG L/48 cannon
Engine: Maybach HI120TRM	

◀ Schwere Panzerspähwagen (SdKfz 234/1)

110.Panzer-Aufklärungs-Abteilung

The replacement for the earlier eight-wheeled SdKfz 231, the SdKfz 234 series was easier to build and had much better protection. The 2cm (0.7in) armed SdKfz 234/1 entered service on the Eastern Front in the summer of 1944.

Specifications

Crew: 4	Speed: 80km/h (50mph)
Weight: 11.56 tonnes (10.47 tons)	Range: 900km (559 miles)
Length: 6.0m (19ft 8in)	Radio: FuG Spr Ger 'a'
Width: 2.40m (7ft 10.5in)	Armament: 1 x 20mm (0.7in) KwK
Height: 2.10m (6ft 10.5in)	L/55 cannon; 1 x 7.92 mm (0.3in)
Engine: Tatra 103 12-cylinder (220hp)	MG (coaxial)

13th Infantry Division (motorized)

The 13th Infantry Division was one of the German Army's first motorized infantry divisions. It was officially formed as a basic infantry division at Magdeburg in October 1934.

ORIGINALLY KNOWN AS THE *Wehrgauleitung Magdeburg*, it was given the cover name *Infanterieführer* IV to hide its existence, which was illegal under the terms of the Treaty of Versailles. During the transition period, the *Reichswehr Wehrkreiskommandos* that had controlled the old divisions were upgraded to corps, and the commanders and divisional staffs all moved up to corps level. Without staffs, it made little sense to simply rename the original seven divisions, especially when they would be broken up to provide the core units for the new divisions of the greatly expanded *Wehrmacht Heeres*.

Twenty-one new divisions were created, with each of the seven original *Wehrgauleitung* that controlled the *Reichswehr* divisions being split into three. Each *Wehrgauleitung* was named after the city in which it made its headquarters. These 21 *Wehrgauleitungen* were the true foundation for the first divisions of the new German Army. The regimental units of the *Reichswehr* divisions were used to form the organic units of the new divisions.

Troops for the new formation came through the expansion of the 9.*(Preussisches) Infanterie-Regiment* of the Berlin-based 3rd Division of the *Reichswehr* and the 12.*Infanterie-Regiment* of the *Reichswehr's* 4th Division, from Dresden. The divisional command structure was all new, however.

Wehrmacht is announced

Once the Nazis announced that Germany was throwing off the shackles of Versailles, the need for cover names for *Wehrmacht* units (which had been in clandestine existence for more than a year) was gone, and *Infanterieführer* IV was given its true name as the 13.*Infanterie-Division* on 15 October 1935.

Divisional History	Formed
Wehrgauleitung Magdeburg/Infanteriefürher IV	1934
13.Infanterie-Division	1935
13.Infanterie-Division (mot)	1937
13.Panzer-Division	1940

INSIGNIA

The Sunwheel was an ancient runic symbol sacred to many pagan societies. It was used by the 13th Division both when an infantry and a Panzer unit.

Commanders

Generalleutnant Moritz von Faber du Faur
September 1939

General der Infanterie Paul Otto
September 1939 – November 1939

Generalleutnant Friedrich-Wilhelm von Rotkirch und Panthen
November 1939 – October 1940

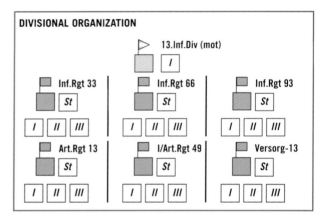

DIVISIONAL ORGANIZATION

13.Inf.Div (mot)
I

Inf.Rgt 33 — St — I | II | III
Inf.Rgt 66 — St — I | II | III
Inf.Rgt 93 — St — I | II | III
Art.Rgt 13 — St — I | II | III
I/Art.Rgt 49 — St — I | II | III
Versorg-13 — St — I | II | III

The development of the Panzer arm in this period meant that it was necessary to introduce motorized divisions that would be able to keep up with the German Army's new armoured spearheads. The 13th Infantry Division was motorized in 1937, and was redesignated as the 13.*Infanterie-Division (mot)* on 2 October of that year.

Motorization

Trucks and other vehicles transporting soldiers, towing guns, and carrying equipment and supplies greatly increase the mobility of infantry units. Motorization provides no tactical advantage in actual combat, because softskin vehicles are vulnerable to artillery and smallarms fire, but it ensures that infantry and their support weapons can get to the battlefield much more quickly.

▶ **France, 1940**

As with most armed forces, the *Wehrmacht* was unprepared for the rapid development in armoured warfare. The standard *Heer* anti-tank weapon in 1939 was the 3.7cm (1.5in) Pak. This was a good enough weapon for its time, but by 1940 its utility was questionable, and by 1941 it was obsolete.

▶ **Leichter Zugkraftwagen 3t (SdKfz 11)**

Artillerie Regiment 13 / I Bataillon / 1.Batterie

The SdKfz 11 was a Hanomag design introduced in 1937. It was the standard three-tonne (2.9-ton) prime-mover, and provided the chassis for the SdKfz 251.

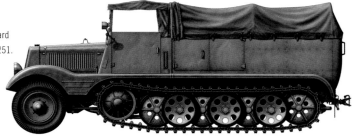

Specifications

Crew: 1 plus 8 troops	Height: 1.62m (5ft 4in)
Weight: 7.1 tonnes (6.46 tons)	Engine: 6-cylinder petrol (100hp)
Length: 5.48m (18ft 0in)	Speed: 53km/h (32.9mph)
Width: 1.82m (5ft 11.5in)	Range: 122km (75.8 miles)

 # Poland and France
SEPTEMBER 1939 – MAY 1940

The 13th Infantry Division (mot) was brought from peacetime levels to full combat strength in July and August of 1939, ready for the invasion of Poland.

THE 13TH DIVISION WAS ASSIGNED TO the XIV Corps, part of General Walter von Reichenau's powerful Tenth Army. As a key unit in General Karl von Rundstedt's Army Group South, Tenth Army formed up in Silesia and occupied Bohemia, from where it would form the southern arm of the huge German pincer movement that would encircle and destroy the Polish field armies. Driving eastwards towards Krakow and Warsaw, the leading units would turn north to meet Guderian's Panzers, which formed the spearhead of General von Bock's Army Group North.

By 5 September, Reichenau's spearheads were less than 50km (31 miles) from Warsaw. The 13th Division fought hard to support the Panzers, but its reputation was severely damaged when on 8 and 9 September, troops from the division massacred civilians in the village of Drzewica, going on to attack medical columns clearly marked with red crosses and then using other civilians as human shields while attacking Polish army positions.

After the Polish campaign, the division was withdrawn into the General Staff Reserve, refitting and recuperating at Dillenburg, about 80km

I Bataillon, Infanterie-Regiment 66 (mot)	Strength
HQ:	
motorcycles	4
sidecars	2
cars	7
light trucks	1
three-tonne (2.9-ton) trucks	4
Infantry companies:	3
motorcycles	3
sidecars	2
cars	1
trucks towing AT gun	1
three-tonne trucks	3
Heavy company:	
motorcycles	7
sidecars	5
cars	4
light trucks	1
medium trucks	4
medium trucks towing Pak36	4

▲ **France, 1940**

Germans advance across a railway line. Motorization meant that men could be carried to the battlefield more quickly, but once there they dismounted to fight.

fought at Amiens before driving through central France towards Lyons.

The division returned to Germany to refit at the end of July, joining Army Group B's reserve in Poland in September.

Conversion to Panzer division

On 11 October 1940, the 13th Infantry Division (mot) was upgraded to become the 13th Panzer Division. At the end of 1940, it was occupied with forming up and re-equipping in Romania, serving as a trials and training unit in the first months of 1941. In May it was assigned to XXXXVIII Corps, part of 1.*Panzergruppe*, which was a spearhead formation for von Rundstedt's Army Group South in the opening stages of Operation *Barbarossa*. Over the next six months, the division was to play its part in the battles

(50 miles) to the east of Cologne. In May, it was transferred to von Rundstedt's Army Group A, where it remained in reserve for the surprise German offensive through the Ardennes. Thrown into battle at Laon, it took part in the drive towards the Channel, reaching the coast at Calais.

Once the British had been forced off the Continent at Dunkirk, the 13th Division was transferred to Kleist's *Panzergruppe*, part of Army Group B, for the Battle of France. The division

The *Tascheinwerfer*, or blackout headlight, was fitted to all German vehicles. This example bears the tactical symbols for a motorized infantry platoon attached to a Panzer division, but it was a standard symbol that would have been carried by all such units in motorized formations.

▼ **Morris Umbauwagen Kfz 12**

Artillerie Regiment 13 / I Bataillon / 1.Batterie

German victories before 1941 netted a huge stock of captured vehicles, which were pressed into military service. *Umbau* means altered or converted, referring to the German military bodywork fitted to this British light truck.

Specifications

Crew: 1	Height: 1.85m (6ft 1in)
Weight: 0.99 tonnes (0.9 tons)	Engine: four-cylinder, 3.5 litre (213ci)
Length: 4.80m (15ft 9in)	Speed: 75km/h (47mph)
Width: 1.80m (5ft 11in)	Range: 225km (136 miles)

at Uman, Kiev and Rostov. Over the winter, it was thrown into the defensive battles at Taganrog, before returning to Rostov for the opening of the summer offensive towards the Caucasus.

After the catastrophe at Stalingrad, the division was part of the general German retreat from the Caucasus, fighting in the battles around Krivoi Rog and Cherkassy over the winter. In the summer of

1944, it was with Army Group South Ukraine, where it was destroyed in the Soviet summer offensive.

In October 1944, the 13th Panzer Division was rebuilt in eastern Hungary. In January 1945, attached to the IX SS Corps, it was thrown into the battle to relieve Budapest, where it was again destroyed. Survivors were used in the formation of the short-lived *Feldherrnhalle* 2 Panzer division.

▶ Leichte Lkw Opel Blitz 2.0-12 (1t)

66.Inf.Reg (mot) / I Bataillon / 2.Kompanie

Light trucks like this 1-tonne (0.98-ton) Opel were used by a wide variety of motorized units, between two and four being assigned to the logistics train of virtually every kind of company in a motorized division.

Specifications

Crew: 1	Engine: Opel 1920cc 6-cylinder petrol
Weight: 3.29 tonnes (3 tons)	(36hp)
Length: 6.02m (19ft 9in)	Speed: 80km/h (50mph)
Width: 2.27m (7ft 5in)	Range: 410km (255 miles)
Height: 2.18m (7ft 2in)	Radio: None

◀ Schwere Panzerspähwagen 6-Rad (SdKfz 231)

13.Aufklarungs-Bataillon / Spähpanzerwagen-Kompanie

The armoured car company of the motorized reconnaissance battalion generally had three light platoons and one heavy platoon, which was equipped with SdKfz 231s.

Specifications

Crew: 4	(60-80hp)
Weight: 5.9 tonnes (5.35 tons)	Speed: 70km/h (43mph)
Length: 5.57m (18 ft 7in)	Range: 300km (186 miles)
Width: 1.82m (5ft 11.5in)	Radio: FuG Spr Ger 'a'
Height: 2.25m (7ft 4.5in)	Armament: 1 x 20mm (0.7in)
Engine: Daimler-Benz, Büssing-	cannon; 1 x coaxial 7.62mm
NAG or Magirus petrol	(0.3in) MG

▼ 15-cm schwerer Infanteriegeschütz 33

33.Inf.Reg.(mot) / 14.Infanteriegeschütz-Kompanie

Infantry battalions were provided with their own artillery equipment for close-range fire support. The infantry gun company was equipped with four light 7.5cm (3in) guns, and a pair of much heavier 15cm (5.9in) sIG 33 weapons. Introduced into service in 1936, the sIG 33 fired a 29kg (64lb) shell out to 4700m (5140 yards). Generally firing high-explosive shells, it could also fire anti-armour grenades. However, these had to be muzzle-loaded, and were very inaccurate; they were used mainly against fortifications.

Specifications

Crew: 5	Calibre: 149.1mm (5.9in)
Weight: 1.75 tonnes (1.6 tons)	Muzzle Velocity: 20m/s (790fps)
Length: 1.64m (64.57in)	Range: 5504m (6000 yards)
Ammunition: High explosive or smoke	

14th Infantry Division (motorized)

Formed as a standard infantry formation in Saxony in October 1934, the 14th Division was originally given the title of *Wehrgauleitung Leipzig*.

As PART OF THE DECEPTION plan employed by the National Socialist government, intended to mask the expansion of the armed forces, the formation was given the cover name of *Kommandant von Leipzig*. The nucleus of the division's regiments was provided by the expansion of the 11.*(Sächsisches) Infanterie-Regiment*, which had formed part of the *Reichswehr*'s 4th Infantry Division. It took on its true identity as the 14.*Infanterie-Division* when the *Wehrmacht* was finally brought out of the shadows in October 1935.

For the next four years, the division remained at its peacetime strength, with some of its constituent units being understrength and others existing in cadre form only. In the summer of 1939, it was brought up to full combat strength, reserves having been called up and full equipment being issued.

Invasion of Poland

For *Fall Weiss*, the invasion of Poland, the 14th Infantry Division was ordered to join Reichenau's Tenth Army in southern Silesia. There it became part of *General der Kavallerie* Erich Höpner's XVI Corps, where it served alongside the 1st and 4th Panzer Divisions and the 31st Infantry Division.

XVI Corps, led by the 1st and 4th Panzer Divisions, drove northeast into Poland, rapidly

penetrating towards Warsaw. Between 16 and 20 September, they stopped and then destroyed a Polish counterattack along the River Bzura. Soon, most of the Polish Army had been enveloped by a double encirclement, and resistance came to an end.

In October 1939, the 14th Division was pulled out of Poland, and while its units made combat losses good it was assigned to Fourth Army's reserve as part of Army Goup B in the Eiffel Mountains. In November, the formation was assigned to the XVI Corps of General Walter von Reichenau's Sixth Army,

INSIGNIA

As with most of the early formations of the new *Wehrmacht*, the 14th Division's identification symbol was a simple, easy-to-identify geometric form.

Commanders

Generalleutnant Peter Weyer
September 1939 – June 1940

Generalmajor Lothar Rendulic
June–October 1940

Generalleutnant Friedrich Fürst
October 1940 – June 1942

Generalleutnant Heinrich Wosch
June–September 1942

Generalleutnant Walther Krause
October–December 1942

Generalleutnant Rudolf Holste
January–May 1943

Generalleutnant Hermann Flörke
May 1943 – December 1944

Generalleutnant Erich Schneider
December 1944 – May 1945

DIVISIONAL ORGANIZATION

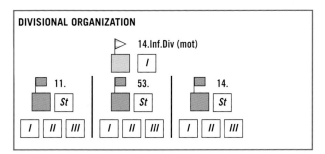

Divisional History	Formed
Wehrgauleitung Leipzig/Kommandant von Leipzig	1934
14.Infanterie-Division	1935
14.Infanterie-Division (mot)	1940
14.Infanterie-Division (*de-motorized*)	1943

▲ **Poland, 1939**
Designed as a light artillery tractor, the distinctive Krupp L2H43 and L2H143 light trucks were often used as personnel carriers in motorized units.

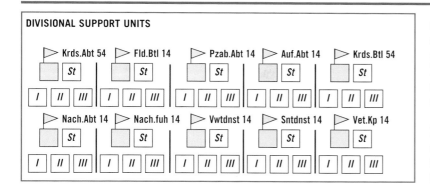

DIVISIONAL SUPPORT UNITS

assault), Liège and Namur. Initial stiff British resistance to the attack of XI Corps along the line of the Dyle River faded as German advances elsewhere forced the Allies to retreat to Dunkirk.

In June, the division remained in Flanders while German forces realigned to continue the offensive into France. Between July and September 1940, the division performed occupation duties in Belgium and Holland, coming under the control of Army Group C.

In September 1940, the division returned to Germany to become fully motorized, and on 15 October the formation officially became the 14. *Infanterie-Division (mot)*.

transferring to XI Corps in the same army in January 1940. During the invasion of the Low Countries, the Sixth Army formed the left flank of Bock's Army Group B, which attacked into the Low Countries in order to lure the British and French northwards into Belgium, leaving their rear vulnerable to Runstedt's attack through the Ardennes.

Sixth Army attacked past the Belgian fortifications at Eben Emael (knocked out in a glider-borne

The stylized straight-armed version of the Iron Cross, the *Balkenkreuz*, was used on vehicles and aircraft. Later in the war, shorter variants with thicker white bands became more common.

▶ **Leichte Panzerspähwagen (2-cm) (SdKfz 222)**

54.Kradschützen-Bn / Spähpanzerwagen-Ko / 1 leichte SpPzw-Zug

The 54th Motorcycle Battalion had one armoured car company and a light armoured car platoon in addition to three motorcycle infantry companies.

Specifications

Crew: 3	Speed: 85km/h (52.8mph)
Weight: 5.3 tonnes (4.8 tons)	Range: 300km (186 miles)
Length: 4.8m (15ft 8in)	Radio: FuG Spr Ger 'a'
Width: 1.95m (6ft 5in)	Armament: 1 x 20mm (0.7in) KwK 30 L/55
Height: 2.00m (6ft 7in)	cannon; 1 x 7.92mm (0.3in) MG (coaxial)
Engine: Horch 3.5L or 3.8L petrol	

▲ **Mittlerer Zugkraftwagen 5t mit 8.8-cm Flak 18 (SdKfz 7)**

14.Art.Regt (mot) / 14.Flak.Bn. / schwere Flak-Batterie

By 1942, standard equipment for army anti-aircraft battalions included one heavy battery with a single platoon of four 8.8cm (3.5in) Flak 18 anti-aircraft guns. They were usually towed by the five-tonne (4.9-ton) SdKfz 7 half-track.

Specifications

Crew: 2	Engine: Maybach HL 62 6-cylinder petrol
Weight: 1.16 tonnes (1.06 tons)	(140hp)
Length: 6.85m (20ft 3in)	Speed: 50km/h (31mph)
Width: 2.40m (7ft 10.5in)	Range: 250km (156 miles)
Height: 2.62m (8ft 7.1in)	Radio: None

✠ Eastern Front
JUNE 1941 – AUGUST 1943

The 14th Division was motorized in October 1940. In the process, it lost *Infanterie-Regiment* 101, which was transferred to the newly formed 18th Panzer Division.

THE DIVISION STAYED ON GERMAN soil for the next eight months, initially as part of Eleventh Army. Motorization was essentially complete by the end of March 1941. In May of that year, the 14th Infantry Division (mot) was assigned as a reserve unit for 3.*Panzergruppe*. Commanded by *Generaloberst* Hermann Hoth, 3.*Panzergruppe* was a tank army in all but name, one of two such formations assigned to Army Group Centre for Operation *Barbarossa*.

The division remained in reserve for the first weeks of the invasion. In July, it was sent to the front to take part in the drive on Bialystock, Minsk and Smolensk. In October, it was involved in the battle for Vyasma, when three German armies destroyed the major Soviet force defending Moscow. As winter closed in, Hoth's Panzers pushed on towards Moscow, reaching Kalinin, northwest of the Soviet capital.

Soviet counteroffensive

Early in December, as the German offensive stalled in the ice, a Soviet counteroffensive forced the invaders back. The 14th Division found itself at Rzhev, in the north of a huge German salient penetrating Soviet-held territory. Elsewhere on the front, the Germans were forced back, but the Rzhev salient held.

For the next year and a half, the 14th Division fought around Rzhev. It was the scene of heavy fighting during the Red Army's Moscow

▸ **Schwere Panzerspähwagen 8-Rad (SdKfz 231)**

Pz. Rgt 1 / II Battalion / 5th Company / 2nd Zug / tank number 4

The heavy platoon of the armoured car company in a motorized division had three SdKfz 231 armoured cars and three SdKfz 232 radio cars.

Specifications

Crew: 4	petrol (150hp)
Weight: 9.1 tonnes (8.3 tons)	Speed: 85km/h (52.8mph)
Length: 5.85m (19ft 2in)	Range: 300km (186 miles)
Width: 2.20m (7ft 2.5in)	Radio: FuG Ger 'a'
Height: 2.35m (7ft 8in)	Armament: 1 x 20mm (0.7in)
Engine: Büssing-NAG 8-cylinder	cannon

▸ **Schwerer Einheits Personenkraftwagen Horch 40 (Kfz 18)**

11.Inf.Regt (mot) / Stab

The powerful 4x4 manufactured by Auto-Union and Horch was the *Wehrmacht*'s standard heavy car chassis. It was used as a troop transport, a field staff car, a light artillery tractor, and with van bodywork as an ambulance.

Specifications

Crew: 1	Engine: Horch 6-cylinder petrol (90hp)
Weight: 2.4 tonnes (2.2 tons)	Speed: 88km/h (55 mph)
Length: 4.44m (14 ft 7in)	Range: 400 km (250 miles)
Width: 1.68m (5ft 6in)	Radio: None usually fitted
Height: 1.73m (5ft 8in)	

counteroffensive in the winter of 1941/42, during Red Army offensives from July through early September 1942, and in the major attempt by the Red Army to pinch out the salient in November and December 1942. Fighting continued into 1943.

Upgrade, downgrade

Early in 1943, it was announced that the the 14th Division would be upgraded to Panzergrenadier status. Plans were put in motion, but before any concrete action could be taken, it was decided to de-motorize the division instead. After losing most of its motor transport, the division became the plain 14th Infantry Division in August/September 1943.

In September 1943, the division joined Ninth Army at Bryansk, transferring to the Third Panzer Army at Vitebsk a month later, where it would remain until May 1944. The division was withdrawn into reserve in June, and so avoided the destruction of Army Group Centre in the massive Soviet offensive of that summer. The 14th Infantry Division ended the war in East Prussia.

Kradschützen-Bataillon 54	Strength
HQ:	
motorcycles	4
sidecars	2
field cars	1
Reconnaissance platoons:	3
motorcycles	1
sidecars	4
field cars	2
Heavy platoon:	
motorcycles	1
sidecars	8
field cars	2
light trucks (Kfz 70)	3

The use of camouflage often meant that the standard black-and-white *Balkenkreuz* was made less obvious, and units would resort to field expedients such as overpainting the cross white to increase visibility.

▶ **Leichter Schützenpanzerwagen 2-cm (SdKfz 250/9)**

14.Panzer-Aufklärungs-Abteilung

In January 1943, the 54th Motorcycle Battalion was renamed as the 14.*Panzer-Aufklärungs-Abteilung*. Later that year, the reconnaissance variant of the SdKfz 250 began replacing the light SdKfz 222 armoured car.

Specifications

Crew: 3	Speed: 60km/h (37mph)
Weight: 6.9 tonnes (6.3 tons)	Range: 320km (199 miles)
Length: 4.56m (14ft 11.5in)	Radio: FuG Spr Ger 'f'
Width: 1.95m (6ft 5in)	Armament: 1 x 20mm (0.7in) KwK 30/38 L/55
Height: 2.16m (7ft 1in)	cannon; 1 x 7.92mm (0.3in) MG (coaxial)
Engine: Maybach HL42TRKM 6-cylinder (100hp)	

▶ **3.7-cm Flak auf mittlerer Zugkraftwagen 8t (SdKfz 7/2)**

14.Inf.Div / 14.Art.Regt

Late in the war, self-propelled Flak units were assigned to most divisions.

Specifications

Crew: 7	6-cylinder (140hp)
Weight: 1.16 tonnes	Speed: 50km/h (31mph)
(1.06 tons)	Range: 250km (156 miles)
Length: 6.55m (21ft 6in)	Armament: Twin 37mm
Width: 2.40m (7ft 10.5in)	(1.5in) Flak 36/37/43 L/89
Height: 3.20m (10ft 6in)	
Engine: Maybach HL62TUK	

Chapter 2

Wartime Motorized Divisions

With the outbreak of war, demand for
mobile formations increased as the *Wehrmacht* expanded.
Initially, the growth was provided by conversion of existing
infantry divisions, many being motorized after the French
campaign at the end of 1940, but a number of new
formations were created, including the elite
Grossdeutschland Division, which emerged from the
expansion of ceremonial and guard units. By 1943, many
of the motorized divisions had become powerful armoured
formations in their own right. To reflect that fact, they
were redesignated as Panzergrenadier, or
armoured infantry, divisions.

◀ **Battle preparations**
German soldiers prepare and fix equipment in the days before the Kursk offensive, July 1943.
Here, a gunner cleans the barrel of a 7.5cm (3in) gun mounted on the front of an Sd Kfz 251/9 halftrack.
The gun provided fire support for a reconnaissance battalion.

Grossdeutschland Division

Grossdeutschland – Greater Germany – was the Nazi ideal of a unified European Germanic state. The name was used for the German Army's premier fighting formation.

THE ORIGINS OF THE *Grossdeutschland* Division went back to the early 1920s. In the unstable political climate of post-war Germany, the *Reichswehr* established a guard unit for Berlin in 1921. Its primary purpose was to defend the Weimar Republic from revolutionaries, but it was also the country's main military ceremonial unit. Disbanded within weeks, the guard unit was almost immediately re-established as the *Kommando der Wachtruppe*. It comprised seven infantry companies, one from each of the seven *Reichswehr* divisions. Based at Moabit Barracks, the *Kommando* performed a daily changing of the guard ceremony for the public.

Adolf Hitler and the Nazis came to power in 1933, but in spite of the rise of the *Leibstandarte-SS* as the *Führer's* personal guard force, the *Wachtruppe* remained in place. Renamed *Wachtruppe Berlin* in 1934, the unit received an eighth company in 1936.

In June 1937, the unit was again renamed, this time to *Wachregiment Berlin*. The recruitment system inherited from the *Reichswehr* was changed, as there were now 21 divisions in the rapidly expanding *Wehrmacht*. Individual soldiers were now posted to the unit for six-month tours of duty, but they still came from all parts of the country. As the *Wachregiment Berlin* provided escorts and honour guards for state visits and major

Commanders

Oberst Wilhelm-Hunert von Stockhausen
June 1939 – August 1941

Oberst Gerhard Graf von Schwerin (acting)
May 1940 (acting)

Oberst Walther Hoernlein
August 1941 – March 1942

Generalmajor Walther Hoernlein
April 1942 – January 1944

General der Panzertruppen Hermann Balck
(temporary) *March–June 1943*

Generalleutnant Hasso von Manteuffel

February 1944 – September 1944

Generalmajor Karl Lorenz
September 1944 – January 1945

Generalmajor Hellmuth Mäder
February 1945 – May 1945

(Grossdeutschland Panzerkorps)

General der Panzertruppen Dietrich von Saucken
November 1944 – March 1945

General der Panzertruppen Georg Jauer
March–April 1945

INSIGNIA

Grossdeutschland infantrymen were distinguished by bearing a script version of the division's 'GD' insignia on their shoulder straps in place of the numbers carried by other troops. However, the vehicle insignia carried through World War II was different: the simple outline of another German military icon, the *Stahlhelm*, or steel helmet.

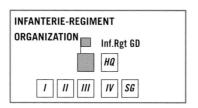

INFANTERIE-REGIMENT ORGANIZATION

Inf.Rgt GD

HQ

| I | II | III | IV | SG |

Divisional History	Formed
Wachregiment Berlin	1921
Kommando der Wachtruppe	1921
Wachtruppe Berlin	1934
Wachregiment Berlin	1937
Infanterie-Regiment Grossdeutschland	1939
Infanterie-Division Grossdeutschland (mot)	1942
Panzergrenadier-Division Grossdeutschland	1943
Panzerkorps Grossdeutschland	1944

▲ **Training**

In this training photograph, an *Unterfeldwebel* (sergeant) from the *Grossdeutschland* regiment with full-helmet camouflage keeps watch for 'enemy' movements.

events like the Olympic Games, individuals posted to the unit were picked for their appearance.

The *Wachregiment* played no part in Germany's military operations before 1939. In January of that year, the *Führer* personally ordered that the *Wachregiment* be renamed as the *Infanterie-Regiment Grossdeutschland*. The unit was officially activated on 14 June 1939, and the occasion was marked by a parade through the streets of the capital. However, the regiment was still working up when Germany invaded Poland. The unit's combat debut came in France in May 1940. Attached to Kleist's *Panzergruppe*, it saw action in the Ardennes and in the Meuse crossing. Near the town of Stonne, the regiment acquitted itself well in heavy fighting with French armoured forces. It also performed well against the British tanks at Arras and in closing the Dunkirk pocket. Transferred south to join the attack across the Seine, it had reached Lyon by the time of the French surrender in June.

▸ Mittlerer Lkw Henschel 33D1

Infanterie-Regiment Grossdeutschland

Motorized infantry formations were basically truck-mounted, using their vehicles as 'battle taxis' to get them into the battle zone but dismounting to fight as regular infantry when actually in combat.

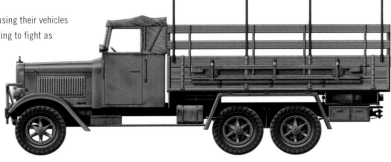

Specifications

Crew: 1	Engine: 10.7 litre (650ci),
Weight: 6.1 tonnes (6 tons)	six-cylinder petrol (100hp)
Length: 7.4m (24ft)	Speed: 60km/h (37mph)
Width: 2.25m (7ft 4in)	Payload: 3 tonnes (2.95 tons) or
Height: 3.2m (10ft 6in)	18 troops

▸ Protz Kw Krupp L2H143 (Kfz 69)

Infanterie-Regiment Grossdeutschland

With its 3.3-litre engine powering the rear four wheels, the Krupp L3H143 was more than powerful enough to tow light artillery or Flak guns. The characteristic nose gave rise to its nickname of 'Krupp Schnauzer'.

Specifications

Crew: 2	Engine: Krupp 3.3L 4-cylinder (60hp)
Weight: 2.45 tonnes (2.23 tons)	Speed: 70km/h (43mph)
Length: 5.10m (16ft 8in)	Range: 450km (280 miles)
Width: 1.93m (6ft 4in)	Radio: None
Height: 1.96m (6ft 5in)	

▸ Mittlerer geländigänger Lkw A-Typ Opel Blitz 3.6 6700A 3t

Infanterie-Regiment Grossdeutschland

Two-wheel-drive standard S-Type trucks like this Opel Blitz were introduced under the Schell programme of 1938. Effective on roads, they lacked off-road capability for which the 4x4 A-Type trucks were developed.

Specifications

Crew: 1	Engine: Opel 6-cylinder petrol
Weight: 3.29 tonnes (3 tons)	(73.5hp)
Length: 6.02m (19ft 9in)	Speed: 80km/h (50mph)
Width: 2.27m (7ft 5in)	Range: 410km (255 miles)
Height: 2.18m (7ft 2in)	Radio: None

The Balkans and *Barbarossa*
APRIL–SEPTEMBER 1941

Following its participation in the German victory parade in Paris, the regiment was expected to take part in Operation *Seelöwe* (Sealion), the abortive invasion of England.

AFTER *SEELÖWE* WAS CALLED OFF, the regiment was moved to the South of France in preparation for Operation *Felix*, the planned invasion of Gibraltar. However, Hitler could not persuade the wily Spanish dictator, Francisco Franco, to support his plans. After the cancellation of *Felix*, the *Grossdeutschland* was moved east to Romania to take part in the Yugoslav campaign then in progress.

Grossdeutschland remained under General Ewald von Kleist's command, forming part of his First Panzer Group alongside the SS Division *Reich* (later to become better known as the SS Panzer Division *Das Reich*). Kleist's *Panzergruppe* – in essence, an armoured army – would attack westwards from southern Romania and northern Bulgaria, directed towards Belgrade.

Advance to Belgrade

As Kleist's Panzers drove west, the *Grossdeutschland* Regiment raced the hard-fighting SS Division *Reich* to be first to reach their objectives. The SS men arrived at the town of Alibunar first, but heavy rains, marshy terrain and muddy roads slowed progress. On 12 April, the Germans reached the Tamis River where it joined the Danube (known as the Dunay in Yugoslavia). The delays in reaching their objectives meant that *Reich* and *Grossdeutschland* were halted on the banks of the Danube while new plans were made.

The 11th Panzer Division and one battalion of the *Grossdeutschland* eventually crossed the river and arrived in the city of Belgrade on 14 May. Much to their chagrin, the Army found Belgrade already in the possession of one SS officer and ten of his men.

SS-*Hauptstürmführer* Fritz Klingenberg, who was the commander of *Reich*'s motorcycle reconnaissance company, had used rubber boats to cross the Danube that morning. Klingenberg quickly realized that the city was very lightly defended. Making contact with staff from the German Embassy, he used an embassy telephone to contact the Mayor of Belgrade. The inventive SS officer claimed to be the forerunner of a powerful assault. He threatened the official with further massive aerial bombardments unless the city was surrendered – neglecting to point out that his radios were not working and that his ten men were all the assault force that there was.

This coup did nothing to improve relations between the *Grossdeutschland* and the SS, which were not good. The SS men fought vigorously and with great dash, but their arrogance rubbed most of the *Wehrmacht* up the wrong way.

Move to 2.*Panzergruppe*

Rivalry with the SS was forgotten when the *Grossdeutschland* Regiment received orders to move north into Poland. There it became assigned to

▶ **Mittlerer/schwerer Einheits Personenkraftwagen (Kfz 18)**

Panzergrenadier-Division Grossdeutschland

The *Wehrmacht* issued its specification for medium and heavy cars in 1935/36. However, confusingly, the same bodywork was often fitted to both medium and heavy chassis.

Specifications	
Crew: 1	Engine: Horch 6-cylinder petrol (90hp)
Weight: 2.4 tonnes (2.2 tons)	Speed: 88km/h (55 mph)
Length: 4.44m (14 ft 7in)	Range: 400 km (250 miles)
Width: 1.68m (5ft 6in)	Radio: None usually fitted
Height: 1.73m (5ft 8in)	

General Heinz Guderian's 2.*Panzergruppe*, the armoured army that would provide the spearhead for Field Marshal Fedor von Bock's *Heeresgruppe Mitte*, or Army Group Centre, in the invasion of the Soviet Union.

Grossdeutschland did not take part in the initial phases of Operation *Barbarossa*. After crossing the border on 27 June 1941, the regiment was quickly moved towards the front, where it joined the battle for Minsk.

Minsk pocket

Guderian's Panzers had raced towards the city, aiming to circle around it to meet up with General Hermann Hoth's 3.*Panzergruppe*, which was coming down from the north. A large proportion of the Soviet frontline forces were isolated in a huge cauldron. Once their supplies had been exhausted, they would have little alternative but to surrender.

After taking part in the battles around Minsk and the creation of the Minsk pocket, *Grossdeutschland* crossed the Dnieper and advanced on Yelnya, where it was involved in heavy fighting against a Soviet

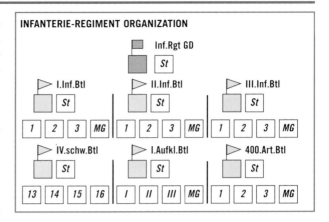

INFANTERIE-REGIMENT ORGANIZATION

counterattack and suffered heavy losses. After the reduction of the Yelnya salient, the regiment might have expected to continue on towards Moscow, but Guderian's *Panzergruppe* was diverted southwards to the Ukraine, where it completed the encirclement of Kiev and helped in the capture more than 600,000 Soviet prisoners of war.

Some *Grossdeutschland* vehicles had a windmill device painted on the side, a reference to a familiar landmark near Stonne in France where the regiment fought its first large scale battle in 1940.

▶ **Schwerer Einheits Kommandokraftwagen Horch 40 (Kfz 21)**

Grossdeutschland Brigade / Stab

The field staff car version of the *Wehrmacht*'s standard heavy car used a universal chassis powered either by a Ford or Auto-Union/Horch V8 engine. Some models were equipped with four-wheel steering.

Specifications

Crew: 1	Engine: Horch 6-cylinder petrol (90hp)
Weight: 2.4 tonnes (2.2 tons)	Speed: 88km/h (55 mph)
Length: 4.44m (14 ft 7in)	Range: 400 km (250 miles)
Width: 1.68m (5ft 6in)	Radio: None usually fitted
Height: 1.73m (5ft 8in)	

▶ **15-cm schwere Infanteriegeschütz**

Schwere Infanteriegeschütz-Kompanie

In France in 1940, the *Grossdeustchland* heavy infantry gun company had two platoons each with two guns. There was also a light company that had six smaller 7.5cm (3in) weapons.

Specifications

Crew: 5	Calibre: 149.1mm (5.9in)
Weight: 1.75 tonnes (1.6 tons)	Muzzle Velocity: 20m/s (790fps)
Length: 1.64m (64.57in)	Range: 5504m (6000 yards)
Ammunition: High explosive or smoke	

Specifications

Crew: 7	(100hp)
Weight: 5.5 tonnes (5 tons)	Speed: 65km/h (40mph)
Length: 4.75m (15ft 7in)	Range: 300km (186 miles)
Width: 2.15m (7ft 1in)	Radio: None
Height: 3.20m (10ft 6in)	Armament: Twin 20mm (0.7in) Flak 38 L/112.5
Engine: Maybach HL42TRKM 6-cylinder	

 2-cm Flak auf leichter Zugkraftwagen 1t (SdKfz 10/5)

Artillerie-Regiment Grossdeutschland / 4.Bataillon / leichte Flak-Batterie

The artillery regiment's self-propelled light Flak battery controlled 12 2cm (0.7in) guns. There was also a medium self-propelled Flak battery with 9 3.7cm (1.5in) weapons, and a heavy battery with 12 towed 8.8cm (3.5in) Flak 18s.

Operation *Typhoon*

OCTOBER–DECEMBER 1941

After mopping up operations around Kiev, the *Grossdeutschland* Regiment was again moved north, to take part in Army Group Centre's final assault on Moscow.

IN ANOTHER GIANT BATTLE OF ENCIRCLEMENT, Hoth and Höppner's Panzers were to bypass Moscow to the north, while Guderian's *Panzergruppe* would pass to the south. The tanks would link up east of Moscow, cutting the Soviet capital off from reinforcements and supplies. Assigned the codename *Taifun* (Typhoon), the German drive on Moscow began on 2 October.

At the beginning of October, *Grossdeutschland* was in position near Roslavl. Advancing eastwards, it took part in the succesful battle to take Bryansk, and by the end of October was advancing slowly towards Tula, southwest of Moscow. By 18 November, the regiment had fought its way through Tula and was advancing towards Ryazan.

'General Winter'

Each advance was getting harder. October had seen the onset of the *rasputitza* – incessant autumn rains that turned dirt roads into bottomless mud, and

which brought movement to a near standstill. The *rasputitza* lasted for four weeks. Then on 7 November, the temperature plunged and the liquid mud turned rock hard.

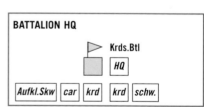

BATTALION HQ

Krds.Btl

HQ

Aufkl.Skw | car | krd | krd | schw.

The German advance began again with breakthroughs in the south as well as towards Moscow. However, daytime temperatures around Moscow varied from -5ºC (23ºF) to -12ºC (10ºF) and the Germans found it increasingly hard to go on fighting in the thin uniforms they had worn all through the baking heat of summer. Supplies of every kind were simply failing to arrive at the front, where battalions were reduced to a fraction of their authorized strength. Panzer divisions counted themselves lucky to have 50 tanks still running.

The Soviets launched a massive counterattack on 5 December. Unable to dig proper defences in the iron ground, many undermanned German units were devastated; the few German tanks still in working order struggled to operate in the conditions and their fuel was out of reach hundreds of kilometres behind the front line.

It seemed as though the *Wehrmacht* might suffer the fate of Napoleon's Grand Army, melting away in the Russian winter. Yet Hitler's iron determination stopped the headlong retreat and destruction of his hopes. *Grossdeutschland* fought a bitter series of defensive battles around Yefremov and Tula, where it would remain on the defensive until April 1942.

▼ **Schützenpanzerwagen-Kompanie / Kraftrad-Bataillon *Grossdeutschland***

By 1942, the key reconnaissance assets of the motorcycle battalion of motorized infantry divisions was provided by armoured cars and half-tracks.

HQ with two SdKfz 250/3

Heavy platoon with four SdKfz 250/7 mortar carriers and three SdKfz 250/1

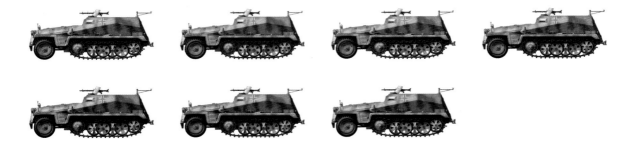

Three reconnaissance platoons each with one SdKfz 250/10 and two SdKfz 250/1

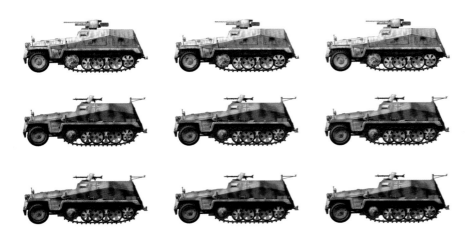

▶ **15-cm sIG 33 auf selbsfahrlafette 38(t) Ausf K (SdKfz 138/1)**

Grenadier-Regiment Grossdeutschland / schwere Infanteriegeschütz-Kompanie

Sometimes called the Bison, but more acurately designated *Grille* (Cricket), the version of the 15cm (5.9in) sIG 33 infantry gun mounted on a PzKpfw 38(t) chassis served with Panzergrenadier divisions on all fronts from 1943 until the end of the war.

Specifications

Crew: 4	Engine: Praga EPA 6-cylinder (125hp)
Weight: 9.4 tonnes (8.6 tons)	Speed: 42km/h (26mph)
Length: 4.60m (15ft 1in)	Range: 250km (155 miles)
Width: 2.12m (6ft 11.5in)	Radio: FuG Ger 'a'
Height: 2.40m (7ft 6in)	Armament: 1 x 150mm (5.9in) sIG 33

▶ **Panzerjäger 38(t) fur 7.62-cm Pak 36(r) (SdKfz 139)**

Grenadier-Regiment Grossdeutschland / Panzerjäger-Kompanie

Known as the Marder III, this self-propelled tank-hunter mounted a powerful captured Soviet gun.

Specifications

Crew: 4	Speed: 42km/h (26mph)
Weight: 11.76 tonnes (10.67 tons)	Range: 185km (115 miles)
Length: 5.85m (19ft 2in)	Radio: FuG Spr 'd'
Width: 2.16m (7ft 0in)	Armament: 1 x 76.2mm (3in) FK296
Height: 2.50m (8ft 2in)	anti-tank gun
Engine: Praga EPA or EPA/2	

Infantry Division *Grossdeutschland*

JANUARY–DECEMBER 1942

Fighting hard against a determined enemy, the *Grossdeutschland* Regiment managed to hold its defensive positions around Tula for more than four months.

THE SOVIET WINTER OFFENSIVE had cost the regiment dearly. Early in February, what remained of the regiment's 2nd Battalion was disbanded, and surviving troops were used to reinforce the other battalions. Later in the month, what was left of the regiment's two grenadier battalions were merged, but losses had been so high that even this combined unit was under strength. After more than nine months of heavy fighting, *Grossdeutschland* was pulled out of the line and reinforced. The disbanded battalions were reinstated and the regiment was allowed a few weeks' rest. Much bigger changes were afoot, however.

On 1 Apr 1942, refitting in the area around Orel, the regiment was expanded dramatically, as it was upgraded to become a motorized infantry division, the *Infanterie-Division Grossdeutschland (mot)*. The original regiment became the 1.*Infanterie-Regiment Grossdeutschland*. A second regiment, 2.*Infanterie-Regiment Grossdeutschland*, had been raised in Berlin and sent to Russia. Further enhancements to the formation included a Panzer battalion, an assault gun battalion and increased Flak, artillery and engineer components. The upgrade to divisional status also brought with it increased support echelons and greater logistic capabilities.

The veterans of GD.1, as the 1st Infantry Regiment came to be known, had very little time for their fellows in GD.2. Unusually, the division had not provided an experienced cadre when the new regiment was formed, and there was little contact between the units. Resentment continued until the end of the war, which was exacerbated when Karl Lorenz of GD.1 was promoted to command the division in 1944, since he obviously favoured his previous command.

1942 Summer Offensive

In the wake of its expansion and reorganization, the *Grossdeutschland* Infantry Division (mot) was assigned to the XLVIII *Panzerkorps* for the opening phases of *Fall Blau* (Plan Blue). This was the plan for Germany's 1942 summer offensive in Russia, which called for an attack on the Volga River at Stalingrad followed by a drive to capture the vital oilfields of the Caucasus. The division took part in the successful attacks to cross the upper Don River and to capture Voronezh. Fortunately, the division was not sent to Stalingrad. In August, it was pulled back to the north bank of the Donets and held as a mobile reserve.

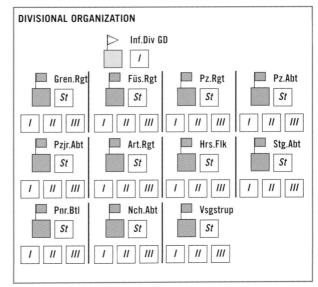

DIVISIONAL ORGANIZATION

▶ **Panzerkampfwagen IV Ausf G (SdKfz 161/1)**
Panzer-Truppe GD / 3rd Company / 3rd Zug / tank number 2

In 1942, *Grossdeutschland*'s Panzer troop had three medium Panzer companies. In 1943, a Tiger battalion and Panther battalion were added to the Panzer IVs.

Specifications

Crew: 5	Speed: 40km/h (24.9mph)
Weight: 25.9 tonnes (23.5 tons)	Range: 210km (130.5 miles)
Length: 6.62 (21ft 8in)	Radio: FuG5
Width: 2.88m (9ft 5in)	Armament: 1 x 75mm (3in) KwK
Height: 2.69m (8ft 10in)	40/43; 2 x 7.92mm (0.3in) MG
Engine: Maybach HL120TRM	(one hull-mounted, one coaxial)

▶ **2-cm Flak 38 auf gepanzerten leichter Zugkraftwagen 1t (SdKfz 10/5)**
Grenadier-Regiment Grossdeutschland / leichte Flak Kompanie (SF)

Introduced as early as 1938, the self-propelled 2cm (0.7in) Flak gun was issued to both Army and *Luftwaffe* Flak units. Originally unarmoured, later versions had an armoured cab and an armoured shield for the exposed Flak 38 gun.

Specifications

Crew: 7	6-cylinder (100hp)
Weight: 5.5 tonnes (5 tons)	Speed: 65km/h (40mph)
Length: 4.75m (15ft 7in)	Range: 300km (186 miles)
Width: 2.15m (7ft 1in)	Radio: None
Height: 3.20m (10ft 6in)	Armament: Twin 20mm (0.7in)
Engine: Maybach HL42TRKM	Flak 38 L/112.5

A further reorganization followed that autumn. On 1 October 1942, the 1st Infantry Regiment was renamed *Grenadier-Regiment Grossdeutschland,* while the 2nd Infantry Regiment became *Füsilier-Regiment Grossdeutschland.*

After the massive Soviet offensive (known as Operation *Uranus*) led by Generals Vatutin and Yeremenko trapped General Friedrich Paulus' German Sixth Army in Stalingrad in November, the Grenadier Regiment was involved in heavy winter fighting with the rest of the division near Rzhev. Continued Soviet pressure prevented any respite from the fighting, and units were being worn to the bone. Nevertheless, the exhausted *Grossdeutschland* Division managed to take part in *Generalfeldmarschall* Erich von Manstein's abortive Operation *Wintergewitter,* the failed attempt to relieve Stalingrad.

▶ **leichter Schützenpanzerwagen 3.7-cm Pak (SdKfz 250/10)**

Pz.Aufkl.Bn GD / SPW Aufklärungs-Kompanie / 1.Zug

The SdKfz 250/10 was used by platoon commanders in the half-track companies of armoured reconnaissance battalions. Armed with a 3.7cm (1.5in) Pak 35/36, it provided fire support for the machine-gun-armed vehicles of the platoon.

Specifications	
Crew: 4	(100hp)
Weight: 6.3 tonnes (5.67 tons)	Speed: 60km/h (37.3mph)
Length: 4.56m (14ft 11.5in)	Range: 320km (199 miles)
Width: 1.95m (6ft 5in)	Radio: FuG Spr Ger 1
Height: 1.97m (6ft 6in)	Armament: 1 x 7.92mm (0.3in) MG
Engine: Maybach HL42TRKM 6-cylinder	

▶ **leichter Funkpanzerwagen (SdKfz 250/3)**

Pz.Aufkl.Bn GD / Schützenpanzerwagen-Aufklärungs-Kompanie

Entering large scale service from 1941, the SdKfz 250 was built in more than a dozen variants. The *Funkpanzerwagen* was used primarily to communicate with and to control *Luftwaffe* air support units.

Specifications	
Crew: 4	(100hp)
Weight: 5.35 tonnes (4.87 tons)	Speed: 60km/h (37.3mph)
Length: 4.56m (14ft 11.5in)	Range: 320km (199 miles)
Width: 1.95m (6ft 5in)	Radio: FuG Spr Ger 1
Height: 1.66m (5ft 5in)	Armament: 1 x 7.92mm (0.3in) MG
Engine: Maybach HL42TRKM 6-cylinder	

▶ **7.5-cm Pak 40/3 auf PzKpfw 38(t) Ausf H (SdKfz 138)**

Panzerjäger-Bataillon Grossdeutschland / schwere Kompanie (SF)

Issued to Panzerjäger units from late 1942, this tank-hunter featured a Pak 40 mounted on the hull of a Panzer 38(t) Ausf H. In September, the division's heavy tank-hunter company had nine guns on strength.

Specifications	
Crew: 4	Speed: 35km/h (22mph)
Weight: 10.8 tonnes (9.8 tons)	Range: 240km (150 miles)
Length: 5.77m (19ft 11in)	Radio: FuG Spr Ger 1
Width: 2.16m (7ft 1in)	Armament: 1 x 75mm (3in) Pak 40/3 L/46
Height: 2.51m (8ft 3in)	anti-tank gun; 1 x 7.92mm (0.3in) MG
Engine: Praga EPA 6-cylinder (140hp)	

Panzergrenadier-Division *Grossdeutschland*

JANUARY–JUNE 1943

In January and February of 1943, *Grossdeutschland* and XLVIII Panzer Corps, along with II SS Panzer Corps took part in the Battle of Kharkov, the third fought around that city.

THE DIVISION FOUGHT ALONGSIDE the SS Divisions *Leibstandarte SS Adolf Hitler, Das Reich* and *Totenkopf* during these battles. After the fall of Kharkov, in one of the last successful battles fought by the *Wehrmacht* in the East, the division was pulled back into reserve and refitted.

During this process, the 1st Battalion of the *GD* Division's Grenadier Regiment was re-equipped with SdKfz 251 armoured half-tracks. The Fusilier Regiment did not receive such vehicles until the spring of 1944. A further enhancement of the division's fighting power came with the addition of a company of PzKpfw VI Tiger I heavy tanks.

The increased strength brought about a change of status, in common with other motorized infantry formations. From June 1943, the division became the *Panzergrenadier-Division Grossdeutschland*.

REGIMENTAL HQ

▢	PzGren.Rgt GD
▨	*HQ*

spw	mot	mot	hv

▶ **15-cm schwere Panzerhaubitze auf Geschützwagen III/IV (SdKfz 165)**

GD Artillerie-Regiment / II.Bataillon / 3.Batterie

Known as the *Hummel* (Bumble Bee), this heavy self-propelled artillery piece was issued to the *Grossdeutschland* Panzergrenadier Division in the summer of 1943.

Specifications

Crew: 6	Speed: 42km/h (26mph)
Weight: 26.5 tonnes (24 tons)	Range: 215km (133.6 miles)
Length: 7.17m (23ft 6in)	Radio: FuG Spr 1
Width: 2.97m (9ft 8in)	Armament: 1 x 150mm (5.9in) sFH
Height: 2.81m (9ft 2in)	18/1 L/30; 1 x 7.92mm (0.3in) MG
Engine: Maybach HL120TRM (265hp)	

▶ **Panzerkampfwagen V Ausf A (SdKfz 171)**

Panzer Regiment Grossdeutschland / I Abteilung / Stab

Grossdeutschland was one of the first formations to be equipped with the PzKpfw V Panther.

Specifications

Crew: 5	Speed: 46km/h (28.6mph)
Weight: 50.2 tonnes	Range: 200km (124.3 miles)
(45.5 tons)	Radio: FuG5
Length: 8.86 (29ft 0in)	Armament: 1 x 75mm (3in)
Width: 3.4m (11ft 2in)	KwK42 L/70; 2 x 7.92mm
Height: 2.98m (9ft 10in)	(0.3in) MG (one hull-mounted,
Engine: Maybach HL230P30	one coaxial)

▶ **Sturmgeschütz 7.5-cm Sturmkanone 40 Ausf F/8 (SdKfz 142/1)**

Sturmgeschütz-Bataillon Grossdeutschland / 1.Batterie

The *Grossdeutschland* Sturmgeschütz Company was expanded to battalion strength in 1942, and it was re-equipped with the Ausf F/8 variant of the StuG.

Specifications

Crew: 4	Speed: 40km/h (24.9mph)
Weight: 25.6 tonnes (23.2 tons)	Range: 140km (87 miles)
Length: 6.77m (22ft 2in)	Radio: FuG15 or FuG16
Width: 2.92m (9ft 8in)	Armament: 1 x 75mm (3in)
Height: 2.15m (7ft 0in)	StuK40 L/48 cannon
Engine: Maybach HL120TRM	

▼ **Sturmgeschütz (Assault Gun) Battalion *Grossdeutschland* 1943**

From late in 1941, the *Grossdeutschland* Regiment had its own assault gun detachment, which continued to serve with the formation as it became a motorized division in 1942 and a Panzergrenadier division in 1943. Each Sturmgeschütz battery consisted of three assault gun platoons of two StuGs supported by an armoured ammunition carrier. By late in 1943, the batteries had grown from the six-gun units seen here to a total of eleven guns per battery.

1st Battery

2nd Battery

3rd Battery

Kursk and after

JULY–DECEMBER 1943

The redesignation of the division meant that its main units also received new names, becoming *Panzergrenadier-Regiment Grossdeutschland* and *Panzerfüsilier-Regiment Grossdeutschland*.

THE NEWLY RE-EQUIPPED DIVISION was sent to Army Group South, where it joined the Fourth Panzer Army commanded by *Generaloberst* Hermann Hoth. It was to play a major part in Operation *Zitadelle*, or Citadel, the titanic series of German attacks intended to pinch off the Kursk salient, a huge bulge in the front line where Soviet forces projected into German-held territory. Army Group Centre would attack from the north with a massively reinforced Panzer group, while Army Group South would strike northwards from the opposite side of the salient with even stronger forces.

New tanks

During the build-up period, a battalion of new Panther Ausf D tanks came under the operational control of *Grossdeutschland*. Attached to XLVIII Panzer Corps alongside the 3rd and 11th Panzer Divisions, the division was on the left flank of the main attack in the south, supporting the powerful central thrust by the II SS Panzer Corps.

The Panzers had to break through little more than 100km (62 miles) to cut off all Soviet units in the salient. Further exploitation might take them back to the Don at Voronezh and bring the *Wehrmacht* into a position to threaten Moscow.

Name	Strength
Panzer-Regiment Grossdeutschland July 1943:	
PzKpfw II	4
PzKpfw III	27
PzKpfw IV	68
PzKpfw VI	15
PzBefwg	8
Flammpanzer	14

The Red Army was ready and waiting for the German attack. It had been building up its forces for months. German losses on the first day were reminiscent of those on the Western Front in 1916. By nightfall on 5 July, 200 Panzers had been knocked out and 220 German aircraft shot down – and in the days that followed, the cost increased proportionately.

Whole regiments were wiped out before the leading formations broke clear of the defence belts – only to run into the waiting Russian armour and infantry. Hoth's Panzers and Kempf's motorized infantry faced the Sixth Guards Army with the Seventh Guards Army on their left – all ready and waiting, all dug in behind belt after belt of murderous anti-tank defences. By 12 July, Hoth's Panzer army

HQ COMPANY

Pz.Rgt GD

HQ

| I | II | III |

▲ **Leichter Gepanzerte Munitionskraftwagen (SdKfz 252)**

Sturmgeschütz-Bataillon Grossdeutschland

Built to provide ammunition support for Sturmartillerie batteries, the SdKfz 252 had a fully enclosed body. It generally towed the *Sonder Anhänger* 3 1/1 trailer to increase the amount of ammunition it could supply to frontline units.

Specifications

Crew: 2

Weight: 5.73 tonnes (5.2 tons)

Length: 4.70m (15ft 5in)

Width: 1.95 (6ft 5in)

Height: 1.80m (5ft 11in)

Engine: Maybach HL42TRKM

Speed: 65km/h (40.3mph)

Range: 320km (199 miles)

Radio: FuG15 or FuG16

Armament: 1 x 7.62mm (0.3in) MG

▲ Operation *Citadel*

Grossdeutschland was part of the most powerful armoured force the *Wehrmacht* had ever assembled, fighting alongside the II SS Panzer Corps at Kursk.

had reached the Prokhorovka area, only 30km (18.6 miles) from their start line. Here they encountered the Fifth Guards Tank Army in the largest and most bloody tank action of the whole battle. The same day, to the north of the bulge, Army Group Centre was attacked by Soviet forces bent on liberating Orel, and

the offensive had to be called off. *Grossdeutschland* was heavily engaged on the southern flank of the salient. The new Panthers were a disaster, suffering from engine fires. Many broke down before reaching the battle. Despite this, the division fought on until it was pulled back to Tomarovka on 18 July 1943.

Withdrawal and retreat

After the disaster at Kursk, the *Grossdeutschland* Panzergrenadier Division was transferred back to Army Group Centre, and resumed its role as mobile reserve. *GD* saw heavy fighting around Karachev before being transferred back to XLVIII Panzer Corps in late August. For the rest of 1943, *Grossdeutschland* was engaged in the withdrawal from the eastern Ukraine, fighting at Kharkov, Belgorod and, finally, on the River Dnieper, At the end of the year, it was in action against strong Red Army attacks east of Krivoi Rog. It was during this period that the *Grossdeutschland* Division became known as *die Feuerwehr*, or Fire Brigade.

▶ Schwerer Panzerspähwagen (Funk) 8-Rad (SdKfz 232)

Pz.Aufkl.Bn Grossdeutschland / Panzerspähwagen-Kompanie

The communications variant of the heavy armoured car carried an FuG11 or 12 command link radio with a wireless range of 50km (31 miles) or a voice range of 10km (6.2 miles). It also carried a vehicle-to-vehicle set, the FuG Spr Ger 'a'.

Specifications

Crew: 4	Speed: 85km/h (52.8mph)
Weight: 9.1 tonnes (8.3 tons)	Range: 300km (186 miles)
Length: 4.67m (15ft 4in)	Radio: FuG12 plus FuG Spr Ger 'a'
Width: 2.2m (7ft 2in)	Armament: 1 x 20mm (0.7in) KwK
Height: 2.35m (7ft 8in)	30/38 L/55 cannon; 1 x 7.92mm
Engine: Büssing-NAG L8V	(0.3in) MG (coaxial)

▶ Panzerkampfwagen IV Ausf H (SdKfz 161/2)

Pz.Rgt GD / II.Bataillon / 6.Kompanie / 1.Zug / tank number 1

In 1944, the GD Panzer Regiment had one four-company battalion of Panthers, one four-company battalion of Panzer IVs and a three-company battalion of Tigers.

Specifications

Crew: 5	Speed: 38km/h (23.6mph)
Weight: 27.6 tonnes (25 tons)	Range: 210km (130.5 miles)
Length: 7.02m (23ft 0in)	Radio: FuG5
Width: 2.88m (9ft 5in)	Armament: 1 x 75mm (3in) KwK
Height: 2.68m (8ft 10in)	40/43; 2 x 7.92mm (0.3in) MG
Engine: Maybach HL120TRM	(one hull-mounted, one coaxial)

▼ *Grossdeutschland* Panzer Regiment, 3rd Battalion, 9th Company

Although in 1943 and 1944, *Grossdeutschland* was nominally a Panzergrenadier division, it was equipped with more tanks than most full Panzer divisions. That panzer strength included a battalion of *Panzerkampfwagen* VI Tiger heavy tanks, divided into three *Zugen*, or platoons.

HQ *Zug*

1st *Zug*

2nd *Zug*

3rd *Zug*

Specifications

Crew: 5	Speed: 38km/h (23.6mph)
Weight: 62.8 tonnes (57 tons)	Range: 140km (87 miles)
Length: 8.45 (27ft 8in)	Radio: FuG5
Width: 3.7m (12ft 1in)	Armament: 1 x 88mm (3.5in) KwK 36 L/56; 2 x
Height: 2.93m (9ft 7in)	7.92mm (0.3in) MG (one hull-mounted, one
Engine: Maybach HL210P45 (700hp)	coaxial)

▲ Panzerkampfwagen VI Tiger 1 Ausf E (SdKfz 181)

Pz.Rgt GD / III.Bataillon

Most Tigers were operated by independent heavy battalions, but a few elite formations (including *Grossdeutschland*) had their own Tiger battalions.

Retreat from Russia

JANUARY–JULY 1944

The German Army was outnumbered and outgunned. The best that that its weary soldiers could hope for was that the long Soviet supply lines would force Stalin's men to halt and regroup.

JANUARY 1944 BROUGHT NO RESPITE for Hitler's hard-pressed Eastern legions. Since the Battle of Kursk the previous summer, the Red Army had been inexorably driving westwards, all along the thousands of kilometres of front. Apart from a few local counterattacks, there was little that the German Army could do but fall back.

In early January of 1944, the *Grossdeutschland* Division was fighting defensive battles at Krivoi Rog in the Ukraine. Over the next six months, the division was used in its 'fire brigade' role,

being moved from crisis to crisis across the front. Late in January 1944, part of the division was used in the relief of the Cherkassy pocket, while other divisional units fought a number of battles from the Dniester to northern Bessarabia.

Following a major Soviet offensive in March, the *Grossdeutschland* Division was moved to Kirovgrad before retreating to the southwest. By the end of March, the Germans had been pushed back to the

ORGANIZATIONS

▭	Arm.Flk.Abt GD
▭	HQ
flk	flk	lt

 The *Grossdeutschland* vehicle insignia, the Stahlhelm, was painted in different colours and mounted on different geometrical shapes by individual units within the division.

▶ **Panzerkampfwagen IV Ausf H (SdKfz 161/2)**

Pz. Rgt 1 / II Battalion / 8th Company / 4th Zug / tank number 2

The Ausf H was the largest series of Panzer IVs, 3774 being built between April 1943 and June 1944. *Grossdeustschland* had four 17-strong companies of the type.

Specifications

Crew: 5	Speed: 38km/h (23.6mph)
Weight: 27.6 tonnes (25 tons)	Range: 210km (130.5 miles)
Length: 7.02m (23ft 0in)	Radio: FuG5
Width: 2.88m (9ft 5in)	Armament: 1 x 75mm (3in) KwK
Height: 2.68m (8ft 10in)	40/43; 2 x 7.92mm (0.3in) MG (one
Engine: Maybach HL120TRM	hull-mounted, one coaxial)

▶ **Panzerkampfwagen V Panther Ausf D (SdKfz 171)**

Pz. Rgt GD / I Battalion / HQ Company

One battalion of Panthers served alongside the Panzer IV battalion.

Specifications

Crew: 5	Speed: 46km/h (28.6mph)
Weight: 47.4 tonnes	Range: 200km (124 miles)
(43 tons)	Radio: FuG5
Length: 8.86m (29ft 0in)	Armament: 1 x 75mm (3in)
Width: 3.4m (11ft 2in)	KwK 42 L/70; 2 x 7.92mm
Height: 2.95m (9ft 8in)	(0.3in) MG (one hull-
Engine: Maybach HL230P30	mounted, one coaxial)

Romanian border. In April, the division was in action at Jassy as it covered the retreat into Bessarabia.

In May, most of the division was re-equipped with new vehicles, including *Schützenpanzerwagen* armoured half-tracks. The fusilier regiments were downsized from four battalions to three. By now, *Grossdeutschland* was probably the best-equipped division in the *Wehrmacht*.

The division returned to action at Podul. After a brief rest in early July, it was again committed to heavy fighting in northern Romania. The division was then transferred to East Prussia.

Armee-Flak-Abteilung *Grossdeutschland*	Strength
1 Battery:	
8.8cm (3.5in) Flak	6
2cm (0.7in) Flak	3
2 battery:	
8.8cm (3.5in) Flak	6
2cm (0.7in) Flak	3
Light battery:	
towed 3.7cm (1.5in) Flak	9
SdKfz 10 with quad 2cm (0.7in) Flakvierling	3

▶ *Grossdeutschland* Panzer Regiment, 1st Battalion, 1st Company

From 1943, Panzer regiments were equipped with one battalion of Panthers and one battalion of Panzer IVs. Nominal strength of each of the companies in the battalion was 17 tanks, though later in the war it was not uncommon for the numbers to be reduced to 14 or even 10 tanks. However, as a spearhead formation, *Grossdeutschland* was supplied more copiously than less prestigious divisions, and in December 1944 it was still operating with 17-tank companies. The division's Tiger battalion was withdrawn, however, becoming corps level assets with the formation of Panzerkorps *Grossdeutschland* at the end of 1944.

HQ *Zug*

1st *Zug*

2nd *Zug*

3rd *Zug*

Panzerkorps *Grossdeutschland*

NOVEMBER 1944 – APRIL 1945

The *Grossdeutschland* Division arrived in East Prussia in the autumn of 1944, after more than three years of almost continuous action on the central and southern fronts.

OVER THE NEXT MONTHS, the *Grossdeutschland* Panzergrenadier Division was involved in heavy fighting in both East Prussia and the Baltic States, suffering immense casualties at Memel. In November 1944, while the *GD* retained its status as a Panzergrenadier division, new units were assigned and several attached units were expanded, enough to form a second division. As a result, the *Grossdeutschland* Division became the lead formation in a corps, the *Panzerkorps Grossdeutschland*. In addition to absorbing the *Grossdeutschland* Division, the newly formed corps also incorporated the *Brandenburg* Panzergrenadier Division.

By March 1945, the Panzergrenadier Division *Grossdeutschland*, as part of the *GD* Panzer Corps, had been reduced to around 4000 men. These escaped by ferry from the collapsing Memel bridgehead. They landed at Pillau and were put straight back into combat. Other units attached to the corps at this stage included the remnants of the 21st Panzer Division, a *Kampfgruppe* from the *Brandenburg* Division, a *Kampfgruppe* from the 1st Fallschirm-Panzer-Division *Hermann Göring* and another from the 20th Panzergrenadier Division.

By 25 April 1945, the corps had ceased to exist, having been completely destroyed in the battles around Pillau. Of the survivors, a few hundred were able to make their way to Schleswig-Holstein and surrendered to British forces. The majority were forced to surrender to the Russians.

Panzerkorps Grossdeutschland
Corps troops:
Arko 500
Stab-Pionier-Regiment 500
Korps-Füsilier-Regiment Grossdeutschland
schwere Panzer-Abteilung Grossdeutschland
Artillerie-Regiment 500
Panzer-Pionier-Bataillon 500
Panzer-Korps-Nachrichten-Abteilung 500
Panzer-Feldersatz-Regiment Grossdeutschland
Versorgungs-Regiment 500

CORPS ORGANIZATION

Pz.K GD / I

Stab 615 — St / I II III

Cor-Troop — St / I II III

21.Pz.Div — St / I II III

Pz.Brand — St / I II III

Fall.Gör — St / I II III

20.Pz.Div — St / I II III

▶ **Mittlerer Schützenpanzerwagen Ausf A (SdKfz 251/1)**

Grenadier-Regiment Grossdeutschland / I.Panzergrenadier-Bataillon

In 1944, the *Grossdeutschland* Grenadier Regiment had one battalion equipped with half-tracks and one motorized *Jäger* battalion.

Specifications

Crew: 2 plus 12 troops	Engine: Maybach HL42TUKRM
Weight: 9.9 tonnes (9 tons)	Speed: 53km/h (33mph)
Length: 5.98m (19ft 7in)	Range: 300km (186 miles)
Width: 2.1m (6ft 11in)	Radio: FuG Spr Ger 1
Height: 1.75m (5ft 8in) or 2.16m	Armament: 1/2 x 7.62mm
(7ft) including MG shield if fitted	(0.3in) MG

▶ 2-cm Flakvierling auf Fahrgestell Zgkw 8t (SdKfz 7/2)

Heeres-Flak-Bataillon Grossdeutschland

As Allied airpower began to make itself felt, German formations were given greatly enhanced anti-aircraft protection. The Flak battalion's light SP battery had three Flakvierlings.

Specifications

Crew: 7	6-cylinder (140hp)
Weight: 1.16 tonnes (1.06 tons)	Speed: 50km/h (31mph)
Length: 6.55m (21ft 6in)	Range: 250km (156 miles)
Width: 2.40m (7ft 10.5in)	Radio: None
Height: 3.20m (10ft 6in)	Armament: Quad 20mm (0.7in)
Engine: Maybach HL 62 TUK	Flak 38

▶ Jagdpanzer 38(t) Hetzer (SdKfz 138/2)

Aufklärungs-Bataillon Grossdeutschland / 1. (Hetzer) Schwadron

Developed using the components of the Czech Panzer 38, the Hetzer was an excellent light tank destroyer. In the summer of 1944, it equipped one squadron of the *Grossdeutschland* Division's Reconnaissance Battalion.

Specifications

Crew: 4	Speed: 42km/h (26mph)
Weight: 17.4 tonnes (15.75 tons)	Range: 177km (110 miles)
Length: 6.38m (20ft 11in)	Radio: FuG5 plus FuG Spr 1
Width: 2.63m (8ft 7in)	Armament: 1 x 75mm (3in) PaK39 L/48
Height: 2.17m (7ft 1in)	anti-tank gun; 1x 7.92mm (0.3in) MG
Engine: Praga AC/2	

Specifications

Crew: 5	Speed: 46km/h (28.6mph)
Weight: 49.4 tonnes (44.8 tons)	Range: 200km (124 miles)
Length: 8.86m (29ft 0in)	Radio: FuG5
Width: 3.42m (11ft 2in)	Armament: 1 x 75mm (3in) KwK 42 L/70;
Height: 2.98m (9ft 9in)	2 x 7.92mm (0.3in) MG (one hull-mounted,
Engine: Maybach HL230P30	one coaxial)

▲ Panzerkampfwagen V Panther Ausf A (SdKfz 171)

Panzer-Regiment Grossdeutschland / I.Bataillon

The division's Panther tanks were all allocated to the 1 Company of the I Battalion.

Führer-Begleit Division

The origins of the *Führer-Begleit* Division date back to the pre-war rivalry between the Army and the SS over who would provide the *Führer*'s personal bodyguard.

ORIGINALLY, THE ARMY provided the Chancellery Guards for ceremonial and protection duties in Berlin, but when the Nazis came to power in 1933 these were soon replaced as Hitler's personal guard by the *Leibstandarte SS Adolf Hitler*.

Hitler was determined that the SS should prove itself in battle, so on the outbreak of World War II he sent the bulk of the *Leibstandarte* into combat. To replace them he ordered the establishment of an elite bodyguard battalion, the *Führer-Begleit* Battalion, whose task it was to protect the *Führer* whenever he left Berlin to tour the front. The first commander of the unit was *Oberst* Erwin Rommel.

A second *Führer-Begleit* unit was formed by the elite *Grossdeutschland* Regiment. The *Führer-Begleit-Abteilung* was a fully motorized formation that took over *Führer* protection duties in the field, while the original bodyguard battalion remained in Berlin and declined in importance.

From 1941, the *Führer-Begleit-Abteilung* moved to Hitler's eastern headquarters in Prussia, the *Wolfsschanze*. It was strengthened by the addition of a heavy Flak battery, which was transferred from the *Luftwaffe Flak-Regiment Hermann Göring*.

The Flak protection of the *Führer*'s headquarters rapidly grew when the 604th Flak Regiment was assigned at the end of 1942. The unit was redesignated as the *Führer-Flak-Bataillon*, and two further batteries were assigned to the unit from the *General Göring* Regiment of the *Luftwaffe*. Two

Commanders

Oberst Otto-Ernst Remer *November 1944*	Generalmajor Otto-Ernst Remer *January 1945*

Divisional History	Formed
Führer-Begleit-Bataillon	1939
Führer-Begleit-Regiment	1944
Führer-Begleit-Brigade	1944
Führer-Begleit-Division	1945

railway Flak platoons were also under the orders of the *Führer* headquarters, though they were never officially part of the *Begleit* organization.

Combat experience

The *Führer-Begleit-Abteilung* maintained its links with its parent formation, the *Grossdeutschland* Regiment, and continued to use the *Stahlhelm* unit insignia. Experienced troops from *Grossdeutschland* were rotated through the protection unit, and elements of the *Begleit-Abteilung* were detached to serve in combat on the Eastern Front.

In June 1944, the *Abteilung* was redesignated as the *Führer-Begleit-Regiment*. At the same time, the *Abteilung* included a light/medium Panzer company, an infantry support company and three motorized infantry companies.

In November of that year, the *Führer-Begleit-Brigade* was formed. The core was provided by the

▶ **Mercedes Benz G4 W31**

Führer-Begleit-Bataillon

The original purpose of Adolf Hitler's escort battalion was to protect the *Führer* whenever he left Berlin to visit operational areas. The big Mercedes G4 convertible was one of Hitler's favourite transports on such occasions.

Specifications

Crew: 1	Engine: 5.4L 8-cylinder petrol (110hp)
Weight: 3.7 tonnes (3.37 tons)	Speed: 67km/h (42mph)
Length: 4.80m (15ft 9in)	Range: 368km (228 miles)
Width: 1.87m (6ft 1.5in)	Radio: None
Height: 1.90m (6ft 2in)	

Führer-Begleit-Regiment, with additional troops and equipment being transferred from the *Grossdeutschland* Panzer Corps.

The new brigade was commanded by *Oberst* Otto Remer. He had been passing through Berlin on 20 July 1944 when news of Hitler's assassination reached the city. Ordered by the anti-Hitler conspirators to put Goebbels, the Propaganda Minister, under arrest, Remer was persuaded by the minister to phone the *Wolfsschanze*. Having spoken to the *Führer*, Remer realized the attempt on Hitler's life had failed, and he mobilized troops in Berlin to counter the attempt by the conspirators to seize control. His new command was a reward for his loyalty to the *Führer*.

Führer-Begleit-Brigade

The brigade was ordered westwards to take part in the upcoming offensive in the Ardennes. The Panzer inventory included two companies of Panthers and one of Jagdpanthers, and other units included a Panzergrenadier battalion, a fusilier battalion and a bicycle battalion. Its original artillery complement was provided by the Flak guns of the Führer-Flak Battalion, but by the beginning of December these had been reinforced by a Sturmgeschütz detachment and two battalions of half-track-towed 10.5cm (4.1in) and 15cm (5.9in) field howitzers.

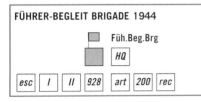

▶ **Mittlerer Pionierpanzerwagen (SdKfz 251/7)**

Führer-Begleit-Brigade / Brigadestab / Pionier-Kompanie

As a brigade, the formation did not have a dedicated pioneer battalion. However, for the Battle of the Bulge, the Brigade Staff had a half-track pioneer company attached, which would become the 124th Pioneer Battalion in 1945.

Specifications

Crew: 7 or 8	6-cylinder (100hp)
Weight: 8.9 tonnes (8.7 tons)	Speed: 50km/h (31mph)
Length: 5.80m (19ft 0in)	Range: 300km (186 miles)
Width: 2.10m (6ft 11in)	Radio: FuG Spr Ger 1
Height: 2.70m (8ft 10in)	Armament: 1/2 x 7.62mm
Engine: Maybach HL42TUKRM	(0.3in) MGs

▶ **Mittlerer Schützenpanzerwagen 7.5-cm (SdKfz 251/9)**

99.Panzergrenadier-Regiment / I.Bataillon / 4.Kompanie

When the brigade was expanded to form the *Führer-Begleit* Division in 1945, the 1st Battalion's heavy company was equipped with a platoon of 7.5cm (3in) armed SdKfz 251/9s. The six vehicles provided fire support to the regular half-track companies.

Specifications

Crew: 3	HL42TUKRM
Weight: 9.4 tonnes	Speed: 53km/h (33mph)
(8.53 tons)	Range: 300km (186 miles)
Length: 5.98m (19ft 7in)	Radio: FuG Spr Ger 'f'
Width: 2.83m (9ft 4in)	Armament: 1 x 75mm (3in)
Height: 2.07m (6ft 10in)	KwK L/24 gun
Engine: Maybach	

Führer-Begleit Brigade
FEBRUARY 1945

The *Führer-Begleit* Brigade was assigned to Hasso von Manteuffel's Fifth Panzer Army in the Ardennes, and saw action at Bastogne against the US 101st Airborne Division.

AFTER THE FAILURE of the Ardennes offensive, the brigade was upgraded to a division. The *Führer-Begleit* Division, with its sister formation the *Führer-Grenadier* Division, was sent to the Eastern Front to help defend the Vistula against the advancing Red Army. In March 1945, the division was moved south to Silesia, where it suffered heavy casualties before being encircled and destroyed in the Spremberg pocket in April 1945. Survivors who managed to break out of the pocket retreated westwards, where they were taken into captivity by the Americans.

DIVISIONAL SUPPORT ORGANIZATION 1945

Füh.Beg.Div — I

Pz.Art 120	Pzjr.Abt 673	Pz.Pnr.Btl 120
St	St	St
I II III	I II III	I II III

Fld.Btl 120	Pz.Nch.Abt 120	Pz.Kom 120
St	St	St
I II III	I II III	I II III

▶ **Panzerkampfwagen V Panther Ausf A (SdKfz 171)**

Panzer-Regiment 102 / I.Bataillon

In February 1945, the 1st Battalion of the *Grossdeutschland* Panzer Regiment was transferred to the *Führer-Begleit* Division, where it became the 1st Battalion, 102nd Panzer Regiment.

Specifications

Crew: 5	Speed: 46km/h (28.6mph)
Weight: 50.2 tonnes	Range: 200km (124 miles)
(45.5 tons)	Radio: FuG5
Length: 8.86m (29ft 0in)	Armament: 1 x 75mm (3in)
Width: 3.4m (11ft 2in)	KwK42 L/70; 2 x 7.92mm
Height: 2.98m (9ft 10in)	(0.3in) MG (one hull-
Engine: Maybach HL230P30	mounted, one coaxial)

▶ **Panzerkampfwagen IV Ausf H (SdKfz 161/2)**

Panzer Regiment 102 / II.Bataillon

In January 1945, ahead of the 1st Battalion, the 2nd Battalion of the *Grossdeutschland* Panzer Regiment was renamed the 2nd Battalion, 102nd Panzer Regiment, *Führer-Begleit* Division. It had the standard late-war composition, with two companies of Panthers and two of Panzer IVs.

Specifications

Crew: 5	Speed: 38km/h (23.6mph)
Weight: 27.6 tonnes (25 tons)	Range: 210km (130.5 miles)
Length: 7.02 (23ft 0in)	Radio: FuG5
Width: 2.88m (9ft 5in)	Armament: 1 x 75mm (3in) KwK
Height: 2.68m (8ft 10in)	40/43; 2 x 7.92mm (0.3in) MG
Engine: Maybach HL120TRM	(one hull-mounted, one coaxial)

Führer-Grenadier Brigade

The *Führer-Grenadier* Division was an offshoot of the *Führer-Begleit-Abteilung*, Hitler's bodyguard unit based at his Prussian headquarters, the *Wolfsschanze*.

DURING THE WAR, a *Führer-Begleit* unit of battalion status was created by drawing men from *Infantry-Regiment Grossdeutschland*. This unit, the *Führer-Begleit-Abteilung*, began to send detachments to the Eastern Front to gain combat experience, and eventually a reinforced *Führer-Grenadier* Battalion was formed to control the guard troops.

In July 1944, the battalion was enlarged to brigade size. Theoretically the *Führer-Grenadier* Brigade, emerging from the *Grossdeutschland* Division and the *Führer-Begleit* Brigade, should have been one of the best *Wehrmacht* formations.

In fact, this brigade had suffered severe losses in East Prussia during its single commitment as a unit. It had not been fully refitted when it was sent westwards to take part in the Ardennes offensive.

Poorly trained

Replacements, drawn from the same pool as those for the *Grossdeutschland* Division and the *Führer-Begleit* Brigade, were hand-picked from the younger classes of recruits, but at this stage in the war the German Army had little chance to give them thorough training and they were thrown into battle nearly raw.

The *Führer-Grenadier* Brigade numbered some 6000 men, had a rifle regiment mounted on armoured half-tracks and trucks, a reconnaissance battalion, an assault gun battalion, and a mixed tank battalion made up of Mark IVs and Panthers. Attached to Seventh Army during Operation *Wacht am Rhein*, the brigade served alongside 79th Volksgrenadier Division. These two formations were cast into battle as General George S. Patton's Third US Army arrived from the south, threatening the flanks of the German advance.

However, the *Führer-Grenadier* Brigade was sent in piecemeal against the two divisions of the US III Corps. The brigade took particularly heavy losses while trying to secure a crossing over the Sure River at Heiderscheid.

Commanders

Oberst Hans-Joachim Kahle *July 1944*	Generalmajor Erich von Hassenstein *February 1945*
Generalmajor Hellmuth Mäder *January 1945*	

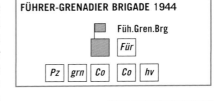

FÜHRER-GRENADIER BRIGADE 1944

Füh.Gren.Brg — Für — Pz | grn | Co | Co | hv

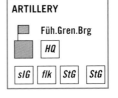

ARTILLERY

Füh.Gren.Brg — HQ — sIG | flk | StG | StG

Divisional History	Formed
Führer-Grenadier-Bataillon (reinforced)	1943
Führer-Grenadier-Brigade	1944
Führer-Grenadier-Division	1945

▶ **Mittlerer Schützenpanzerwagen Ausf D (SdKfz 251/1)**

I.Bataillon (SPW) / 2.Kompanie

The four companies of the 1st Battalion of the *Führer-Grenadier* Brigade's infantry regiment were equipped with half-tracks.

Specifications

Crew: 2 plus 12 troops	Engine: Maybach HL42TUKRM
Weight: 9.9 tonnes (9 tons)	Speed: 53km/h (33mph)
Length: 5.98m (19ft 7in)	Range: 300km (186 miles)
Width: 2.1m (6ft 11in)	Radio: FuG Spr Ger 1
Height: 1.75m (5ft 8in) or 2.16m	Armament: 1/2 7.62mm
(7ft) including MG shield	(0.3in) MG

▶ **Mittlerer Schützenpanzerwagen Ausf C 7.5-cm (SdKfz 251/9)**

99.Panzergrenadier-Regiment / I.Bataillon (SPW) / 4.Kompanie

The fire-support variant of the SdKfz 251 was developed in 1943 after the upgrading of early Panzer IVs left a supply of obsolete KwK 37 short-barrelled guns. No longer effective as tank guns, they were used as short-range infantry-support weapons.

Specifications	
Crew: 3	Speed: 53km/h (33mph)
Weight: 9.4 tonnes (8.53 tons)	Range: 300km (186 miles)
Length: 5.98m (19ft 7in)	Radio: FuG Spr Ger 'f'
Width: 2.83m (9ft 4in)	Armament: 1 x 75mm (3in) KwK
Height: 2.07m (6ft 10in)	L/24 gun
Engine: Maybach HL42TUKRM	

▶ **2-cm Flak 38 auf gepanzerten leichter Zugkraftwagen 1t (SdKfz 10/5)**

Luftwaffe-Flak-Bataillon

Their origins as Hitler's protection force meant that both the *Führer-Begleit* and the *Führer-Grenadier* formations were well supplied with anti-aircraft artillery.

Specifications	
Crew: 7	6-cylinder (100hp)
Weight: 5.5 tonnes (5 tons)	Speed: 65km/h (40mph)
Length: 4.75m (15ft 7in)	Range: 300km (186 miles)
Width: 2.15m (7ft 1in)	Radio: None
Height: 3.20m (10ft 6in)	Armament: Twin 20mm
Engine: Maybach HL42TRKM	(0.7in) Flak 38 L/112.5

Führer-Grenadier Division

JANUARY 1945

The *Führer-Grenadier* Division was created in January 1945. It was based around the units of the *Führer-Grenadier* Brigade which had survived the Battle of the Bulge.

Established at Cottbus in Saxony, northeast of Dresden, the division was built using the *Panzergrenadier-Ersatz- und Ausbildungs-Brigade Grossdeutschland*, the *Grossdeutschland* replacement formation. The Panzer strength of the new division was provided by *Panzer-Regiment* 101, which was created out of the *Führer-Grenadier* Brigade's 3rd Battalion. In early February 1945, the regiment's tank strength was concentrated into one battalion, with two companies each of 14 PzKpfw V Panthers and two companies equipped with PzKpfw IVs. On 15 February the division received 10 Jagdpanthers, and two days later took delivery of another 16 Panthers.

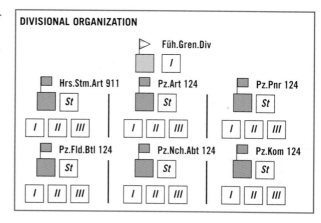

DIVISIONAL ORGANIZATION

Füh.Gren.Div

Hrs.Stm.Art 911   Pz.Art 124   Pz.Pnr 124

Pz.Fld.Btl 124   Pz.Nch.Abt 124   Pz.Kom 124

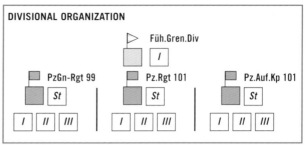

DIVISIONAL ORGANIZATION

Füh.Gren.Div
I

PzGn-Rgt 99 — St — I | II | III

Pz.Rgt 101 — St — I | II | III

Pz.Auf.Kp 101 — St — I | II | III

▲ **Battle of the Bulge**

Loaded with ammunition, a Panzergrenadier turns to face the camera at the beginning of the Ardennes offensive, December 1944.

The division was thrown into action on the Vistula and was used to plug the 40km (24.9-mile) gap that had emerged between Army Group North and Army Group Centre. The division took part in Operation *Sonnenwende*, a counterattack into the Soviet spearheads heading for the Oder.

Battles on the Oder

In March, surviving units were sent to join XXXIX Panzer Corps, part of Seventeenth Army at Lauban. They took part in the first German counterattacks at Kustrin, aimed at throwing back the Red Army bridgeheads across the Oder and relieving troops trapped there by the Soviets; the operation failed to prevent the Soviet capture of the fortress.

In April 1945, the division joined II Corps of Sixth SS Panzer Army, which was preparing to defend Vienna. Badly battered after the fighting on the Oder, the division could do little to stem the Soviet attacks and at the end of April was in full retreat with the rest of the Sixth SS Panzer Army. When the war ended in May, the few survivors surrendered to the Americans. They were later turned over to the Russians.

Specifications

Crew: 2	Engine: Maybach HL62 6-cylinder (140hp)
Weight: 1.16 tonnes (1.06 tons)	Speed: 50km/h (31mph)
Length: 6.85m (20ft 3in)	Range: 250km (156 miles)
Width: 2.40m (7ft 10.5in)	Radio: None
Height: 2.62m (8ft 7.1in)	

▲ **Mittlerer Zugkraftwagen 5t (SdKfz 7) mit 8.8-cm Flak 18**

Luftwaffe-Flak-Bataillon

The mixed *Luftwaffe* Flak battalion attached to the *Führer-Grenadier* Division had three heavy batteries, each with four 8.8cm (3.5in) Flak guns. The batteries also had three 2cm (0.7in) guns for self-protection against low-flying fighter-bombers.

Sizilien Panzergrenadier Division

It was only a question of time following the German surrender in Tunisia before the Allies eventually attacked Sicily, and the Axis scrambled to create a force to defend the island.

FORMED ON 14 MAY 1943, the *Sizilien* Division was an ad hoc organization initially incorporating the remains of the 15th Panzer Division, most of which had been lost in North Africa. Established in eastern Sicily, it took on strength *Panzer-Abteilung 215*, together with assorted 'march battalions' made up from elements of units destined for North Africa but which had not yet transferred across the Mediterranean before the Allied victory in Tunisia. It was commanded by *Oberst* Ernst-Günther Baade.

As a non-standard division, the unit also had a non-standard organization. Component parts included the *Regimental Gruppe Ens*, under the command of *Oberst* Ens. Later to be formally entitled the 104th Panzergrenadier Regiment (Reinforced), it consisted of three rifle battalions each of three rifle companies, one heavy weapons company, one engineer platoon, one anti-tank platoon and one platoon of infantry guns.

Oberst Fullreide's *Regimental Gruppe Fullreide* (later the 129th Panzergrenadier Regiment) had a similar structure, but its 3rd Battalion, based at Comiso, also had a small formation of tanks. *Oberst*

Divisional History	Formed
Division Sizilien	1943
15.Panzer-Division	1943
15.Panzergrenadier-Division	1943

▶ **Panzerkampfwagen IV Ausf H (SdKfz 161/2)**

Panzer-Bataillon 215

The *Sizilien* Division's Panzer Battalion was created from Army troops in Italy, which had originally been on their way to North Africa before the fall of Tunisia.

Commanders

Generalmajor Eberhard Rodt
June 1943 – February 1944

Generalleutnant Eberhard Rodt
February 1944 – April 1945

INSIGNIA

 Few Wehrmacht formations used stars or celestial objects as their divisional symbol. One of the few which did was the 15th Panzergrenadier Division.

 Formed in Sicily after the fall of *Panzerarmee Afrika*, the original three-pointed star was supplemented by a five-pointed star that was easier to apply.

 Variants of the star were applied in the field. Single-colour vehicles had a simple outline: camouflaged vehicles needed the symbol to be painted on a panel.

Körner's *Regimental Gruppe Koerner* (later the 115th Panzergrenadier Regiment) was the division's third regimental formation.

Armour and artillery

Also under divisional command was an armoured reconnaissance battalion (which may have had as many as 40 Panzer IIIs and IVs), the 33rd Engineer Battalion, the 33rd Flak Battalion (which later became the 315th Flak Battalion), the 999th Signal Company and miscellaneous service units. Elements of the Flak battalion were deployed individually or in small groups to protect major roads.

Specifications

Crew: 5

Weight: 27.6 tonnes (25 tons)

Length: 7.02 (23ft 0in)

Width: 2.88m (9ft 5in)

Height: 2.68m (8ft 10in)

Engine: Maybach HL120TRM

Speed: 38km/h (23.6mph)

Range: 210km (130.5 miles)

Radio: FuG5

Armament: 1 x 75mm (3in) KwK 40/43; 2 x 7.92mm (0.3in) MG (one hull-mounted, one coaxial)

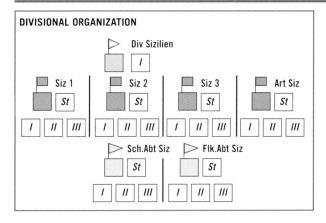

DIVISIONAL ORGANIZATION

battalion of 210mm (8.3in) mortars. The latter was held in Army Reserve until the middle of July, when it was attached to *Gruppe Fullreide.*

In June 1943, the division, commanded from the 5th of that month by *Generalmajor* Eberhard Rodt, took control of the 2nd Company of *schwere Panzer-Abteilung* 504 and its 17 Tiger tanks. The unit was assigned as the 4th Company of *Panzer-Abteilung* 215 at Gierga. However, in the course of forming up, the division was ordered to western Sicily and was instructed to transfer its Tigers to the control of the *Hermann Göring* Division. On 1 July 1943, the division was provisionally renamed the 15th Panzer Division, which had been destroyed in Tunisia.

Against the Americans

Following the Allied landings in Sicily, the division was assigned to XIV Panzer Corps, which was nominally under the control of the Sixth Italian Army. It was thrown into action against the Americans at Licata. Two days later, on 15 July 1943, the division was given its definitive title when it became known as the 15th Panzergrenadier Division.

The division's artillery units formed the *Artillerie-Regiment Sizilien* (later 33rd Artillery Regiment). One battalion was assigned to support each of the regimental groups, and a further battalion was detached to served with *Gruppe Smaltz*, which was under the control of the *Luftwaffe's Fallschirm-Panzer-Division Hermann Göring*. Other artillery assets included one Nebelwerfer (rocket) regiment, one battalion of 150mm (5.9in) mortars, and one

⚙ 15th Panzergrenadier Division
JULY 1943

Descended from the 33rd Infantry Division, the 15th Panzer Division was destroyed in Tunisia. Its traditions were passed on to the 15th Panzergrenadier Division in Sicily.

ON 10 JULY 1943, British and American forces invaded Sicily. The Seventh US Army, under General George S. Patton, attacked through the west. The British Eighth Army under General Bernard Montgomery was to drive up the east coast. It was the largest amphibious operation of the war to date. Over 160,000 men, 14,000 vehicles, 600 tanks and 1800 guns were landed from 2500 ships.

On paper, the Axis forces in Sicily were strong. The Italian Sixth Army could field 230,000 men and 1500 guns. But the units were not motorized, and the difficult terrain and poor roads would hinder attempts by the defenders to concentrate their forces against any Allied thrust. However, the Italians were supported by two German formations: the *Hermann Göring* Division and the newly formed 15th

Panzergrenadier Division. Resistance to the landings was mixed. Some Italian formations fought hard, but others melted away. The Germans, however, fought with exemplary professionalism. Divided into small *Kampfgruppen*, German rearguards tenaciously held up vastly larger forces. Sharp counterattacks won local victories that kept the Allies off-balance. German reinforcements also arrived, including the elite 1st Fallschirmjäger Division and the 29th Panzergrenadier Division.

Montgomery was determined that the British would win the battle for Sicily, with the Seventh US Army providing only a supporting role. The main British thrust would be towards Messina up the eastern coast of the island. Montgomery decided to launch an attack around the western flank of Mount

Etna – in the process cutting off the route of advance of General Omar Bradley's US II Corps. Bradley was forced to move troops around the US 1st Infantry Division, freeing further German forces to counter the British. The 15th Panzergrenadier Division, which had been confronting the Americans, moved to link up with the *Hermann Göring* Division.

By the end of July, the British were within striking distance of Adrono, a key position on the new German defensive line, and threatened to cut off the 15th Panzergrenadier Division in Troina. Fighting fiercely, the division managed to bring the British advance to a halt.

Outflanked by Patton

While Montgomery's Eighth Army made slow progress up the eastern side of the island, the dynamic General Patton was sent on a roundabout route to the north coast. Once past Palermo, he turned eastwards and raced towards Messina.

Clearly, Sicily was lost to the Axis, and Hitler conceded that only a timely withdrawal would avoid a second Tunisia debacle. Stubborn defensive fighting held the Allies back until the beginning of August, when Field Marshal Kesselring ordered the evacuation to begin. On 11 August, every available vessel was employed to ferry the remaining defenders to the mainland.

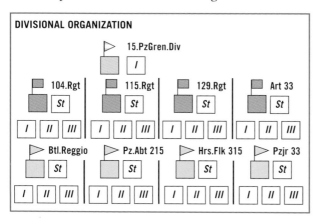

DIVISIONAL ORGANIZATION

15.PzGren.Div / I

104.Rgt / St / I II III
115.Rgt / St / I II III
129.Rgt / St / I II III
Art 33 / St / I II III

Btl.Reggio / St / I II III
Pz.Abt 215 / St / I II III
Hrs.Flk 315 / St / I II III
Pzjr 33 / St / I II III

▶ **Panzerkampfwagen III Ausf G (SdKfz 101)**
Panzer-Abteilung 215 / Stab

By the time the 15th Panzergrenadier Division had been founded, tanks like this Panzer III were largely obsolete. However, they survived as command tanks in Panzer battalions, regiments and brigades.

Specifications

Crew: 4	Speed: 40km/h (24.9mph)
Weight: 22.4 tonnes (20.3 tons)	Range: 165km (102.5 miles)
Length: 5.41m (17ft 8in)	Radio: FuG5
Width: 2.95m (9ft 9in)	Armament: 1 x 37mm (1.5in) KwK L/46
Height: 2.44m (8ft)	or 50mm (2in) KwK L/38 gun; 2 x
Engine: Maybach HL120TRM petrol	7.92mm (0.3in) MG

▶ **Panzerkampfwagen IV Ausf F1 (SdKfz 161)**
Panzer-Abteilung 215

The F1 variant of the Panzer IV was the last to be equipped with a short 7.5cm (3in) gun. Some were still in service in 1943, though a few were converted to F2 standard with the long KwK 40 L/43 cannon.

Specifications

Crew: 5	Speed: 40km/h (24.9mph)
Weight: 25.9 tonnes (23.5 tons)	Range: 210km (130.5 miles)
Length: 5.92m (19ft 5in)	Radio: FuG5
Width: 2.84m (9ft 4in)	Armament: 1 x 75mm (3in) KwK 37
Height: 2.68m (8ft 9.5in)	L/24 gun; 2 x 7.92mm (0.3in) MG
Engine: Maybach HL120TRM	(one hull-mounted, one coaxial)

▶ **PzKpfw VI Tiger I Ausf E (SdKfz 181)**

Schwere Panzer-Abteilung 504 / 2.Kompanie

The Tigers of the 50th Heavy Panzer Battalion were assigned to the 15th Panzergrenadier Division in July 1943, but had been detached from direct service with the division by August of that year.

Specifications

Crew: 5	Engine: Maybach HL210P45
Weight: 62.8 tons (57 tonnes)	Speed: 38km/hr (23mph)
Length: 8.45m (27.7ft)	Range: 140km (87miles)
Width: 3.7m (12ft)	Radio: FuG5
Height: 2.93m (9.6ft)	

 # Italian Campaign
SEPTEMBER 1943 – MAY 1944

Following the withdrawal from Sicily, the 15th Panzergrenadier Division was assigned to the XIV Corps of the German Tenth Army in southern Italy.

THE BRITISH EIGHTH ARMY under Montgomery had landed in the toe of Italy and was now driving up the peninsula to link up with an amphibious landing at Salerno. The initial landing appeared to be a success. But the Allies failed to expand or reinforce their beachhead, while the Germans rushed in every mechanized formation they could scrape together. Despite frequent air attacks that necessitated night marches, and a

gasoline shortage that was never fully overcome, within a week of the landing the Germans had six Panzer or Panzergrenadier divisions opposing four Allied infantry divisions. On 12 September, the Germans commenced an all-out attack, supported by strong *Luftwaffe* elements. The attack almost succeeded, but the Allies held on and the Germans had to retreat northwards to an immensely strong set of defences known as the Gustav Line. After the

Name	Strength
Panzer-Abteilung 215:	
Panzer III	6
Panzer IV	46
PzBefwg III	1

▼ **Mittlerer Schützenpanzerwagen Ausf B (SdKfz 251/2)**

Nebelwerfer-Regiment 71 / II.Bataillon

The 71st Nebelwerfer Regiment was on its way to Africa in 1943. The 2nd Battalion, equipped with self-propelled launchers, was still in Sicily when Tunisia fell, and was used on the island to support the 15th Panzergrenadier Division.

Specifications

Crew: 2 plus 12 troops	Speed: 53km/h (33mph)
Weight: 9.9 tonnes (9 tons)	Range: 300km (186 miles)
Length: 5.98m (19ft 7in)	Radio: FuG Spr Ger 1
Width: 2.1m (6ft 11in)	Armament: 6 x 280mm (11in) or
Height: 1.75m (5ft 8in) or 2.16m	320mm (12.6in) unguided rockets;
(7ft) including MG shield if fitted	1/2 7.92mm (0.3in) MG
Engine: Maybach HL42TUKRM	

fighting at Salerno, the 15th Panzergrenadier Division was deployed to the Rapido River to the south of Monte Cassino. Veteran troops and strong positions ensured that Allied attempts to pierce the line at Cassino were incredibly costly. The 15th Division mauled several US Army attacks over the next months before the French managed a

breakthrough. The German forces retreated in good order to the first of a further series of lines of defence.

The 15th Panzergrenadier Division was withdrawn from the line at the end of May, moving into Tuscany to regroup. However, after the Allied invasion of Normandy in June 1944, the battle-tested formation received orders to move to France.

▶ Mittlerer Lkw Typ S Opel Blitz 3t

15.Panzergrenadier-Division

Owned by General Motors from the 1920s, the Opel factory was taken over by the German Government in 1940. The many variants of the Opel Blitz proved to be tough and reliable under the harshest of conditions.

Specifications	
Crew: 1	Engine: Opel 6-cylinder petrol
Weight: 3.29 tonnes (3 tons)	(73.5hp)
Length: 6.02m (19ft 9in)	Speed: 80km/h (50mph)
Width: 2.27m (7ft 5in)	Range: 410km (255 miles)
Height: 2.18m (7ft 2in)	Radio: None

▶ Krankenkraftwagen Phänomen-Granit 1500S (Kfz 31)

1. / Krankenkraftwagenzug 33

This ambulance has a late standard house-type body fitted to a standard 1.5-tonne (1.47-ton) S-Type 4x2 chassis built by Phänomen, a long-established automotive company based at Zwickau in Saxony.

Specifications	
Crew: 1	Engine: Horch 3.5L or 3.8L V8 petrol
Weight: 1.89 tonnes (1.72 tons)	(82 or 92hp)
Length: 5.05m (16ft 7in)	Speed: 120km/h (74mph)
Width: 1.79m (5ft 10in)	Range: 400km (248 miles)
Height: 1.69m (5ft 6.5in)	Radio: None

▶ Gross Nachrichtkraftwagen Krupp L3H163 (Kfz 72)

Nachrichten-Abteilung 99

The wooden-bodied Kfz 72 van was used for a variety of roles, and was seen as a communications workshop, a telephone exchange, a radio van, a command vehicle, a printing vehicle and a meteorological van.

Specifications	
Crew: 8	Engine: Hwa526D 6.2L diesel
Weight: 5.5 tonnes (5 tons)	Speed: 70km/h (43.4mph)
Length: 6.00m (19ft 8in)	Range: 330km (205 miles)
Width: 2.00m (6ft 6in)	Radio: Various, depending on
Height: 2.76m (9ft 1in)	deployment

▼ Panzer-Abteilung 215

When formed in July 1943, the 15th Panzergrenadier Division controlled three medium Panzer companies and a single heavy Panzer company equipped with Tiger tanks. The medium companies still operated a small number of Panzer IIIs, but the bulk of the battalion's strength was provided by long-barrelled PzKpfw IV Ausf F2 and Ausf G tanks.

Mittlerer Panzer-Kompanie-Stabzug

Mittlerer Panzer-Kompanie

☆ France

JULY–OCTOBER 1944

The Allied invasion of Normandy, combined with the massive Soviet summer offensive in the East, forced the *Wehrmacht* high command into a wholesale rearrangement of its forces.

IN JULY 1944, THE 15TH Panzergrenadier Division was in Florence in Tuscany, recovering from a year of hard combat in Sicily and Italy. With German forces under Field Marshal Albert Kesselring showing every sign of being able to hold the Allies in their step-by-step struggle up the Italian peninsula, it was decided that the tough, battle-hardened 15th Panzergrenadier Division might be better used in France, where Allied armies were on the point of breaking out of Normandy.

In August 1944, the division was moving out of the South of France when the Battle of Normandy came to an end. Surviving German forces in northern France were in full retreat, and fast-moving American armies were sweeping through central France, threatening to cut the division off. The 15th Panzergrenadier Division, now under orders from the German First Army of Army Group B, made a fighting withdrawal northwards into Lothringen (the German name for Lorraine).

Defensive duties

Once in Lorraine, the division was reassigned to the LXVI Army Corps of the German Nineteenth Army,

part of Army Group G. In October, the division was transferred to LVIII Corps of 5.*Panzerarmee*, also assigned to Army Group G. It was thrown into the defence of the Saarland, Adolf Hitler's first territorial acquisition only a decade before.

After the exhilarating sweep across France, Allied armies had stalled near the German border. General Courtney Hodges' First US Army had just started what was to become the bloody battle for the Hürtgen Forest, and General George S. Patton's Third US Army was encountering increasing resistance in the approaches to the Saarland. As part of Fifth Panzer Army, the 15th Division played a full part in slowing the Allied advance.

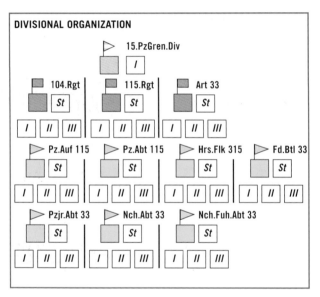

DIVISIONAL ORGANIZATION

▲ **Leichte Personenkraftwagen (Kfz 1)**
33.Aufklärungs-Abteilung

As more VW Kubels were produced, they began supplementing and eventually replacing motorcycles and sidecars in divisional motorcycle battalions and reconnaissance units.

Specifications

Crew: 1	Engine: Volkswagen 998cc petrol (24hp). Later
Weight: 0.64 tonnes (0.58 tons)	Volkswagen 1131cc petrol (25hp)
Length: 3.73m (12 ft 3in)	Speed: 100km/h (62mph)
Width: 1.60m (5ft 3in)	Range: 600km (375 miles)
Height: 1.35m (4ft 5in)	Radio: None

▶ **Jagdpanther (SdKfz 153)**
Panzerjäger-Kampftruppe

Early in 1945, the 15th Panzergrenadier Division operated with a non-standard anti-tank troop, which had 18 Jagdpanthers, three Jagdpanzer IVs, five StuGs, eight towed Pak 40s and eight 8.8cm (3.5in) Flak guns.

Specifications

Crew: 5	Engine: Maybach HL230P30
Weight: 50.7 tons (46 tonnes)	Speed: 46km/hr (29mph)
Length: 9.9m (32.5ft)	Range: 160km (99miles)
Width: 3.42m (11ft)	Radio: FuG5 plus FuG2
Height: 2.72m (9ft)	

▶ **Leichter Spähpanzerwagen (SdKfz 222)**

33.Aufklärungs-Abteilung / Stabkompanie / Spähpanzerwagen-Zug

In France, the 15th Panzergrenadier Division maintained a single armoured car platoon as part of the reconnaissance battalion's staff company. It had at least three SdKfz 221/222s, although these were becoming obsolete.

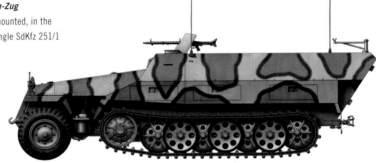

Specifications

Crew: 3	Speed: 85km/h (52.8mph)
Weight: 5.3 tonnes (4.8 tons)	Range: 300km (186 miles)
Length: 4.8m (15ft 8in)	Radio: FuG Spr Ger 'a'
Width: 1.95m (6ft 5in)	Armament: 1 x 20mm (0.7in) KwK 30 L/55
Height: 2.00m (6ft 7in)	cannon; 1 x 7.92mm (0.3in) MG (coaxial)
Engine: Horch 3.5L or 3.8L petrol	

▶ **Mittlerer Kommandopanzerwagen I Ausf C (SdKfz 251/1)**

33.Aufklärungs-Abteilung / Stabkompanie / Spähpanzerwagen-Zug

Although the bulk of the division's Panzergrenadiers were truck-mounted, in the summer of 1944 the division's reconnaissance battalion had a single SdKfz 251/1 half-track in the armoured car platoon of its staff company.

Specifications

Crew: 2 plus 12 troops	(7ft) including MG shield if fitted
Weight: 9.9 tonnes (9 tons)	Engine: Maybach HL42TUKRM
Length: 5.98m (19ft 7in)	Speed: 53km/h (33mph)
Width: 2.1m (6ft 11in)	Range: 300km (186 miles)
Height: 1.75m (5ft 8in) or 2.16m	Radio: FuG Spr Ger 1

 # From the Ardennes to the end
DECEMBER 1944 – APRIL 1945

Although exhausted after months of fighting, the 15th Panzergrenadier Division was to play a major part in *Wacht am Rhein*, Germany's last major offensive in the West.

THREE GERMAN ARMIES had been created for Operation *Wacht am Rhein*, Hitler's surprise attack through the Ardennes. By mid-December, they had been marshalled under a cloak of secrecy opposite a thinly occupied strip of front weakly held by the US VIII Corps.

In the north was the Sixth SS Panzer Army under *Obergruppenführer* Sepp Dietrich. In the middle section of the front waited the Fifth Panzer Army under the experienced young Panzer commander General Hasso von Manteuffel. To the south, flanking the main attack formations, was the German Seventh Army under General Erich Brandenberger.

Initial results, as German Panzers smashed through thin Allied lines, were impressive, but all too quickly the assault began to grind to a halt, faced by fuel shortages and stubborn American resistance. One of the most stubborn examples of that resistance was at the Belgian town of Bastogne, held by the US 10th Armored and 101st Airborne Divisions.

Attack on Bastogne

The main assault on Bastogne was carried out by elements of the 15th Panzergrenadier Division, which attacked early in the morning of Christmas Day 1944. One group of Panzer IVs almost broke through into the town, but were beaten off. The Americans fought on while other German formations bypassed Bastogne, and on 26 December elements of Patton's Third Army, which had been fighting its way northwards, arrived and lifted the siege.

With the failure of the Ardennes offensive, the 15th Panzergrenadier Division took part in the general German withdrawal. Early in 1945, the division fought in the Netherlands and in the Reichswald, attached to 1. *Fallschirmarmee*. In February and March, it was in northern Holland, before retreating across the border into the Emsland. The division surrendered to the British in Wesermünde, near Cuxhaven, in April 1945.

▶ Panzer-Abteilung 115

During the winter of 1943/44, the 15th Panzergrenadier Division's 215th Panzer Battalion was redesignated as the 115th Panzer Battalion. Originally operating with Panzer IIIs and Panzer IVs, it had been re-equipped with assault guns by August of 1944. A single Panzer III command tank remained in service with the battalion HQ company. This remained the standard formation until the end of the war.

Stab Kompanie

Kompanie

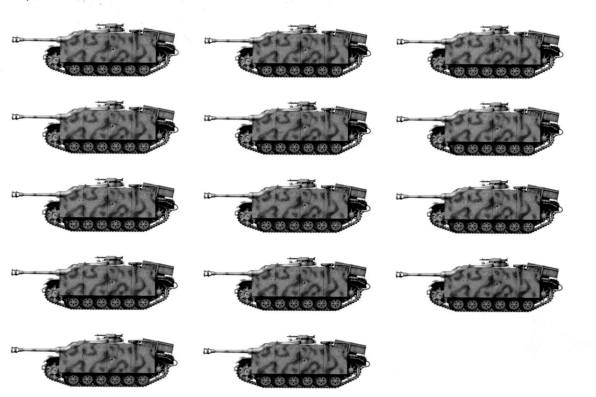

▶ **Leichte Zugkraftwagen 3t (SdKfz 11)**

Artillerie-Regiment 33

The SdKfz 11 was the German Army's standard three-tonne (2.9-ton) artillery
tractor. It was the main prime-mover for the 10.5cm (4.1in) lFH 18.

Specifications

Crew: 1 plus 8 troops	Engine: 6-cylinder petrol (100hp)
Weight: 7.1 tonnes (6.46 tons)	Speed: 53km/h (32.9mph)
Length: 5.48m (18ft 0in)	Range: 122km (75.8 miles)
Width: 1.82m (5ft 11.5in)	Radio: None
Height: 1.62m (5ft 4in)	

Specifications

Crew: 1 plus 26 passengers	Engine: Opel 6-cylinder petrol (73.5hp)
Weight: 3.29 tonnes (3 tons)	Speed: 80km/h (50mph)
Length: 6.02m (19ft 9in)	Range: 410km (255 miles)
Width: 2.27m (7ft 5in)	Radio: None
Height: 2.18m (7ft 2in)	

▼ **Mittlerer Kraftomnibus Opel Blitz 3.6-47S**

15.Panzergrenadier-Division / Divisionstab

The Blitz 3.6-47S, known as the *Wehrmachts-Omnibus*, carried 26 passengers, but
could quickly be converted into an ambulance or a command vehicle.

◀ **Mittlerer Lkw Henschel 33D1**

15.Panzergrenadier-Division / Divisionstab

The motor pool of the divisional headquarters had eleven
trucks, including six medium-capacity vehicles like the
Henschel 33D1.

Specifications

Crew: 1	Engine: 10.7 litre (650ci),
Weight: 6.1 tonnes (6 tons)	six-cylinder petrol (100hp)
Length: 7.4m (24ft)	Speed: 60km/h (37mph)
Width: 2.25m (7ft 4in)	Payload: 3 tonnes (2.95 tons) or
Height: 3.2m (10ft 6in)	18 troops

16th Infantry Division (motorized)

The 16th Infantry Division was one of the first formations to be formed in the newly established *Wehrmacht* after Germany threw off the shackles of the Versailles Treaty.

THE DIVISION WAS FORMED in October 1934 in Münster, and was given the cover name of *Kommandant von Münster*. Following the unveiling of the new *Wehrmacht* in 1935, it was given its definitive designation as the 16th Infantry Division in October of that year.

Part of the first wave (*Erste Welle*) of German mobilization, the division was part of the standing army in 1939. It saw no action in Poland, since it formed part of the Fifth Army in Army Group C, the relatively weak force left on the lower Rhine to guard against any attack by Anglo-French forces.

After a brief period with the Sixth Army, the division was transferred in December 1939 to VI Corps, Twelfth Army, which was part of Army Group A. Based in the Eifel region, it formed part of the huge build-up of German forces in the West, ready for the invasion of the Low Countries and France.

Battle for France

Under the command of General Gerd von Rundstedt, Army Group A was responsible for the powerful attack through the Ardennes which would cut off the Allied field armies as they advanced into Belgium. As a standard infantry division, the 16th lacked the mobility to keep up with the Panzer divisions that smashed through the French defences and raced across northern France. As a result, it played a supporting role, isolating and taking French positions left helpless in the wake of the rampaging German armoured forces.

INSIGNIA

The original emblem of the 16th Infantry Division was an old German runic symbol, the *Dreipass* or *Triskeles*. This was a three-legged sunwheel.

Late in 1942, on the Kalmuch Steppe, the divisional HQ was 'adopted' by a stray greyhound, or *Windhund*, which became the divisional symbol.

Placed in reserve in June 1940, the division was returned to Sennelager in Germany in August, where it was split up to form the nucleus of two new divisions. The staff and bulk of the divisional units became the 16th Panzer Division, while the remainder of the division absorbed the staff and elements of the 228th Infantry Division and became the 16th Infantry Division (motorized). After completing its training in December, the new motorized division was sent to western France, where it continued to work up while undertaking occupation duties.

In April 1941, the division was transferred to XXXXVI Corps, part of the Second Army, which was

▼ **France, 1940**

In a northern French town, two German infantrymen make their way warily down a street, ignoring the pleas of a wounded French soldier.

Commanders

Generalmajor Gotthard Heinrici *October 1937*	Generalleutnant Siegfried Henrici *November 1941*
Generalleutnant Heinrich Krampf *February 1940*	Generalmajor Gerhard Graf von Schwerin *November 1942*
Generalmajor Hans-Valentin Hube *June 1940*	Generalmajor Wilhelm Crisollo *May 1943*
General der Infanterie Friedrich-Wilhelm von Chappus *November 1940*	Generalmajor Gerhard Graf von Schwerin *June 1943*
Generalleutnant Siegfried Henrici *March 1941*	Generalmajor Günther von Manteuffel *January 1944*
Generalleutnant Johannes Streich *October 1941*	Generalmajor Karl Stingl *March 1944*

rapidly being assembled in Hungary for the Balkans campaign. The *Wehrmacht* had no plans to invade the Balkans, but Italy's ill-advised attack on Greece had come unstuck, and Hitler had to send troops to help his fellow dictator, Mussolini.

Balkans and Russia

The Germans forced the Yugoslav Government to allow its forces transit, but when the Yugoslav Government was overthrown by an anti-German uprising, plans for the *Wehrmacht* to pass through Yugoslavia on its way to Greece became a full-scale invasion and conquest of the country. The Second

Army struck south out of Hungary into Croatia, and the 16th Division ended the campaign at Sarajevo in Bosnia-Herzegovina.

Withdrawn to Germany to rest and refit, the 16th Division missed the start of the invasion of Russia, Operation *Barbarossa*, in June 1941. However, once brought back up to strength, it was sent to join von Rundstedt's Army Group South. The division fought against the Soviets in the Ukraine, at Dubno and Nikolayev, where it aided in helping to break the Stalin Line.

In September 1941, the division was involved in the giant battle of encirclement at Kiev, and by November it had advanced into the region around Kursk. The Soviet winter offensive that started at Moscow in December 1941 was to continue with a series of attacks up and down the front. Although the German lines bent, they did not break, and by the spring of 1942 the situation had stabilized enough for the *Führer* and the German high command to consider the aims of their next summer offensive.

Divisional History	Formed
Kommandant von Münster	1934
16.Infanterie-Division	1935
16.Infanterie-Division (mot)	1940
16.Panzergrenadier-Division	1943

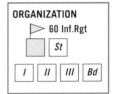

ORGANIZATION

60 Inf.Rgt

St

| I | II | III | Bd |

▶ **Panzerkampfwagen II Ausf B/C (SdKfz 121)**

Panzer-Abteilung 116 / leichte Panzer-Kompanie

Motorized infantry divisions began to receive tank battalions in 1941. In 1942, *Panzer-Abteilung* 116 had ten Panzer IIs on strength in 1942, and there were four remaining when the formation became a Panzergrenadier division in June 1943.

Specifications

Crew: 3

Weight: 9.8 tonnes (8.9 tons)

Length: 4.81m (15ft 10in)

Width: 2.22m (7ft 4in)

Height: 1.99m (6ft 6in)

Engine: Maybach HL62TR (140hp)

Speed: 40km/h (24.9mph)

Range: 200km (124.3 miles)

Radio: FuG5

Armament: 1 x 20mm (0.7in) KwK 30 or 38

L/55 cannon; 1 x 7.92mm (0.3in) MG (coaxial)

▶ **Panzerkampfwagen III Ausf J (SdKfz 141/1)**

Panzer Abteilung 116

During the drive towards the Caucasus in 1942 and in the battles around Stalingrad, the bulk of the 16th Division's tank strength was provided by 35 Panzer IIIs armed with long 5cm (2in) guns.

Specifications

Crew: 4

Weight: 22.4 tonnes (20.3 tons)

Length: 5.41m (17ft 8in)

Width: 2.95m (9ft 9in)

Height: 2.44m (8ft)

Engine: Maybach HL120TRM petrol

(300hp)

Speed: 40km/h (24.9mph)

Range: 165km (102.5 miles)

Radio: FuG5

Armament: 1 x 50mm (2in) KwK L/38

gun; 2 x 7.92mm (0.3in) MG (one

coaxial, one hull-mounted)

Race for the Caucasus
SUMMER 1942

The German summer offensive of 1942 had two main objectives. After destroying Soviet forces on the Don, at Stalingrad, the *Wehrmacht* would turn south towards the Caucasus oilfields.

EARLY SUCCESSES IN THE INITIAL attack in the Voronezh sector led Hitler to order that both main objectives be attacked simultaneously, rather than in sequence. As a result, the Sixth Army commanded by General Paulus drove for Stalingrad while Army Group A advanced on the Caucasus.

The 16.*Infanterie-Division (mot)* was attached to III Corps of Kleist's First Panzer Army, fighting south and east towards Aramvir and Maikop at the foot of the Caucasus. However, a gap began to open between Kleist's Panzers and the Sixth Army that was targeted on Stalingrad.

Farthest advance

The 16.*Infanterie-Division (mot)* was sent to an area south of Stalingrad to fill the gap between Kleist's First Panzer Army and Hoth's Fourth Panzer Army, which had been moved from the Stalingrad drive down to the Caucasus and back again. The 16th Division advanced into the Kalmuck Steppe, and a divisional reconnaissance unit, *Aufklärungs-Abteilung 341*, pushed to within 32km (20 miles) of Astrakhan on the Caspian Sea, the most easterly point reached by any German unit.

Windhund

In November, the division acquired a new nickname. A patrol found a stray, starving female greyhound, or *Windhund*. The divisional commander, *Generalmajor* Gerhard Graf von Schwerin, decided to adopt the dog and the troops named her Sascha.

To the men of the division, Sascha was an ideal symbol of their rapid advances in the summer, and when von Schwerin suggested that the new divisional symbol, or *Truppenkennzeichen*, should be the *Windhund*, his proposal was accepted with enthusiasm by the troops.

DIVISIONAL ORGANIZATION

16.Inf.Div / I

60.Rgt — St — I / II / III
156.Rgt — St — I / II / III
Art.Rgt 146 — St — I / II / III

Pz.Abt 116 — St — I / II / III
Pz.Auf 116 — St — I / II / III
Hrs.Flk 218 — St — I / II / III

Pzjr.Abt 228 — St — I / II / III
Pnr.Btl 675 — St — I / II / III

▶ **Mittlerer Funk Kraftwagen (Kfz 15/2)**

Nachrichten-Abteilung 228

The Kfz 15 was one of the standard vehicles used by communications battalions of motorized divisions. Typically, the battalion would have more than 30 such cars in its telephone and radio platoons.

Specifications	
Crew: 1	Engine: Mercedes-Benz 6-cylinder petrol
Weight: 2.4 tonnes (2.2 tons)	(90hp)
Length: 4.44m (14ft 7in)	Speed: 88km/h (55mph)
Width: 1.68m (5ft 6in)	Range: 400km (250 miles)
Height: 1.73m (5ft 8in)	Radio: Various depending on deployment

▶ Mittlerer Lkw Typ S Opel Blitz 3t

16.Infanterie-Division (mot)

Each infantry squad in a motorized division had a medium truck for transport. With four squads per platoon and three platoons per company, twelve trucks were needed as troop carriers for each company.

Specifications

Crew: 1	Engine: Opel 6-cylinder petrol
Weight: 3.29 tonnes (3 tons)	(73.5hp)
Length: 6.02m (19ft 9in)	Speed: 80km/h (50mph)
Width: 2.27m (7ft 5in)	Range: 410km (255 miles)
Height: 2.18m (7ft 2in)	Radio: None

▶ Mittlerer Lkw A-Typ Opel Blitz 3.6-6700 mit 2-cm Flak 38

Heeres-Flak-Abteilung 281

The 16th Infantry Division had a single light Flak battery in its Flak battalion. It was armed with twelve 2cm (0.7in) Flak guns, which were usually towed but which could also be mounted on trucks.

Specifications

Crew: 1	(73.5hp)
Weight: 3.29 tonnes (3 tons)	Speed: 80km/h (50mph)
Length: 6.02m (19ft 9in)	Range: 410km (255 miles)
Width: 2.27m (7ft 5in)	Radio: None
Height: 2.18m (7ft 2in)	Armament: Twin or quad 20mm
Engine: Opel 6-cylinder petrol	(0.7in) Flak 38 cannon

Destroyed in the East
1943–1944

Once the massive Soviet counteroffensive isolated the German Sixth Army at Stalingrad, the 16th Division was attached to the Fourth Panzer Army in its unsuccessful relief attempt.

AFTER THE BRUTAL AND FIERCE battles for Stalingrad, the 16.*Infanterie-Division (mot)*, having managed to avoid encirclement, took part in defensive operations in the southern sector, fighting against the Soviet offensives of the winter of 1942/43. The division played a full part in the German defensive operations after the Soviet offensives threatened to smash the German front, helping to hold a line of retreat open as the German forces in the Caucasus, under the command of Kleist, were forced to withdraw into the Ukraine. The 16.*Infanterie-Division (mot)* then took part in the fighting withdrawal to the Mius River.

The 16.*Infanterie-Division (mot)* was transferred to the newly reconstituted Sixth Army in the spring of 1943. In May and June of 1943, the division was redesignated as the 16.*Panzergrenadier-Division* in line with the *Führerbefehl* reorganizing all motorized infantry formations. The new Panzergrenadier division did not participate in the Battle of Kursk, but it did fight in the retreat from the Mius River and suffered heavy casualties during the winter fighting in the southern Ukraine around Zaporozhe and in the Dnieper battles.

Losses were so heavy that the remnants of the

division were almost completely non-effective in combat. Early in 1944, the 16th Panzergrenadier-Division was transferred to France.

Rebuilt as a Panzer division

At the end of March 1944, the formation was reorganized as the 116th Panzer Division. The non-standard divisional number came from the division's own 116th Panzer Battalion, since there was already a 16th Panzer Division (which had already been formed out of the 16th Infantry Division in 1940). The new division absorbed the 179th Reserve Panzer Division in the process.

Upon its formation, the 116th Panzer Division was immediately sent to the Pas-de-Calais for an expected Allied amphibious invasion, and it was on the north bank of the Seine on 6 June 1944. In August, it took part in Operation *Lüttich*, the German counteroffensive at Mortain, which resulted in the largest tank battle of the Normandy campaign. By the 21st of that month, after breaking out of the Falaise pocket, the 'Greyhound Division' was down to only 600 men, 12 tanks and no artillery. It was the

Panzer-Abteilung 116:	Strength
Panzer III Befehlswagen	1
Panzer II	4
Panzer III	32
Panzer III (short-barrel 75mm/3in)	5
Panzer IV (long barrel)	11

sole German formation garrisoning Aachen on 13 September 1944, when the US 3rd Armored Division began its assault on the *Westwall*. The 116th Panzer Division was withdrawn for refitting and then recommitted, but failed to save the city.

Final acts

The Greyhound Division fought in the ferocious Battle of the Hurtgen Forest, and then took part in the Battle of the Bulge, again sustaining heavy casualties. It was caught in the Wesel pocket, but managed to escape across the Rhine. It surrendered with the final collapse of Army Group B in the Ruhr pocket in April 1945.

▼ Schwere Kraftrad 750-cc mit Seitenwagen
Panzergrenadier-Regiment 60 / Stab Kompanie

Motorcycles were part of the standard equipment in most headquarters companies and detachments within a division. The Stab, or headquarters, company of 60th Panzergrenadier Regiment would have had at least 20 solo motorcycles and 12 or more motorcycles with sidecars.

Specifications	
Crew: 2	Engine: BMW 750cc petrol (26hp)
Weight: 0.67 tonnes (0.61 tons)	Speed: 92km/h (57mph)
Length: 2.4m (7ft 10in)	Range: 340km (211 miles)
Width: 1.73m (5ft 8in)	Radio: None
Height: 1m (3ft in)	Armament: 1 x 7.92mm (0.3in) MG (if fitted)

▶ 7.5-cm Pak 40 Auf Fahrgestell PzKpfw II Marder II
Panzerjäger-Abteilung 228

Based on the Panzer II chassis, the Marder II tank-hunter entered service in July 1942. It remained on frontline service with Panzerjäger detachments until the end of the war in 1945.

Specifications	
Crew: 3 or 4	Speed: 40km/h (24.9mph)
Weight: 11 tonnes (10 tons)	Range: 200km (124.3 miles)
Length: 6.36m (20ft 10in)	Radio: FuG5
Width: 2.28m (7ft 6in)	Armament: 1 x 75mm (3in) PaK 40/2 anti-tank
Height: 2.2m (7ft 2.5in)	gun; 1 x 7.92mm (0.3in) MG (top-mounted)
Engine: Maybach HL62TR (140hp)	

▲ **Battle of the Bulge**
German Panzergrenadiers smile for the camera following the limited success of the German offensive in the Ardennes, January 1945.

▶ **Leichte Nachricht Kraftwagen Stöwer 40 (Kfz 2)**
Nachrichten-Abteilung 16
The Stöwer Kfz 2 was a version of the standard *leichte Einheits Personenkraftwagen* design. It was used as a radio or telephone car, and as a maintenance vehicle for the communications battalion.

Specifications

Crew: 1	Engine: Stöwer AW2 or R180W petrol (50hp)
Weight: 1.81 tonnes (1.65 tons)	Speed: 100km/h (62.5mph)
Length: 3.58m (11ft 9in)	Range: 500km (311 miles)
Width: 1.57m (5ft 2in)	Radio: None
Height: 1.78 (5ft 10in)	

▶ **2-cm Flak auf Zgkw 1t (SdKfz 7/4)**
Panzergrenadier-Regiment 60 / I.Bataillon / Flak-Kompanie (SF)
Although the division had an Army Flak battalion attached, the three Panzergrenadier battalions in each of the two Panzergrenadier regiments had their own self-propelled light anti-aircraft company with 2cm (0.7in) Flak.

Specifications

Crew: 7	6-cylinder (140hp)
Weight: 1.16 tonnes (1.06 tons)	Speed: 50km/h (31mph)
Length: 6.55m (21ft 6in)	Range: 250km (156 miles)
Width: 2.40m (7ft 10.5in)	Radio: None
Height: 3.20m (10ft 6in)	Armament: Quad 20mm (0.7in)
Engine: Maybach HL62TUK	Flak 38

18th Infantry Division (motorized)

The 18th Infantry Division had the usual history of such formations, beginning as a standard infantry unit before successively becoming motorized and then partly armoured.

T HIS UNIT WAS FORMED in October 1934 in Liegnitz as the *Wehrgauleitung Liegnitz*. Shortly after the unit was established, it was given the cover name *Infanteriefübrer* III. The organic regimental units of this division were formed by the expansion of the 8.(*Preussisches*) *Infanterie-Regiment* of the 3.*Division* of the *Reichswehr*, based in Berlin, and the 12.*Infanterie-Regiment* of the 4.*Division* of the *Reichswehr*, based in Dresden.

With the formal announcement of the creation of the *Wehrmacht* (which had covertly been in place for over a year) on 15 October 1935, the cover name *Infanteriefübrer* III was dropped and the unit became offically known as the 18.*Infanterie-Division*. In

INSIGNIA

The 18th Infantry Division's symbol was inspired by the ancient runic writing system, but was not one of the letters of the original runic alphabets.

The Eagle was a popular Nazi symbol and was used in a variant of the 18th Division's insignia, though it is unlikely to have been applied in combat.

August 1939, the division was brought up to full mobilization strength, ready for the attack on Poland.

In September 1939, the 18th Infantry Division was attached to XI Corps of the Tenth Army, part of Army Group South. Tenth Army, under the command of General Walter von Reichenau, assembled in German Silesia, from where it would drive through the heart of Poland to the Polish capital, Warsaw.

After the fall of Poland, the 18th Division was part of the general movement of forces to western Germany, where it went into Sixth Army reserve while resting and refitting.

With Army Group B

In January 1940, having been brought back up to combat strength, the division was assigned to IV Corps of the Sixth Army. It formed part of General von Bock's Army Group B, which attacked the Low Countries in May 1940. The division advanced into Holland before moving south into Flanders. This attack successfully drew the Allied armies out of their fortified positions along the French border, leaving them vulnerable to the surprise attack by von Rundstedt's Army Group A through the Ardennes.

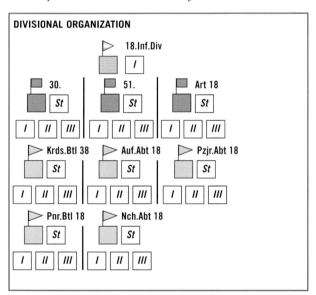

DIVISIONAL ORGANIZATION

18.Inf.Div / I

30. St / I II III
51. St / I II III
Art 18 St / I II III

Krds.Btl 38 St / I II III
Auf.Abt 18 St / I II III
Pzjr.Abt 18 St / I II III

Pnr.Btl 18 St / I II III
Nch.Abt 18 St / I II III

Commanders

Generalleutnant Friedrich-Karl Cranz
August 1939 – March 1941

Generalmajor Friedrich Herrlein
March–December 1941

Generalleutnant Werner von Erdmannsdorff
December 1941 – June 1943

General der Infanterie Werner von
Erdmannsdorff *June–August 1943*

Generalleutnant Karl Zutavern
August 1943 – April 1944

General der Artillerie Curt Jahn
April–May 1944

Generalleutnant Karl Zutavern
May–September 1944

Generalleutnant Dr Hans Bölsen
September–December 1944

Generalmajor Josef Rauch
January 1945 – May 1945

Divisional History	Formed
Wehrgauleitung Liegnitz/Infanteriefübrer III	1934
18.Infanterie-Division	1935
18.Infanterie-Division (mot)	1940
18.Panzergrenadier-Division	1943

After the fall of France, the division was employed on occupation duties with the Second Army. In October, the division was returned to Germany where it was to undergo motorization. Now known as the 18.*Infanterie-Division (mot)*, it was assigned to the XXXXVI Corps of the Eleventh Army.

▶ **Infantry Mortars**

Mortars were an important part of infantry equipment. Every infantry and reconnaissance company had at least two 8cm (3.1in) Granatwerfer 34 in its trucks or half-tracks, and most heavy companies had up to eight weapons.

▼ **Schwerer Einheits Kommandokraftwagen Horch 40 (Kfz 18)**

18.Infanterie-Division (mot)

The command variant of the standard *Wehrmacht* heavy car was used by senior officers at divisional level and higher as a personal transport in the field.

Specifications	
Crew: 1	Engine: Horch 6-cylinder petrol (90hp)
Weight: 2.4 tonnes (2.2 tons)	Speed: 88km/h (55 mph)
Length: 4.44m (14ft 7in)	Range: 400km (250 miles)
Width: 1.68m (5ft 6in)	Radio: None usually fitted
Height: 1.73m (5ft 8in)	

 # Barbarossa

JUNE 1941

The men of the 18th Division spent the winter of 1940/41 receiving new equipment and training for their new role as motorized infantrymen.

IN MAY 1941, THE NEW MOTORIZED division was assigned to General Hermann Hoth's 3rd Panzer Group. Pretty much an armoured army, 3.*Panzergruppe* was one of two such formations assigned to Field Marshal Fedor von Bock's Army Group Centre for the German invasion of the Soviet Union, Operation *Barbarossa*.

Attacking to the north and south of the Pripet Marshes, Bock's Panzer spearheads raced towards the city of Minsk. Guderian's 2.*Panzergruppe* would swing up from the south to meet Hoth's spearheads sweeping down from the north. In this way, the Soviet frontline forces would be cut off in a huge

cauldron. Once they had run out of supplies, the only option would be to surrender.

By 24 June, less than three days after the attack had begun, 17th Panzer Division had arrived at Slonim, more than 140km (87 miles) from the border and midway to the Germans' first objective. On the afternoon of the 27th, the division's leading tanks reached Minsk, where they encountered the spearheads of Hoth's 3.*Panzergruppe*, which had driven 350km (217 miles) in five days.

Hoth and Guderian continued to drive their Panzers and motorized infantry eastwards, eyes firmly set on ultimately taking Moscow. Hitler had other ideas, however. He ordered Guderian southwards to link up with von Rundstedt's Army Group South, the aim being to eliminate the huge Soviet army around Kiev. The attack on Moscow was halted, and several units from Army Group Centre were transferred to Army Group North, whose attack on Leningrad had stalled just short of the objective.

Driving up the west bank of the Volkhov, the leading German tank units reached Ishora, only

17km (10.5 miles) from the centre of Leningrad. The motorized infantry swung up to the east towards the River Neva and the shores of Lake Ladoga. The former capital of Russia was now surrounded.

But not yet occupied: the two leading divisions were soon enmeshed in a labyrinth of anti-tank ditches and straggling earthworks thrown up by the desperate Leningraders while the Germans had paused to regroup. By the evening of 10 September,

▼ Panzerjäger-Abteilung 18

In 1941, the standard organization for the *Panzerjäger-Abteilung* of a motorized infantry division included both 3.7cm (1.5in) platoons and 5cm (2in) platoons as seen here. A self-propelled heavy company had been added by the summer of 1942. When upgraded in June 1943, the 18th Panzergrenadier Division's 118th Panzerjäger Battalion was fully equipped with self-propelled tank-destroyers. After the division was wiped out with Army Group Centre in the summer of 1944, it was rebuilt as a *Kampfgruppe*. When it was expanded to full division size in January 1945, its *Panzerjäger-Abteilung* fielded two batteries of StuGs and one of towed 7.5cm (3in) Pak 40s.

Medium platoon

Light platoon

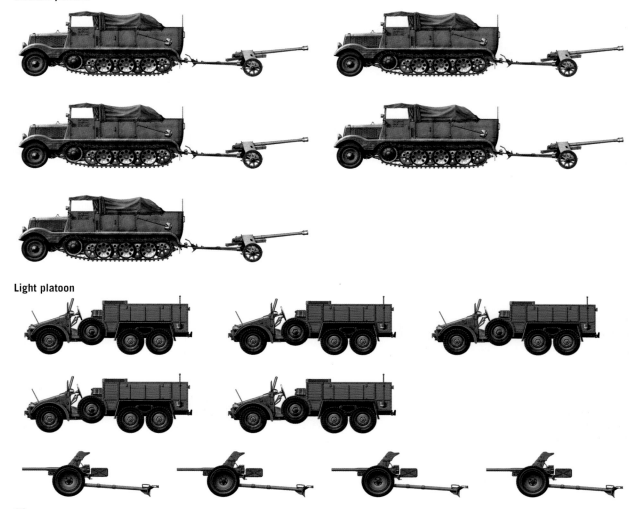

German units had reached the Dugerdorf Heights, 10km (6.2 miles) southeast of the city.

However, so many Panzers had been hit or had broken down that the momentum of the attack had been dissipated. German infantry crept up on their left during the following day, entered the Leningrad suburbs of Slutsk and Pushkin, and in the evening occupied the Summer Palace of the Tsars at Krasnoye Selo. But the impetus had gone.

The 18th Infantry Division (mot) was transferred from 3.*Panzergruppe* to the Sixteenth Army, part of Army Group North. Moving north from Minsk to the Volkhov Front, southeast of Leningrad, it was to continue in the fierce but indecisive fighting for Leningrad for the next year and a half, before being transferred back to Army Group Centre in the autumn of 1943, by which time it had been renamed the 18.*Panzergrenadier-Division*.

▶ Protz Kw Krupp L2H143 (Kfz 69)

Panzergrenadier Regiment 30 / I Bataillon / schwere Kompanie / Flak Zug

The prime-mover (light artillery tractor) variant of the Krupp Protz was given the designation Kfz 69. Manufactured between 1937 and 1942, approximately 7000 L2H43s and L2H143s were built.

Specifications

Crew: 2	Engine: Krupp 3.3L 4-cylinder (60hp)
Weight: 2.45 tonnes (2.23 tons)	Speed: 70km/h (43mph)
Length: 5.10m (16ft 8in)	Range: 450km (280 miles)
Width: 1.93m (6ft 4in)	Radio: None
Height: 1.96m (6ft 5in)	

▶ Schwere geländegängige gepanzerte Personenkraftwagen (SdKfz 247)

Panzer-Aufklärungs-Abteilung 118 / Stab

The SdKfz 247 was an armoured staff car initially based on the Krupp L2H143 chassis, though later variants used the standard 4x4 heavy car chassis. They were issued to the commanders of the reconnaissance battalions of Panzer and motorized units.

Specifications

Crew: 2	Engine: Krupp M304 3.3L 4-cylinder petrol
Weight: 4.6 tonnes (4.2 tons)	(60hp)
Length: 4.60m (15ft 2in)	Speed: 70km/h (43mph)
Width: 1.90m (6ft 3in)	Range: 390km (242 miles)
Height: 1.70m (5ft 7in)	Radio: Various

▶ Krankenkraftwagen Phänomen Granit 25H (Kfz 31)

18.Krankenkraftwagenzug / 1.Gruppe

Medical units attached to infantry and Panzergrenadier divisions usually included two medical companies and two or three ambulance platoons. Each ambulance platoon consisted of three *Gruppen*, or sections, with five ambulances.

Specifications

Crew: 1	Engine: Horch 3.5L or 3.8L V8 petrol
Weight: 1.89 tonnes (1.72 tons)	(82 or 92hp)
Length: 5.05m (16ft 7in)	Speed: 120km/h (74mph)
Width: 1.79m (5ft 10in)	Range: 400km (248 miles)
Height: 1.69m (5ft 6.5in)	Radio: None

Destroyed with Army Group Centre
JUNE 1943 – JULY 1944

The 18th Infantry Division (mot) was redesignated as the 18th Panzergrenadier Division on 23 June 1943. After refitting, it rejoined Army Group Centre at Jelna, near Smolensk, in October.

IN NOVEMBER 1943, the division was in action on the Orscha sector, moving to Bobruisk in February. In spite of Soviet victories elsewhere, the Germans held the Red Army off on the central front until July of 1944.

Operation *Bagration*

However, the *Wehrmacht* had no answer to the titanic Soviet summer offensive known as Operation *Bagration*. In less than two months, Army Group Centre had been torn apart and the Germans had been pushed back to the Polish border. In the process, the 18th Panzergrenadier Division had been almost

totally destroyed in the Bobruisk pocket. What few scraps of the division that survived were attached to the 105th Panzer Brigade.

Name	Strength
Panzer-Aufklärungs-Abteilung 118:	
SdKfz 222 light armoured cars	12
SdKfz 223 light armoured cars	6
Kfz 69 lt trucks towing 7.5cm (3in) leichtes IG	2
Kfz 70 lt trucks towing 2.8cm (1.1in) sPzB 41	3
SdKfz 10 half-trks towing 7.5cm (3in) PAK 40	3

▶ **Panzerjäger 38(t) für 76.2-mm Pak 36(r) (SdKfz 139)**
Panzerjäger-Abteilung 118
Several hundred Marder IIIs, equipped with captured Soviet 76.2-mm guns, were sent to Panzerjäger detachments in 1942. By 1943, they were being supplemented by vehicles mounting 7.5-cm Pak 40s.

Specifications	
Crew: 4	Speed: 42km/h (26mph)
Weight: 11.76 tonnes (10.67 tons)	Range: 185km (115 miles)
Length: 5.85m (19ft 2in)	Radio: FuG Spr 'd'
Width: 2.16m (7ft 0in)	Armament: 1 x 76.2mm (3in) FK296
Height: 2.50m (8ft 2in)	anti-tank gun
Engine: Praga EPA or EPA/2	

▶ **7.5-cm Sturmgeschütz 40 Ausf G (SdKfz 142/1)**
Panzer Abteilung 118 / I Kompanie
At the time of its destruction in the summer of 1944, the 18th Division's Panzer battalion was equipped with three companies each with 14 StuG assault guns.

Specifications	
Crew: 4	Speed: 40km/h (24.9mph)
Weight: 26.3 tonnes (23.9 tons)	Range: 155km (96.3 miles)
Length: 6.77m (22ft 2in)	Radio: FuG15 and FuG16
Width: 2.95m (9ft 8in)	Armament: 1 x 75mm (3in) StuG
Height: 2.16m (7ft 0in)	L/48 cannon
Engine: Maybach HL120TRM	

▶ **Mittlerer Lkw Typ S Opel Blitz 3t**

18.Panzergrenadier-Division

Every unit of the German armed forces used a large number of Opel trucks as transports. They became the mainstay of the motorized divisions.

Specifications

Crew: 1	Engine: Opel 6-cylinder petrol
Weight: 3.29 tonnes (3 tons)	(73.5hp)
Length: 6.02m (19ft 9in)	Speed: 80km/h (50mph)
Width: 2.27m (7ft 5in)	Range: 410km (255 miles)
Height: 2.18m (7ft 2in)	Radio: None

▶ **Mittlerer Lkw Henschel L33**

18.Panzergrenadier-Division

Manufactured between 1931 and 1941, the Henschel 33G1 and the very similar Krupp L3H163 and Mercedes LG3000 were built in fairly large numbers to a common military specification in a wide variety of body styles.

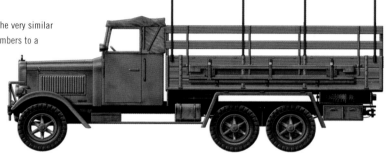

Specifications

Crew: 1	Engine: 10.7 litre (650ci),
Weight: 6.1 tonnes (6 tons)	six-cylinder petrol (100hp)
Length: 7.4m (24ft)	Speed: 60km/h (37mph)
Width: 2.25m (7ft 4in)	Payload: 3 tonnes (2.95 tons)
Height: 3.2m (10ft 6in)	or 18 troops

▽ Division rebuilt – again and again
SEPTEMBER 1944 – MAY 1945

With the formation formally declared destroyed at the end of July 1944, it was not originally intended that the 18th Panzergrenadier Division should be reconstituted.

HOWEVER, THE HIGH COMMAND changed its mind, and the division was ordered to be re-formed on 7 September 1944 at *Truppenübungsplatz* (TrpÜbPl) Neuhammer, a troop training area in Silesia. Known as *Kampfgruppe 18.Pzgren. Div.*, the formation was centred on the independent *Panzer-Brigade* 105. The re-formation was never completed, though, and *Panzer-Brigade* 105 remained independent.

A second attempt to re-form the division was attempted in December 1944 in *Wehrkreis* I (Königsberg Military District), the divisional title being applied to a variety of units thrown together on an ad hoc basis. East Prussia was cut off. The Third

Panzer Army, under *Generaloberst* Erhard Raus, fell back into Königsberg and the Samland peninsula. The beleaguered Germans were joined by the former garrison of Memel, evacuated on 29 January under the guns of the surviving units of the German Navy, including the heavy cruiser *Prinz Eugen*. From the Baltic to southern Poland, improvised *Kampfgruppen* fought desperately, firstly to win time for German forces to make good their escape, and then to break free themselves. As the end drew near, the 18th Panzergrenadier Division had been worn down to almost nothing, and it was again disbanded at the beginning of March 1945 in East Prussia.

The division was re-formed a final time on 21 March 1945, in the region of the Vistula River, mainly from portions of *Panzer-Division Holstein* and *Panzer-Division Schlesien*. The divisional *Stab* (headquarters) was re-formed as *Stab/Division Ulrich von Hutten* on 4 April 1945.

On the morning of 21 April, Zhukov's tanks entered the northern suburbs of Berlin, and Konev's tanks were pressing up from the south. Against the overwhelming might of the Red Army, there was little the defenders could do except make the inevitable Soviet victory as costly as possible. The remnants of the 18th Division continued in combat in the Battle of Berlin. The survivors were still trying to fight their way out of the city on 2 May 1945, when the German capital finally surrendered to the Soviets.

▶ **Jagdpanzer IV/70 (V) (SdKfz 162/1)**
Panzer-Regiment 118 / I.Abteilung / 4.Kompanie (Jagdpanzer)

The 18th Panzergrenadier Division absorbed the armoured units of the Schlesien and Holstein Panzer Divisions when it was rebuilt in the last two months of the war. In March 1945, it received 18 Jagdpanzer IV/70s.

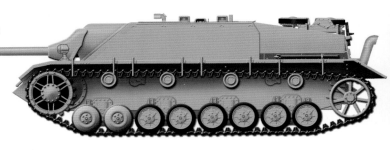

Specifications

Crew: 4	Speed: 35km/h (21.7mph)
Weight: 25.8 tonnes (23.48 tons)	Range: 210km (130.5 miles)
Length: 8.50 (27ft 10.5in)	Radio: FuG5
Width: 3.17m (10ft 5in)	Armament: 1 x 75mm (3in) PaK
Height: 2.85m (9ft 4in)	42 L/70 anti-tank gun; 1 x
Engine: Maybach HL120TRM	7.92mm (0.3in) MG
(300hp)	

▼ **Mittlerer Schützenpanzerwagen Ausf D (SdKfz 251/22)**
Schlesien Panzer Division, later 18th Panzerjäger Battalion

Known as the Kanonen SPW, the SdKfz 251/22 was introduced on Hitler's orders at the end of 1944. The 7.5cm (3in) Pak 40 was mounted minus its wheels into a standard SPW. The hull was slightly cut down to allow the gun to traverse.

Specifications

Crew: 4 or 5	Speed: 50km/h (31mph)
Weight: 8 tonnes (7.28 tons)	Range: 300km (186 miles)
Length: 5.98m (19ft 7in)	Radio: None
Width: 2.1m (6ft 11in)	Armament: 1 x 75mm (3in) PaK 40
Height: 2.25m (7ft 4.5in)	L/46 anti-tank gun; 1 x 7.92mm
Engine: Maybach HL42TUKRM	(0.3in) MG (rear-mounted)
6-cylinder petrol (100hp)	

▶ **Panzerkampfwagen IV Ausf H (SdKfz 161/2)**
Panzer-Regiment 118 / I.Abteilung

In early 1945, the 118th Panzer Regiment had three medium Panzer companies consisting of Panzer IVs. Initially, it had only nine Panzer IVs until 26 tanks were delivered in March.

Specifications

Crew: 5	Speed: 38km/h (23.6mph)
Weight: 27.6 tonnes (25 tons)	Range: 210km (130.5 miles)
Length: 7.02 (23ft 0in)	Radio: FuG5
Width: 2.88m (9ft 5in)	Armament: 1 x 75mm (3in) KwK
Height: 2.68m (8ft 10in)	40/43; 2 x 7.92mm (0.3in) MG
Engine: Maybach HL120TRM	(one hull-mounted, one coaxial)

▶ **7.5-cm Sturmgeschütz 40 Ausf G (SdKfz 142/1)**

Panzerjäger-Abteilung 18 / Sturmgeschütz-Batterie

The 18th Panzergrenadier Division was due to receive two batteries of StuGs in September 1944, but the division's reconstruction was delayed and many of the units were transferred to the 105th Panzer Brigade.

Specifications

Crew: 4	Engine: Maybach HL120TRM
Weight: 26.3 tonnes (23.9 tons)	Speed: 40km/h (24.9mph)
Length: 6.77m (22ft 2in)	Range: 155km (96.3 miles)
Width: 2.95m (9ft 8in)	Radio: FuG15 and FuG16
Height: 2.16m (7ft 0in)	Armament: 1 x 75mm (3in) StuG L/48 cannon

▼ **1st Panzer Battalion, 118 Panzer Regiment, April 1945**

Early in March 1945, what was left of the 18th Panzergrenadier Division was disbanded. On 21 March 1945, however, the division was ordered to re-form for the last time, incorporating the short-lived Holstein and Schlesien Panzer Divisions. It began to receive new equipment late in March, including ten powerful Jagdpanzer IVs that joined the eight already in service with the Jagdpanzer Company of the 118th Panzer Regiment. Most were destroyed in the final battles for Berlin.

Jagdpanzer-Kompanie, Panzer-Regiment 118

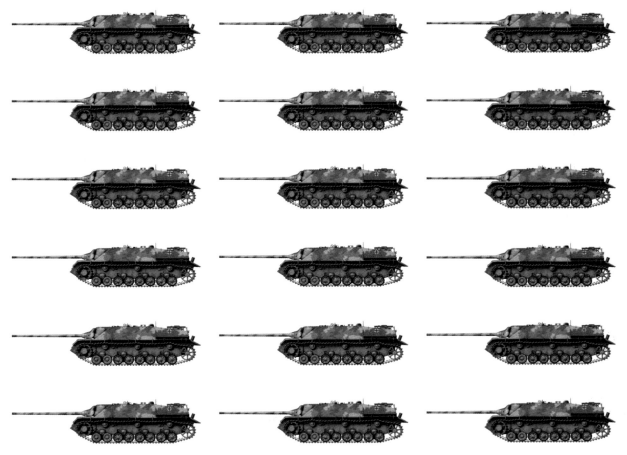

20th Infantry Division (motorized)

Although later in numerical order than several other motorized divisions, the 20th Infantry Division was one of the earliest of its type to be established by the German Army.

ORIGINALLY FORMED IN HAMBURG in October 1934, the 20th Infantry Division was known as the *Wehrgauleitung Hamburg*, before being given the cover name of *Reichswehrdienststelle Hamburg*, which was designed to hide the fact that Germany was re-creating its army in defiance of the terms of the Treaty of Versailles. The core of the the division was formed by the expansion of the 6.*Infanterie-Regiment* of the 2.*Division* of the *Reichswehr*.

As with the other early infantry divisions of the *Wehrmacht Heeres*, most of its its troops marched into battle on foot, and its artillery was largely horse-drawn. Standard infantry divisions were of little use in the new *Blitzkrieg* tactics being evolved by Panzer pioneers like Heinz Guderian. There was no way that soldiers on foot could keep up with fast-moving armoured units, so it was clear that infantry movement would have to be made much faster.

Fortunately, civilian trucks and lorries are readily adaptable to military uses of transporting soldiers, towing guns, and carrying equipment and supplies. Speed of deployment became vital to *Blitzkrieg*. This was particularly true in western Europe, where there was an excellent road network. Motorized infantry units could follow immediately behind the Panzer forces, where they would be used for flank defence and to mop up bypassed enemy strongpoints.

In the autumn of 1937, orders were given that the 20th Infantry Division was to become a fully motorized formation, a process that was completed early in 1938. It was one of the few such formations available for the invasion of Poland in September 1939, when it was assigned to Guderian's XIX Corps, attacking out of West Prussia to cut the Polish

corridor to the Baltic, and then racing in the northern flank of a gigantic pincer movement ending at Brest-Litovsk. After the Polish campaign, the division returned to Germany to recuperate. During that campaign the motorized divisions were found to be somewhat unwieldy, so afterwards the 20th and other motorized divisions were reorganized to reduce their size by about a third, leaving them with six motorized

Commanders

Generalleutnant Max Schwandtner
October 1934 – November 1938

General der Infanterie Mauritz von Wiktorin
November 1938 – November 1940

General der Infanterie Hans Zorn
November 1940 – January 1942

General der Infanterie Erich Jaschke
January 1942 – January 1943

General der Panzertruppen Georg Jauer
January 1943 – December 1944

Generalmajor Georg Scholze
January–May 1945

INSIGNIA

Formed in the port city of Hamburg, the 20th Infantry Division chose to commemorate the link by using an anchor as its divisional symbol.

The 20th Infantry Division (mot) used the triangle-in-a-circle device for much of the course of the war on the Eastern Front.

The dice insignia was used by the 20th Panzergrenadier Division during the defence of the *Reich* in the later stages of the war.

DIVISIONAL ORGANIZATION

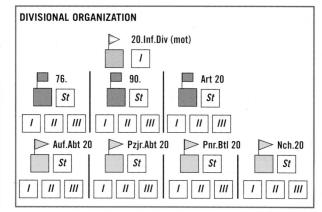

Divisional History	Formed
Wehrgauleitung Hamburg	1934
Reichswehrdienstelle Hamburg	1934
20.Infanterie-Division	1935
20.Infanterie-Division (mot)	1937
20.Panzergrenadier-Division	1943

infantry battalions arranged in two regiments, plus ordinary divisional support units.

War in the West

In November 1939, the division was assigned to the XVI Corps of the Sixth Army. During the invasion of the West, it was one of the few 'fast' formations available to Army Group B, which attacked the Low Countries. In June, it was assigned to Twelfth Army for the Battle of France; after the surrender of France, apart from a period in reserve in Germany, it remained there on occupation duty until April 1941.

Specifications	
Crew: 5	Muzzle Velocity: 520m/s (1706fps)
Weight: 6.3 tonnes (5.7 tons)	Range: 13km (8 miles)
Length: 4.4m (14 ft 5in)	Ammunition: High explosive or smoke
Calibre: 149.1mm (5.9in)	

▲ **15-cm schwere Feldhaubitze 18 (sFH 18)**

58.Artillerie-Regiment (mot) / I.Bataillon

The 20th Artillery Regiment lacked heavy howitzers in Poland. To make up strength, a battalion of the 58th Artillery Regiment, equipped with heavy field howitzers, was attached to the regiment early in 1940.

▶ **schwere Panzerspähwagen 6-Rad (SdKfz 231)**

Aufklärungs-Abteilung 20

Attached to Guderian's XIX Corps, the 20th Infantry Division (mot) had only a detachment of its reconnaissance battalion available during the German invasion of Poland in September 1939.

Specifications	
Crew: 4	Magirus petrol (60–80hp)
Weight: 5.9 tonnes (5.35 tons)	Speed: 70km/h (43.5mph)
Length: 5.57m (18 ft 7in)	Range: 300km (186 miles)
Width: 1.82m (5ft 11.5in)	Radio: FuG Spr Ger 'a'
Height: 2.00m (6ft 6in)	Armament: 1 x 20mm (0.7in)
Engine: Daimler-Benz, Büssing-NAG or	cannon; 1 x 7.62mm (0.3in) MG

 # Invasion of Russia

JUNE 1941

In May 1941, the 20th Infantry Division was sent to Poland, where it went into the reserve pool for Army Group C, to be prepared for the invasion of the Soviet Union.

FOR OPERATION *BARBAROSSA*, THE GERMAN attack on Stalin's USSR, the 20th Infantry Division (mot) was assigned to the XXXIX Corps of General Hermann Hoth's 3.*Panzergruppe*, part of the main strike force of the powerful Army Group Centre. It was evident that together with General Heinz Guderian's 2.*Panzergruppe*, Hoth's Panzer Group was perhaps the most significant force in the entire operation, which was intended to execute the most exciting and spectacular military feat of the century, perhaps of all history. And the first few days seemed to confirm the prospect.

Guderian took his *Panzergruppe* across the River Bug on each side of the fortress of Brest-Litovsk, captured the fortress and then raced with his armoured spearheads towards Minsk. Guderian's path to the city was from the south; Hoth, meanwhile, was to sweep down from the north. The aim was to encircle and trap the Soviet frontline forces within a massive cauldron. By the afternoon of 27 June, the leading tanks of the 17th Panzer Division, part of Guderian's force, arrived at Minsk, linking up with

the spearheads of Hoth's 3.*Panzergruppe*, which had covered 350km (217 miles) in five days.

However, the subsequent diversion of Guderian's Panzers south to take part in the battle for Kiev saw Hoth's divisions too weak to mount the expected advance towards Moscow, so several formations were sent to assist Field Marshal von Leeb's Army Group North, which had surrounded Leningrad but was facing fierce Soviet resistance.

The 20th Infantry Division (mot) was one of the formations moved north, where it arrived in September 1941. Assigned to the Sixteenth Army, it entered combat around Tichwin and Lake Ilmen in October, and it was to remain in the region for over a year, battling with the Soviet Volkhov Front.

ORGANIZATION

76.Pz.Reg

I. St
1 2 3 Hv

II. St
4 5 6 Hv

III. St
7 8 9 Hv

REGIMENTAL ORGANIZATION

76.Pz.Reg
HQ

St Bd Co Pz mc Sn Pi Gn

Specifications

Crew: 7
Weight: 5.5 tonnes (5 tons)
Length: 4.75m (15ft 7in)
Width: 2.15m (7ft 1in)
Height: 3.20m (10ft 6in)
Engine: Maybach HL42TRKM
 6-cylinder (100hp)
Speed: 65km/h (40mph)
Range: 300km (186 miles)
Radio: None
Armament: Twin 20mm (0.7in)
Flak 38 L/112.5

▼ **2-cm Flak auf leichter Zugkraftenwagen 1t (SdKfz 10/5)**
Panzer-Abteilung 5 / Stab / Flak-Zug
The single-barrelled 2cm (0.7in) Flak guns were replaced by Flakvierlings in 1943.

▶ **leichte Panzerspähwagen (SdKfz 222)**
Panzer-Aufklärungs-Abteilung 120 / leichte Spähpanzerwagen-Kompanie
When formed in 1943, the Panzergrenadier Reconnaissance Battalion lacked heavy armoured cars, having one light armoured car company and three motorcycle companies.

Specifications

Crew: 3
Weight: 5.3 tonnes (4.8 tons)
Length: 4.8m (15ft 8in)
Width: 1.95m (6ft 5in)
Height: 2.00m (6ft 7in)
Engine: Horch 3.5L or 3.8L petrol

Speed: 85km/h (52.8mph)
Range: 300km (186 miles)
Radio: FuG Spr Ger 'a'
Armament: 1 x 20mm (0.7in) KwK 30 L/55
 cannon; 1 x 7.92mm (0.3in) MG (coaxial)

20th Panzergrenadier Division

JULY 1943

The 20th Infantry Division (mot) spent most of 1942 on the Volkhov Front. However, in December of that year it was transferred back to Army Group Centre.

PRESSURE ON THE GERMAN lines at that time was intense: the Soviet attack that had isolated the German Sixth Army at Stalingrad had been the signal for a general series of Red Army offensives across the full length of the Eastern Front. In the north and centre, the German forces had held their positions under severe stress, but in the south Stalingrad fell, Kleist's Panzers were in danger of being cut off in the Caucasus, and Soviet forces were driving westwards.

Two weeks after the liberation of Kharkov, the Red Army was at Pavlograd, only 40km (25 miles) from the Dnieper River – and quite close to Hitler, who was paying a flying visit to Zaporozhe. Hitler had come to confer with his commanders. At quiet moments in the conference, the sound of Russian artillery could just be made out. However, the Soviets in their turn were being overstretched.

Field Marshal Erich von Manstein sprang a trap on 20 February 1943. On the day that the forward Russian patrols reached Pavlograd, Panzers were driving up the west bank of the Donets behind them. In what he dubbed his 'backhand blow', Manstein drove east to cut off all the Russian forces that had broken over the Donets.

By 3 March, the Russians had been forced to abandon nearly 15,500km² (6000 square miles) of their recent gains. The SS Panzer Corps stormed Kharkov in mid-March, and Belgorod was retaken.

Name	Strength
1st Battalion (3 part motorized batteries):	
10.5-cm leFH	9
2nd Battalion (3 part motorized batteries):	
10.5-cm leFH	9
3rd Battalion (3 part motorized batteries):	
15-cm sFH and 3 10-cm K18	6
Attached army battery:	
15.2-cm Russian howitzers	4

Name	Strength
Stab:	
StuG III	3
FlakZug:	
SdKfz 10 with Flakvierling (quad 2-cm)	3
1 StuG Battery:	
StuG III	14
2 StuG Battery:	
StuG III	14
3 StuG Battery:	
StuG III	14

▶ **2-cm Flak 38 auf gepanzerten leichter Zugkraftwagen 1t (Sd Kfz 10/5)**

Heeres Flak Abteilung 284

By 1944, 2-cm (0.8in) flak guns were being replaced by more powerful 3.7-cm (1.5in) guns.

Specifications

Crew: 7

Weight: 5.5 tonnes (5 tons)

Length: 4.75m (15ft 7in)

Width: 2.15m (7ft 1in)

Height: 3.20m (10ft 6in)

Engine: 1 Maybach HL42TRKM 6-

cylinder (100hp)

Speed: 65km/h (40mph)

Range: 300km (186.3 miles)

Radio: None

Armament: Twin 20mm Flak 38

L/112.5

By the end of the month, the four Soviet tank corps strung out between the Donets and Zaporozhe had been annihilated.

In the spring of 1943, the situation had stabilized to some extent, the front running from just west of Rostov in the south, up to Velikiye-Luki west of Moscow (where the 20th had been in the thick of the fighting), then to Leningrad.

In July 1943, the division was caught up in the transformation of the German Army's motorized forces, when it was redesignated as the 20th Panzergrenadier Division. The 5th Panzer Battalion, equipped with assault guns, was added.

▶ 7.5-cm Sturmgeschütz 40 Ausf G (SdKfz 142/1)

Panzer-Abteilung 8

Established in October 1943, the 8th Panzer Battalion went into combat in the Ukraine. The battalion's three companies were *Sturmgeschütz*-equipped.

Specifications

Crew: 4	Speed: 40km/h (24.9mph)
Weight: 26.3 tonnes (23.9 tons)	Range: 155km (96.3 miles)
Length: 6.77m (22ft 2in)	Radio: FuG15 and FuG16
Width: 2.95m (9ft 8in)	Armament: 1 x 75mm (3in) StuG
Height: 2.16m (7ft 0in)	L/48 cannon
Engine: Maybach HL120TRM	

▶ Mittlerer Schützenpanzerwagen 7.5-cm Ausf D (SdKfz 251/9)

Panzergrenadier-Regiment 76

In spite of its change of designation in 1943, it was not until late in 1944 that the 20th Panzergrenader Division's infantry actually became Panzergrenadiers. SdKfz 251/9s provided fire support in the regiment's heavy companies.

Specifications

Crew: 3	HL42TUKRM
Weight: 9.4 tonnes	Speed: 53km/h (33mph)
(8.53 tons)	Range: 300km (186 miles)
Length: 5.98m (19ft 7in)	Radio: FuG Spr Ger 'f'
Width: 2.83m (9ft 4in)	Armament: 1 x 75mm (3in)
Height: 2.07m (6ft 10in)	KwK L/24 gun
Engine: Maybach	

▶ Mittlerer Schützenpanzerwagen 7.5-cm Pak 40 (SdKfz 251/22)

Kampfgruppe Müncheberg

Issued to the Panzerjäger detachments of Panzer divisions, tank-destroyers like this would have been on the 20th Panzergrenadier Division's inventory when the formation was merged with the *Müncheberg* Panzer Division early in 1945.

Specifications

Crew: 4 or 5	Speed: 50km/h (31mph)
Weight: 8 tonnes (7.28 tons)	Range: 300km (186 miles)
Length: 5.98m (19ft 7in)	Radio: None
Width: 2.1m (6ft 11in)	Armament: 1 x 75mm (3in) PaK 40
Height: 2.25m (7ft 4.5in)	L/46 anti-tank gun; 1 x 7.92mm
Engine: Maybach HL42TUKRM	(0.3in) MG (rear-mounted)
6-cylinder petrol (100hp)	

Defence of the Reich
1944–1945

The 20th Panzergrenadier Division switched frequently between army groups in the role of a mechanized 'fire brigade', and ended the war fighting along the Oder River in Silesia.

I N JUNE 1943, the division was transformed from a motorized infantry division to a Panzergrenadier formation. It was attached to XXXXIII Corps, part of the Third Panzer Army with Army Group Centre. It remained there for the rest of the summer, transferring to LIII Corps of Second Panzer Army at Orel in August before being sent to reinforce XII Army Corps of Ninth Army at Bryansk in September.

In the Ukraine
In October, the division moved to Army Group South, fighting with Fourth Panzer Army on the Dnieper, at Zhitomir and at Vinnitsa. In March 1944, the division was assigned to First Panzer Army at Kamenets Podolsk and Brody, before switching

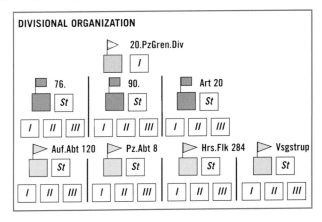

▼ **Fighting the Russian winter**
The 20th Panzergrenadier Division spent much of its existence fighting against the Red Army's winter offensives on the Eastern Front.

back to Fourth Panzer Army at Baranov in August. For the rest of the year, the division fought to stem the Soviet advance through the Ukraine into Poland, holding the line of the Vistula River (known as the Weichsel in German) after the Red Army paused to

◤ On the Oder

SdKfz 251s (centre and left) and an SdKfz 234 (far right) move up to the Oder
River in February 1945, where they would await the final Soviet assault on
northern Germany.

Specifications

Crew: 3	Muzzle Velocity (AP): 990m/s (3248fps)
Weight: 1.5 tonnes (1.37 tons)	Range: AP: 2000m (2190 yards), HE: 7.5km
Length: 3.7m (12 ft 1.5in)	(4.66 miles)
Calibre: 75mm (3in)	Ammunition: Armour-piercing, high explosive

▶ 7.5-cm Panzerabwehrkanone (Pak 40)

Panzer-Aufklärungs-Abteilung 120

Although the divisional Panzerjäger Battalion had become
fully self-propelled over the winter of 1943/44, the Panzerjäger
Platoon of the Reconnaissance Battalion's Heavy Company was
equipped with three towed Pak 40s.

▶ Mittlerer Schützenpanzerwagen Ausf C (SdKfz 251/1)

Panzergrenadier-Regiment 90

The division's motorized infantry regiments – the 20th, 76th and 90th – became Panzergrenadier
regiments on 1 December 1944. However, because production never matched demand, only one
battalion of each would have been equipped with half-tracks.

Specifications

Crew: 2 plus 12 troops	Engine: Maybach HL42TUKRM
Weight: 9.9 tonnes (9 tons)	Speed: 53km/h (33mph)
Length: 5.98m (19ft 7in)	Range: 300km (186 miles)
Width: 2.1m (6ft 11in)	Radio: FuG Spr Ger 1
Height: 1.75m (5ft 8in) or 2.16m	Armament: 1/2 x 7.62mm
(7ft) including MG shield if fitted	(0.3in) MG

regroup. In January 1945, the 20th Division refitted with what reinforcements were available, before being attached to the *Grossdeutschland* Panzer Corps in Silesia in February.

Defence of Berlin

In April 1945, 20th Panzergrenadier Division was sent to the Oder and was attached to the XI SS Army Corps, commanded by *Obergruppenführer* Matthias Kleinheisterkamp. After months of fighting, the division was considerably understrength, with its manpower totalling some 8000 troops and with a Panzer strength of 15 Jagdpanzer IVs and a similar number of Panzer IVs.

Other units in the corps included the remnants of the 9th Fallschirmjäger Division, the 169th, 303rd and 712th Infantry Divisions. The last-mentioned was formed from the *Grossdeutschland* replacement

brigade (*Panzergrenadier-Ersatz-Brigade GD*) and was a division in name only. On 15 April 1945, the 20th Division was transferred to LVI Panzer Corps of Ninth Army. It was combined with the understrength *Müncheberg* Panzer Division (which had been formed in March), to make up a single *Kampfgruppe* commanded by *Generalmajor* Werner Mummert, the *Müncheberg* Division's commander.

The *Kampfgruppe* was sent to delay the Soviet advance across the Seelow Heights. Arriving on 16 April, it was forced back through the city of Müncheberg and continued to retreat back to Berlin. Some troops were cut off and were swept up by XI SS Army Corps, which went into action at Halbe. However, the bulk of what remained of the 20th Panzergrenadier Division – only 1000 men – reached Berlin on 22 April. The survivors were sent to defend Potsdam, surrendering to the Soviets in May 1945.

▶ **PzKpfw V Panther als PzBefWg (SdKfz 171)**

Kampfgruppe Müncheberg

When the *Müncheberg* Panzer Division merged with the 20th Panzergrenadier Division, it had been reinforced with two companies of Panthers that could be fitted with infra-red night-vision equipment.

Specifications

Crew: 5	Speed: 46km/h (28.6mph)
Weight: 49.4 tonnes	Range: 200km (124.4 miles)
(44.8 tons)	Radio: FuG5
Length: 8.86m (29ft 0in)	Armament: 1 x 75mm (3in) KwK
Width: 3.42m (11ft 2in)	42 L/70; 2 x 7.92mm (0.3in)
Height: 2.98m (9ft 9in)	MG (one hull-mounted, one
Engine: Maybach HL230P30	coaxial)

▶ **Mittlerer Schützenpanzerwagen 'Uhu' (SdKfz 251/20)**

Kampfgruppe Müncheberg

The SdKfz 251/20 carried a 60cm (23.6in) infra-red searchlight that could illuminate targets for Panthers with infra-red sights out to a range of 1500m (1640 yards) in total darkness – without the targets knowing about it.

Specifications

Crew: 2 plus 12 troops	Speed: 50km/h (31mph)
Weight: 8 tonnes (7.28 tons)	Range: 300km (186 miles)
Length: 5.98m (19ft 7in)	Radio: FuG Spr Ger 1
Width: 2.1m (6ft 11in)	Armament: 600mm (23.6in)
Height: 1.75m (5ft 8in)	infra-red searchlight
Engine: Maybach HL42TUKRM	

25th Infantry Division (motorized)

The 25th Infantry Division was formed at Ludwigsburg in Swabia to the north of Stuttgart on 1 April 1936 as part of the first expansion of the newly formed German Army, or *Heer*.

IN 1935, TWO YEARS AFTER the Nazi accession to power, Germany announced that it no longer intended to honour the terms of the Treaty of Versailles, and the *Reichswehr* – the limited military force allowed under the treaty – became the *Wehrmacht*. The newly formed *Wehrmacht* would be based on existing land and naval forces, the renamed *Heer* and the *Kriegsmarine*, together with a new independent air force, the *Luftwaffe*.

Army expansion

The *Heer* saw the seven existing *Reichswehr* divisions expanded to become 21 division-sized units in three Army Groups. This was the first stage of expansion; more units were formed in the next months.

INSIGNIA	
	The insignia adopted by the 25th Infantry Division shows the three antlers of the ancient arms of the Duchy of Württemburg.
	During the war, after regional affiliations became less important, the division was assigned one of the newer geometrical insignia.

Divisional History	Formed
25. Infanterie-Division	1936
25. Infanterie-Division (mot.)	1940
25. Panzergrenadier-Division	1943

▼ **Invasion of the Soviet Union, summer 1941**
Motorized infantry deploy from their Sd Kfz 251 half-tracks as they attack a Russian village during the early stages of Operation *Barbarossa*, July 1941.

Commanders

General der Artillerie Christian Hansen
Pre-war – October 1939

General der Infanterie Heinrich Clössner
October 1939 – January 1942

General der Panzertruppen Siegfried Henrici
January 1942 – February 1942

General der Infanterie Anton Grasser
February 1942 – November 1943

Generalleutnant Dr Fritz Benicke
November 1943 – March 1944

Generalleutnant Paul Schürmann
March 1944 – July 1944

Generalleutnant Paul Schürmann
October 1944 – February 1945

Generalleutnant Arnold Burmeister
February 1945 – 8 May 1945

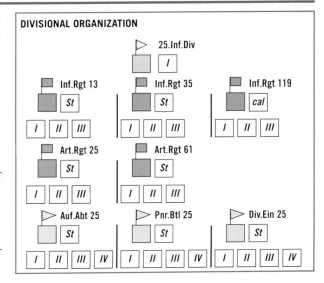

DIVISIONAL ORGANIZATION

The 25th Infantry Division was one of the second wave of divisions to be formed. For the next couple of years, it remained at peacetime levels of manning and equipment, but with the approach of war in 1939 it was brought to its full combat strength as part of the German Army's first wave of wartime mobilization. The division did not take part in the invasion of Poland on 1 September 1939. Instead, it formed part of the skeleton force protecting Germany's western borders and was based in the Saarland as part of the First Army with Army Group C.

Following the conquest of Poland, the 25th Infantry Division was placed in OKH (*Oberkommando des Heeres*/Army high command) reserve, before being attached to Twelfth Army in the Eifel in May 1940, ready to play its part in the attack on the West. Forming part of the general reserve for the initial stages of the attack, it was transferred to the XVIII Corps of Ninth Army, part of Army Group B, for the conquest of France in June 1940.

After seeing combat on the Aisne during the Battle of France, it was transferred to occupation duties under the control of Army Group C, before being returned to Germany at the end of September for motorization. On 15 November 1940, the division was renamed as the 25th Infantry Division (mot), and it began training in its new role.

▲ **15-cm schwere Infanterie (sIG 33)**

13.Infanterie-Regiment / Infanterie-Geschütz-Kompanie (mot) / schwere Zug

Each infantry regiment had a heavy infantry gun platoon with two towed sIG 33s. Originally truck-towed, they were later moved by light SdKfz 10 half-tracks.

Specifications

Crew: 5	Muzzle Velocity: 241m/s (783fps)
Weight: 1.75 tonnes (1.6 tons)	Range: 5504m (6000 yards)
Length: 1.64m (64.57in)	Ammunition: High explosive or smoke
Calibre: 149.1mm (5.9in)	

▶ **Mannschaft Kraftwagen Krupp L2H123 (Kfz 70)**

35. Infanterie Regiment (mot) / I Bataillon

Originally produced in 1936, the Krupp light 6x 4 truck was designed as a prime-mover for light guns. However, it was also widely used as a communications vehicle, a light AA gun platform and as a troop carrier.

Specifications

Crew: 2	Engine: Krupp M304 3.3L 4-cylinder (60hp)
Weight: 2.6 tonnes (2.37 tons)	Speed: 70km/h (43mph)
Length: 4.95m (16ft 3in)	Range: 450km (280 miles)
Width: 1.95m (6ft 5in)	Radio: None
Height: 1.96m (6ft 5in)	

Eastern Front
1941–1942

Motorized formations were intended to provide infantry support to the fast-moving Panzer spearheads, and the 25th Infantry Division (mot) was heavily involved in Operation *Barbarossa*.

INITIALLY ATTACHED TO GUDERIAN'S 2.*Panzergruppe* with von Bock's Army Group Centre, the division was transferred to von Kleist's 1.*Panzergruppe* before the opening of the campaign. Based around Zamosc, 1.*Panzergruppe* provided the spearhead of von Rundstedt's Army Group South, driving into the Ukraine when the invasion started in June 1941.

The division formed part of the *Panzergruppe's* mobile reserve, along with 16.*Infanterie-Division* (mot), 25.*Infanterie-Division* (mot), 13.*Panzer-Division*, 16.*Panzer-Division* and the *Leibstandarte SS Adolf Hitler*. It went into action with von Mackensen's III Army Corps at Zhitomir in July. In August, the division took part in the massive battles of encirclement at Uman and around Kiev, which saw more than half a million Soviet prisoners taken.

ORGANIZATION

Pz.Rgt 35

St

Pz | mc | sig | Pio

REGIMENTAL ORGANIZATION

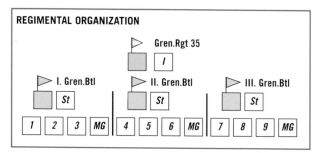

Gren.Rgt 35

I

I. Gren.Btl | II. Gren.Btl | III. Gren.Btl

St | St | St

1 | 2 | 3 | MG | 4 | 5 | 6 | MG | 7 | 8 | 9 | MG

In September 1941, the division was transferred back to Army Group Centre for the drive on Moscow, and in October it came under the control of XXXXVIII Corps of Guderian's 2.*Panzergruppe*, which had been renamed 2.*Panzerarmee*, for the attack on Bryansk.

Attack on Moscow

Assigned the codename *Taifun* (Typhoon), the German drive on Moscow began on 2 October. The Soviets had concentrated huge forces to bar the road to their capital, but these were smashed yet again. In two more great battles of encirclement, another 650,000 Soviets were captured.

The attack was delayed by the *rasputitza*, the bottomless mud caused by the autumn rains, which lasted for four weeks. Then, on 7 November, the temperature plummeted and the liquid mud turned rock hard. The German advance began again with breakthroughs in the south as well as towards Moscow. However, on 5 December, with the spires of the Kremlin visible through German binoculars, the Soviets launched a massive counteroffensive that drove the *Wehrmacht* back. The German troops, inadequately equipped for the Russian winter, fought desperately for survival, gradually slowing the Soviet offensives and eventually bringing them to a stop.

In February 1942, the 25th Division was transferred to the LIII Corps, which had come to a

▶ **8.8-cm Panzerabwehrkanone 43/41**

25.Artillerie-Regiment / I.Bataillon / 3.Batterie

One of the most powerful anti-tank guns of the war, the Pak 43 used the same tube as the tank gun on the massive King Tiger.

Specifications

Crew: 5

Weight: 6.4 tonnes (5.8 tons)

Length: 9.20 (30ft 2in) with carriage

Calibre: 88mm (3.5in) L/71

Muzzle Velocity (AP): 1130m/s (3707fps)

Range (AP): Over 2km (1.24 miles)

Ammunition: Armour-piercing or high explosive

halt around Bryansk and Orel. For the next year, the 25th Infantry Division (mot) remained with Army Group Centre, fighting a continual series of holding actions around Bryansk while the main weight of Germany's offensive plans in the Soviet Union shifted south to the Ukraine. That did not mean that the division avoided heavy fighting, however. The Soviets launched massive offensives in January/February 1942, June/July 1942 and February 1943, all of which were repelled by tough German resistance.

▶ Mittlerer Zugkraftwagen 8t (SdKfz 7)

25.Artillerie-Regiment / III.Bataillon / 3.Batterie

The SdKfz 7 was the German Army's standard heavy artillery prime-mover, used to tow K18s and the 8.8cm (3.5in) Flak gun. Early in 1944, the 25th Panzergrenadier Division had three K18s as well as two heavy 220mm (8.6in) French howitzers.

Specifications

Crew: 2	6-cylinder (140hp)
Length: 6.85m (20ft 3in)	Weight: 1.16 tonnes (1.06 tons)
Width: 2.40m (7ft 10.5in)	Speed: 50km/h (31mph)
Height: 2.62m (8ft 7.1in)	Range: 250km (156 miles)
Engine: Maybach HL62	Radio: None

▶ Mittlerer Pionierpanzerwagen (SdKfz 251/7)

25.Pionier-Abteilung / 1.Panzer-Pionier-Kompanie

The engineer battalion attached to motorized and Panzergrenadier divisions had one half-track company and two motorized companies. The SdKfz 251/7 carried light bridges, mines and other specialist combat engineer material.

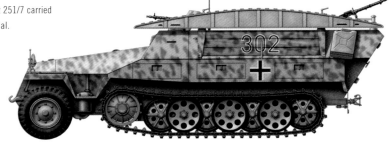

Specifications

Crew: 7 or 8	6-cylinder (100hp)
Weight: 8.9 tonnes (9.1 tons)	Speed: 50km/h (31mph)
Length: 5.80m (19ft 0in)	Range: 300km (186 miles)
Width: 2.10m (6ft 11in)	Radio: FuG Spr Ger 1
Height: 2.70m (8ft 10in)	Armament: 1/2 x 7.62mm
Engine: Maybach HL42TUKRM	(0.3in) MGs

25th Panzergrenadier Division
JUNE 1943 – JUNE 1944

The reorganization of Germany's motorized divisions in the summer of 1943 saw the 25th Infantry Division (mot) upgraded to become the 25th Panzergrenadier Division.

UNTIL THAT TIME, THE DIVISION'S fighting strength had been provided by the three battalions of the 35th Infantry Regiment (mot), the three battalions of the 119th Infantry Regiment (mot), the 25th Motorcycle Battalion, and the towed guns of the three motorized battalions of the 25th Artillery Regiment. The artillery regiment fielded 10.5cm (4.1in) Czech-built Skoda howitzers, 10.5cm (4.1in) leFH light howitzers, 15cm (5.9in) sFH heavy howitzers and a small number of 10cm (3.9in) K18 long-range cannon. In the summer of 1943, the 25th Artillery Regiment also had two French 220mm (8.6in) heavy howitzers and one 105mm (4.1in) French gun on strength.

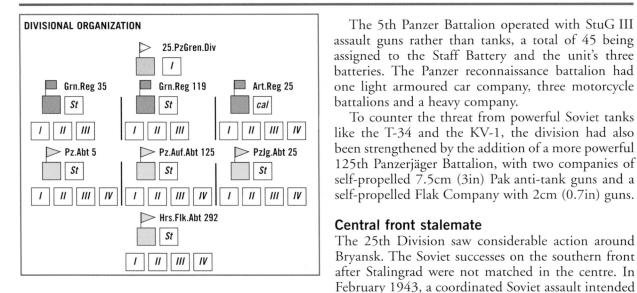

DIVISIONAL ORGANIZATION

25.PzGren.Div
I

Grn.Reg 35 — St — I | II | III

Grn.Reg 119 — St — I | II | III

Art.Reg 25 — cal — I | II | III | IV

Pz.Abt 5 — St — I | II | III | IV

Pz.Auf.Abt 125 — St — I | II | III | IV

PzJg.Abt 25 — St — I | II | III | IV

Hrs.Flk.Abt 292 — St — I | II | III | IV

The upgrade to Panzergrenadier division status saw the addition of the 5th Panzer Battalion and the conversion of the 25th Motorcycle Battalion into the 125th Panzer Reconnaissance Battalion.

The 5th Panzer Battalion operated with StuG III assault guns rather than tanks, a total of 45 being assigned to the Staff Battery and the unit's three batteries. The Panzer reconnaissance battalion had one light armoured car company, three motorcycle battalions and a heavy company.

To counter the threat from powerful Soviet tanks like the T-34 and the KV-1, the division had also been strengthened by the addition of a more powerful 125th Panzerjäger Battalion, with two companies of self-propelled 7.5cm (3in) Pak anti-tank guns and a self-propelled Flak Company with 2cm (0.7in) guns.

Central front stalemate

The 25th Division saw considerable action around Bryansk. The Soviet successes on the southern front after Stalingrad were not matched in the centre. In February 1943, a coordinated Soviet assault intended to destroy the German forces at Orel and in the Rzhev salient was negated by the German evacuation of the salient, which shortened German defensive lines enabling them to halt the Soviet offensive.

▶ **7.5-cm Pak 40 auf PzKpfw 38(t) Marder III (SdKfz 138)**
125.Panzerjäger-Abteilung

The three companies of the 25th Panzergrenadier Division's tank-destroyer battalion were each equipped with 12 self-propelled Pak 40s mounted on Panzer II chassis or, as here, on Panzer 38(t)s.

Specifications

Crew: 4	Speed: 35km/h (22mph)
Weight: 10.8 tonnes (9.8 tons)	Range: 240km (150 miles)
Length: 5.77m (19ft 11in)	Radio: FuG Spr Ger 1
Width: 2.16m (7ft 1in)	Armament: 1 x 75mm (3in) Pak 40/3 L/46
Height: 2.51m (8ft 3in)	anti-tank gun; 1 x 7.92mm (0.3in) MG
Engine: Praga EPA 6-cylinder (140hp)	

▶ **Mittlerer Personenkraftwagen Skoda Typ 952 (Kfz 15/1)**
25.Nachrichten-Abteilung / Fernsprech-Kompanie (mot)

The standard Kfz 15 body was used by telephone (*Fernsprech*) and radio (*Funk*) engineers. The rear of the vehicle housed lockers for equipment and tools, and it was also fitted with a towing hook for light equipment trailers.

Specifications

Crew: 1	Engine: Skoda 3.1L petrol (80-85hp)
Weight: 2.4 tonnes (2.2 tons)	Speed: 100km/h (62mph)
Length: 4.8m (15 ft 9in)	Range: 400km (250 miles)
Width: 1.80m (5ft 9in)	Radio: Various depending on deployment
Height: 1.72m (5ft 3in)	

In July and August 1943, the Soviets succeeded in stopping the massive German offensive at Kursk. In tandem with the ensuing counteroffensive into the Ukraine, the Soviets launched Operation *Suvorov* against Army Group Centre in August. Progress was slow, but the Red Army forced the German line back on a broad front, capturing Smolensk and the important rail junction at Nevel.

However, the Germans had time to build a strong defensive line, the *Ostwall*, which stretched from Vitebsk through Orscha to Mogilev. The 25th Division took part in the unsuccessful attempt to defend Smolensk, and by the end of the year the formation was in a strong defensive position at Orscha. Further Soviet offensives against Gomel and Orscha in November 1943 and against Vitebsk in February 1944 were unsuccessful against the strong *Ostwall* defences.

Army Group Centre was much more successful in holding off the Red Army than Army Group South, in part because the terrain was more heavily forested and easier to defend; competently led German units had time to prepare effective field fortifications, while Soviet leadership had been uninspired.

▼ 25.Panzergrenadier-Division / 5.Panzer-Abteilung / Sturmgeschütz-Batterie

When the division was upgraded to Panzergrenadier status in the summer of 1943, it was given *Panzer-Abteilung 5*, which was established from the *Panzer-Ersatz-Abteilung 5*. Many of its men were veterans of the fighting in North Africa, the original 5th Panzer Regiment having been part of the 21st Panzer Division. The 5th Panzer Abteilung finally joined up with the newly formed 25th Panzergrenadier Division near the end of October. The battalion was equipped with three Sturmgeschütz companies and a Flak platoon. Each StuG company's nominal strength was 14 assault guns.

Stab

1st *Zug*   2nd *Zug*   3rd *Zug*

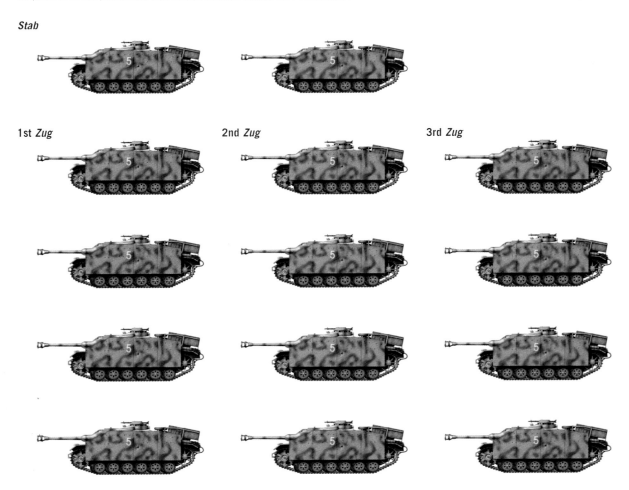

Destroyed with Army Group Centre
JULY 1944

In 1943 and in the first half of 1944, the 25th Panzergrenadier Division played its part in Army Group Centre's stubborn defence against a series of Soviet offensives.

THIS WAS ALL TO CHANGE in the summer of 1944. In spring, the Red Army assembled massive forces all along the front lines in central and southern Russia. The Soviets carried out a masterful deception campaign to convince the Germans that the main Soviet summer offensive would be launched against Army Group Northern Ukraine. The German high command moved Panzer units south from the central front while the massive Soviet build-up opposite Army Group Centre was not detected.

Operation *Bagration*

Operation *Bagration* was launched on 22 June 1944. Over 2.5 million soldiers and 6000 tanks in 185 Soviet divisions smashed into German positions along nearly 1000km (620 miles) of front. The 500,000-strong Army Group Centre was annihilated, and 350,000 Germans were killed or captured in the greatest German defeat of the war. Soviet forces liberated Minsk and Byelorussia by the end of August, crossing the pre-war border and advancing into East Prussia and Poland by the end of the year.

The 25th Panzergrenadier Division was caught in the maelstrom. Attacked by overwhelming Soviet forces at Minsk, the division was destroyed. The handful of survivors who reached safety were used to form the nucleus of Panzer Brigade 107, which was

▲ **Panzer reconnaissance**

The SdKfz 250/3 communications half-track was used by the HQ section of light armoured reconnaissance companies from 1942 to 1945.

sent to the Western Front in September 1944. It was immediately thrown into action to stop the Allied forces driving northwards to relieve the parachute troops at Arnhem. After suffering losses in heavy fighting around Venlo, the brigade was withdrawn to become part of the re-forming 25th Division.

▲ **Leichte Personenkraftwagen (Kfz 1)**

125.Panzer-Aufklärungs-Abteilung / leichte Aufklärungs-Kompanie (mot)

Although some reconnaissance units were still using motorcycles in 1944, most had been replaced by the Kfz 1 Kübelwagen.

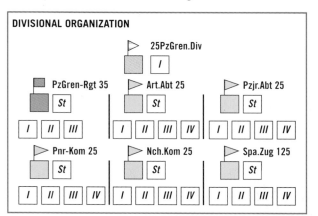

DIVISIONAL ORGANIZATION

25PzGren.Div — I

PzGren-Rgt 35 — St — I / II / III

Art.Abt 25 — St — I / II / III / IV

Pzjr.Abt 25 — St — I / II / III / IV

Pnr-Kom 25 — St — I / II / III / IV

Nch.Kom 25 — St — I / II / III / IV

Spa.Zug 125 — St — I / II / III / IV

Specifications	
Crew: 1	Engine: Volkswagen 998cc petrol (24hp). Later
Weight: 0.64 tonnes (0.58 tons)	Volkswagen 1131cc petrol (25hp)
Length: 3.73 (12 ft 3in)	Speed: 100km/h (62mph)
Width: 1.60m (5ft 3in)	Range: 600km (375 miles)
Height: 1.35m (4ft 5in)	Radio: None

▲ **Leichte Panzerspähwagen (2-cm) (SdKfz 222)**

125.Panzer-Aufklärungs-Abteilung / leichte Spähpanzerwagen-Kompanie

When the 25th Panzergrenadier Division was destroyed in the summer of 1944, its armoured car company was equipped with light SdKfz 221 and 222 vehicles.

Specifications

Crew: 3	Speed: 85km/h (52.8mph)
Weight: 5.3 tonnes (4.8 tons)	Range: 300km (186 miles)
Length: 4.8m (15ft 8in)	Radio: FuG Spr Ger 'a'
Width: 1.95m (6ft 5in)	Armament: 1 x 20mm (0.7in) KwK 30 L/55
Height: 2.00m (6ft 7in)	cannon; 1 x 7.92mm (0.3in) MG (coaxial)
Engine: Horch 3.5L or 3.8L petrol	

5th Panzer Battalion, November 1944	Strength
Flak Platoon:	
3.7cm (1.5in) Flak on sWS half-track	4
1 Panzer Company:	
PzKpfw V Panthers	11
2 Panzer Company:	
PzKpfw V Panthers	11
3 Panzer Company:	
PzKpfw V Panthers	11
1 Panzerjäger Company:	
PzKpfw IV/70	11

▼ **7.5-cm Sturmgeschütz 40 Ausf G (SdKfz 142/1)**

25.Panzerjäger-Abteilung / 1.Sturmgeschütz-Batterie

Late in 1944, some StuGs were fitted with the cast-steel *Saukopf* (Sow's Head) gun mantlet. This offered better protection than earlier plate mantlets.

Specifications

Crew: 4	Speed: 40km/h (24.9mph)
Weight: 26.3 tonnes (23.9 tons)	Range: 155km (96.3 miles)
Length: 6.77m (22ft 2in)	Radio: FuG15 and FuG16
Width: 2.95m (9ft 8in)	Armament: 1 x 75mm (3in) StuG
Height: 2.16m (7ft 0in)	L/48 cannon
Engine: Maybach HL120TRM	

▶ **Panzerjäger IV/70(V) (SdKfz 162/1)**

5.Panzer-Abteilung / 4.Kompanie

The 5th Panzer Battalion had three Panther Ausf G companies and a single company with the Panzer IV/70 tank-destroyer, which had the same gun as the Panther.

Specifications

Crew: 4	Speed: 35km/h (21.7mph)
Weight: 25.8 tonnes (23.48 tons)	Range: 210km (130.5 miles)
Length: 8.50m (27ft 10.5in)	Radio: FuG5
Width: 3.17m (10ft 5in)	Armament: 1 x 75mm (3in) PaK 42
Height: 2.85m (9ft 4in)	L/70 anti-tank gun; 1 x 7.92mm
Engine: Maybach HL120TRM (300 hp)	(0.3in) MG

29th Infantry Division (motorized)

The 29th Infantry Division (mot) was one of the few divisions of the German Army to have been motorized before the outbreak of World War II.

ESTABLISHED IN THE CITY OF ERFURT in central Germany on 1 October 1936, the 29th Infantry Division was based on the 15th Infantry Regiment of the old *Reichswehr* and drew its recruits from the surrounding territory of Thuringia (although Erfurt itself had been Prussian territory since 1806). It was decided to fully motorize the division, a process which took place through 1937.

Motorized divisions were to play an important part in the emerging *Blitzkrieg* theory, since their mobility meant that they could provide the infantry support advancing Panzer formations would need. As a result, the division was already well manned when it was ordered onto a war footing in August 1939.

The 29th Infantry Division (mot) was assigned to XIV Corps of the German Tenth Army for the invasion of Poland. Launching out of Silesia, the division provided a mobile rearguard as von Reichenau's army drove northeast towards Warsaw. The 29th Division took part in the encirclement and destruction of a strong Polish force around Radom, and remained in the area with other XIV Corps formations, clearing up remnants of Polish forces.

In December 1939, following the capitulation of Poland, the 25th Division was transferred to the West as the *Wehrmacht* began reorganizing its forces for the campaign against France and the Low Countries. In May 1940, it was assigned to Sixteenth Army in Luxembourg as part of Army Group A, where it formed part of the strategic reserve, facing the French forces in the Maginot Line. It was quickly moved forward to join Army Group A's race for the Channel.

After Dunkirk, the division was transferred to Guderian's *Panzergruppe* for its breakneck advance through eastern France to the Swiss border. Following the French surrender, the division was transferred to Army Group C, and was employed on occupation duties in eastern France until early in 1941.

In the spring of 1941, the division returned to Germany, where it came under the control of *Wehrkreis* IX in Thuringia. In May, it was transferred to Guderian's 2.*Panzergruppe*, which was preparing for the invasion of Russia.

Commanders

Generalleutnant Joachim Lemelsen
Pre-war

Generalmajor Willibald Freiherr von Langermann und Erlencamp
May 1940

Generalmajor Walter von Boltenstern
September 1940

Generalmajor Max Fremerey
September 1941

Generalmajor Hans-Georg Leyser
September 1942 – January 1943

General der Panzertruppen Walter Fries
March 1943

Generalleutnant Dr Fritz Polack
August 1944 – 24 April 1945

INSIGNIA

The 29th Infantry Division chose the falcon as its insignia, which led to it being nicknamed the *Falke* (Falcon) Division during the war.

As with many other divisions, the *Falke* Division used different versions of its falcon symbol during its nine-year existence.

Operation *Barbarossa*

At the start of the invasion of the Soviet Union, the 29th Division was transferred to Fourth Army. As Guderian's Panzers struck deep into Russia, the Fourth and Ninth Armies were tasked with first containing and then destroying the large pockets of Red Army resistance left behind in the headlong advance.

Over the next months, the division saw action against cut-off Soviet forces at Minsk, Smolensk and

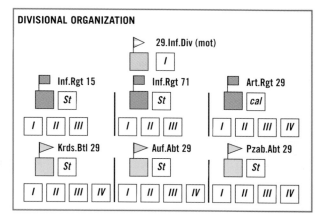

DIVISIONAL ORGANIZATION

Bryansk. At the end of the year, as the Panzers drove on towards Moscow, the 29th Division was sent forward to reinforce Guderian's Panzer Army at Tula. It arrived on 1 December, just days before the massive Soviet counteroffensive that was to drive the Germans away from the gates of Moscow.

Launching their assault on the night of 5/6 December, the Soviet troops under the command of General Georgi Zhukov hammered into the overstretched Germans, driving them back over 80km (50 miles) by the end of the year. The 29th Division, along with the rest of Second Panzer Army, finally came to a halt at Orel, where they managed to hold the Red Army's advance.

▲ **Half-track reconnaissance**

The light SdKfz 250 half-track began supplementing armoured cars in Panzer and Panzergrenadier units from 1941. This is the modernized variant, built from 1943.

Divisional History	Formed
29.Infanterie-Division	1936
29.Infanterie-Division (mot)	1937
29.Panzergrenadier-Division	1943

▶ **Werkstatt Kraftwagen Krupp L3H163 (Kfz 79)**

29.Versorgungs Truppe

Large van-bodied variants of medium trucks were used for a wide variety of tasks, especially for communications, as command posts or, as here, as a workshop for vehicle maintenance units in the divisional support services.

Specifications

Crew: 1 + maintenance section	Engine: 6-cylinder petrol (110bhp)
Weight: 9 tonnes (8.85 tons)	Speed: 45km/h (28mph)
Length: 7.4m (24ft 5in)	Range: not known
Width: 2.5m (8ft 2in)	Payload: workshop equipment
Height: 3m (9ft 9in)	

▶ **Schwere Panzerspähwagen 6-Rad (SdKfz 231)**

29.Aufklärungs-Abteilung / Spähpanzerwagen-Kompanie

The 29th had the mobility to cover large areas of Poland as it protected the rear of the advancing Tenth Army. One of the reconnaissance battalion's roles would have been to locate any combat-effective Polish units bypassed in the advance.

Specifications

Crew: 4	or Magirus petrol (60-80hp)
Weight: 5.9 tonnes (5.35 tons)	Speed: 70km/h (43.5mph)
Length: 5.57m (18ft 7in)	Range: 300km (186 miles)
Width: 1.82m (5ft 11.5in)	Radio: FuG Spr Ger 'a'
Height: 2.00m (6ft 6in)	Armament: 1 x 20mm (0.7in)
Engine: Daimler-Benz, Büssing-NAG	cannon; 1 x 7.62mm (0.3in) MG

✈ *Fall Blau*

JUNE–SEPTEMBER 1942

The German summer Offensive of 1942 had two main objectives: first, to sieze the city of Stalingrad on the Volga, and then to drive on to capture the oilfields of the Caucasus.

THE 29TH INFANTRY DIVISION (MOT) had been transferred to Army Group South in June 1942 after six months of fighting around Orel. In July, it was assigned to Sixth Army on the Don River.

Fall Blau (Plan Blue), the German plan for a knockout offensive in southern Russia, called for all available forces to be concentrated on the southern sector. Their mission was firstly to annihilate the enemy on the Don. Next they were to swing north and take Stalingrad, then follow this up with a combined assault to conquer the Caucasus oil areas. Without that oil, German Panzers would go nowhere. Lastly, they were to capture the passes through the Caucasus Mountains, giving access to the Middle East.

Army Group South, renamed Army Group B, included the Second and Sixth Armies, Fourth Panzer Army and Third Hungarian Army. It was to advance into the bend of the Don River, then on to the Volga at Stalingrad. The other claw in a gigantic pincer movement would be a new formation, Army Group A – comprising First Panzer Army, Seventeenth Army and Third Romanian Army – which would link up with Army Group B somewhere on the steppe west of the Volga, hopefully trapping another vast haul of Soviet prisoners. Having gutted the Soviet armies

again, Army Group A would then lunge south and east to overrun the Soviet oilfields.

On 28 June, the great summer offensive began. Army Group B, under Field Marshal Fedor von Bock, attacked on a 150km (93-mile) front. Two days later,

▲ **Panzerkampfwagen II (SdKfz 121)**

129.Panzer-Abteilung / leichte Panzer-Kompanie / leichte Zug

Although still nominally a motorized infantry unit, the 25th Division had a Panzer battalion attached in 1942. At this time, the bulk of the unit's armoured strength was still provided by Panzer IIs and Panzer IIIs.

Specifications

Crew: 3	Speed: 40km/h (24.9mph)
Weight: 9.8 tonnes (8.9 tons)	Range: 200km (124.3 miles)
Length: 4.81m (15ft 10in)	Radio: FuG5
Width: 2.22m (7ft 4in)	Armament: 1 x 20mm (0.7in) KwK 30 or 38
Height: 1.99m (6ft 6in)	L/55 cannon; 1 x 7.92mm (0.3in) MG (coaxial)
Engine: Maybach HL62TR (140hp)	

▶ **Panzerkampfwagen III Ausf G (SdKfz 141)**

129.Panzer-Abteilung / leichte Panzer-Kompanie / 1.Zug

Although until 1942 tanks were still finished in grey, operational experience meant that most were repainted into less obvious colours in the field. The summer yellow on this Panzer III is fading after hard use.

Specifications

Crew: 4	Speed: 40km/h (24.9mph)
Weight: 22.4 tonnes (20.3 tons)	Range: 165km (102.5 miles)
Length: 5.41m (17ft 8in)	Radio: FuG5
Width: 2.95m (9ft 9in)	Armament: 1 x 37mm (1.5in) KwK L/46
Height: 2.44m (8ft)	or 50mm (2in) KwK L/38 gun; 2 x
Engine: Maybach HL120TRM petrol	7.92mm (0.3in) MG (one coaxial, one
(300hp)	hull-mounted)

129.Panzer-Abteilung, June 1942	Strength
PzIII PzBefwg	2
PzKpfw II	12
PzKpfw III with 5cm (2in) long gun	36
PzKpfw IV with long gun	8

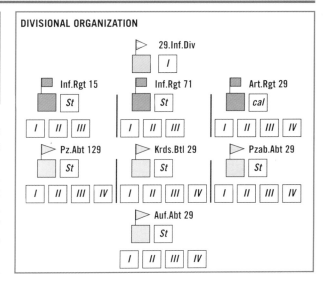

DIVISIONAL ORGANIZATION

Army Group A under Wilhelm List burst over the Donets bend and drove southwards to Proletarskaya and the Caucasus.

The attacks were resoundingly successful. Hoth was in Voronezh by 3 July, though progress was not fast enough to satisfy Hitler and he replaced von Bock with Baron Maximilian von Weichs. Army Group B then poured down the Donets corridor to link up with Kleist's armour pushing on Rostov.

Hitler then gave a directive that arguably cost him the war in the East. He changed the plans for his two army groups. Rather than take Stalingrad and then attack the Caucasus, he opted to move on both objectives simultaneously. Sixth Army reached the banks of the Volga on 23 August, and its commander, General Paulus, began to plan the attacks which he hoped would take the city.

▶ **Panzerkampfwagen IV Ausf F2 (SdKfz 161/1)**
129.Panzer-Abteilung / mittlerer Panzer-Kompanie
In September 1942, as the division approached Stalingrad with the rest of Sixth Army, divisional records showed that the medium Panzer company had eight long-barrel Panzer IVs in its inventory.

Specifications
Crew: 5
Weight: 27.6 tonnes (25 tons)
Length: 7.02 (23ft 0in)
Width: 2.88m (9ft 5in)
Height: 2.68m (8ft 10in)
Engine: Maybach HL120TRM
Speed: 38km/h (23.6mph)
Range: 210km (130.5 miles)
Radio: FuG5
Armament: 1 x 75mm (3in) KwK 40/43; 2 x 7.92mm (0.3in) MGs (one hull-mounted, one coaxial)

▶ **Leichte Personenkraftwagen (Kfz 1)**
71.Infanterie Regiment (mot) / Stab / Nachrichten Zug
Originally designed as a family car for the Nazi Party's *Kraft durch Freude* organization, the Volkswagen 82 chassis proved to be tough and reliable, and saw service with every type of division on all battlefronts.

Specifications
Crew: 1
Weight: 0.64 tonnes (0.58 tons)
Length: 3.73m (12 ft 3in)
Width: 1.60m (5ft 3in)
Height: 1.35m (4ft 5in)
Engine: Volkswagen 998cc petrol (24hp). Later Volkswagen 1131cc petrol (25hp)
Speed: 100km/h (62mph)
Range: 600km (375 miles)
Radio: None

✈ Destroyed at Stalingrad
OCTOBER 1942 – JANUARY 1943

Although the Sixth Army had reached the Volga on 23 August, it took time for General Paulus to prepare his forces to make the final assault on Stalingrad.

THE FIRST ASSAULT was launched on 14 September, by which time the opportunity to take the city easily had passed. The Sixth Army's makeshift attack could have succeeded only if it met an enemy that was not only beaten but whose morale was extremely low. From the very first engagements in the increasingly bitter street fighting, it was clear to the Germans that the Soviets had recovered beyond anyone's expectations.

The 29th Infantry Division (mot), transferred back from Fourth Army to Sixth Army, took part in the series of bitter battles that followed, making repeated attacks into the southern portion of Stalingrad. Soviet soldiers fought for every yard of every street and every alleyway in the city. In Berlin, Hitler was already proclaiming the victory in Stalingrad, and poured as many reinforcements as possible into the inferno. By contrast, the Soviets fed in just enough troops to keep the Germans occupied, and to resist their best efforts.

Russian attack

On 19 November, the last of six major attacks by the Sixth Army had been repulsed, and the weary German troops were licking their wounds. Surprise was near total when the Soviets unleashed massive barrages north and south of Stalingrad. The Soviets had taken in the lessons of *Blitzkrieg* at last. This time, their attack was launched at the weakest part of the Axis line: the thinly held flanks, which were protected only by Romanian and Italian formations.

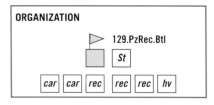

ORGANIZATION

129.PzRec.Btl

St

car | car | rec | rec | rec | hv

Smashed

Sixth Army was cut off. The 29th Division found itself defending the extreme west of German-held territory, in an area between Dmitriyevka and Karpovka, about 25km (15.5 miles) from the centre of Stalingrad. A report sent to Army Group Don by Sixth Army on 28 December recorded that the 29th Infantry Division (mot) was still effective, with six out of eight infantry battalions being combat capable. The artillery regiment still had 30 guns, though there were only three operational anti-tank weapons.

On 9 January, the Soviet Twenty-first Army launched a major attack on Karpovka, which smashed through the extended German lines. In the process, the 29th Infantry Division (mot) was destroyed. Less than a month later, the last German forces in Stalingrad surrendered.

▶ **15-cm sIG 33 auf PzKpfw 38(t) Ausf H (SdKfz 138/1)**

Panzergrenadier Regiment 15 / I Bataillon / sIG Kompanie

Known as the *Grille* (Cricket) or Bison, this vehicle was issued to the heavy infantry gun companies of the Panzergrenadier regiments serving with Panzer and Panzergrenadier divisions.

Specifications

Crew: 5	Engine: Praga EPA/2
Weight: 12.7 tonnes (11.5 tons)	Speed: 35km/h (21.7mph)
Length: 4.61m (15ft 1in)	Range: 185km (115 miles)
Width: 2.16m (7ft 0in)	Radio: FuG16
Height: 2.40 (7ft 10.5in)	Armament: 1 x 150mm (5.9in) sIG 33 gun

▼ Kradschützen or Panzer-Aufklärungs Bataillon / Spähpanzerwagen-Kompanie

Armoured cars in reconnaissance units included both gun-armed vehicles for protection and radio-equipped vehicles whose primary mission was to get intelligence about the enemy back to regimental or divisional headquarters.

schwere Spähpanzerwagen-Zug

leichte Spähpanzerwagen-Zug

leichte Spähpanzerwagen-Zug

leichte Spähpanzerwagen-Zug

29th Panzergrenadier Division

SICILY AND ITALY, JULY 1943 – APRIL 1945

The destruction of the 29th Infantry Division (mot) at Stalingrad in January 1943 was not the end of the formation, since it was ordered to be re-formed in March 1943.

THE REBORN DIVISION incorporated the newly forming 345 Infantry Division, which had been authorized on 24 November 1942 and which had begun assembling its constituent units in France in February 1943. On 1 March 1943, the division was redesignated as the 29th Infantry Division.

Upgraded to Panzergrenadier

The division continued its build-up through the spring, eventually receiving orders to transfer to southern Italy. However, it arrived in Italy under a new designation, having been renamed the 29th Panzergrenadier Division on 23 June 1943. After arriving in Apulia, the division was sent to Sicily after

the Allied invasion, but could do nothing to stop the Anglo-American forces. It was pulled back over the Strait of Messina, where it formed the rearguard of the orderly German retreat up the 'toe' of Italy.

The Allied landings at Salerno on 9 September threatened to cut off the German forces retreating up the Italian Peninsula. The 29th Division broke contact with the British Eighth Army which was advancing through Calabria, racing northwards to the beachhead. There, it was part of a powerful German force that sealed off the Allied landings until remaining German forces in the south of Italy could retreat northwards to the almost impregnable defensive positions of the Gustav Line.

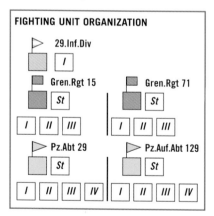

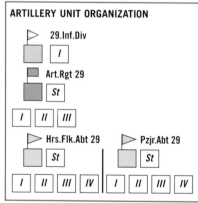

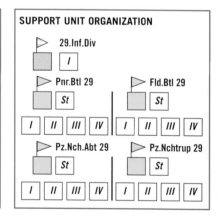

▶ **Mittlerer Lkw A-Typ Opel Blitz 3.6-6700 mit 2-cm Flak 38**

313 Heeres Flak Abteilung / leichte Batterie

The simplest way of providing a unit with self-propelled anti-aircraft guns was to mount the light 2cm (1.8in) Flak 38 onto the loadbed of a cargo truck.

Specifications

Crew: 1

Weight: 3.29 tonnes (3 tons)

Length: 6.02m (19ft 9in)

Width: 2.27m (7ft 5in)

Height: 2.18m (7ft 2in)

Engine: Opel 6-cylinder petrol (73.5hp)

Speed: 80km/h (50mph)

Range: 410km (255 miles)

Radio: None

Armament: Twin or quad 20mm (0.7in) Flak 38 cannon

The 29th Division would continue its fighting retreat northwards for the remainder of the war, being involved in the Anzio battle early in 1944, and in the Po River campaign in 1945.

On 24 April 1945, the 29th Panzergrenadier Division, together with the rest of the LXXVI Panzer Corps, was caught by the British Eighth Army between the Po and the Apennine Mountains and was destroyed. Only a few survivors of the division managed to reach the Po River and swim across it to safety. Even these were rounded up in the next few days, but the division itself no longer existed.

▶ Schwere Spähpanzerwagen 7.5-cm KwK (SdKfz 234/3)

129.Panzer-Aufklärungs-Abteilung / schwere Zug

Six SdKfz 234s armed with short 7.5cm (3in) tank guns were assigned to armoured reconnaissance battalions to provide fire support for the 18 armoured cars in the Spähpanzerwagen company.

Specifications

Crew: 4	Speed: 80km/h (49.7mph)
Weight: 11.50 tonnes (10.47 tons)	Range: 900km (559 miles)
Length: 6.0m (19ft 8in)	Radio: FuG Spr Ger 'a'
Width: 2.40m (7ft 10.5in)	Armament: 1 x 75mm (3in) KwK 51 L/24
Height: 2.21m (7ft 4in)	cannon; 1 x 7.92 mm (0.3in) MG
Engine: Tatra 103 12-cylinder (220hp)	

▶ 7.5-cm Sturmgeschütz 40 Ausf G (SdKfz 142/1)

129.Panzer-Abteilung / Stab-Batterie

The 129th Panzer Battalion was formed in France in March 1943 by detaching personnel from the 345th Division (mot). The battalion was equipped with one HQ battery and three further batteries of assault guns.

Specifications

Crew: 4	Speed: 40km/h (24.9mph)
Weight: 26.3 tonnes (23.9 tons)	Range: 155km (96.3 miles)
Length: 6.77m (22ft 2in)	Radio: FuG15 and FuG16
Width: 2.95m (9ft 8in)	Armament: 1 x 75mm (3in) StuG
Height: 2.16m (7ft 0in)	L/48 cannon
Engine: Maybach HL120TRM	

▶ Leichte Funkpanzerwagen I Ausf B (SdKfz 250/3)

129.Panzer-Aufklärungs-Abteilung / SPW Aufklärungs-Kompanie / Stab

The Light Armoured Reconnaissance Company was equipped with variants of the SdKfz 250. The SdKfz 250/3 was used by the company HQ to communicate with division and for coordinating with *Luftwaffe* close-support aircraft.

Specifications

Crew: 4	(100hp)
Weight: 5.35 tonnes (4.87 tons)	Speed: 60km/h (37.3mph)
Length: 4.56m (14ft 11.5in)	Range: 320km (199 miles)
Width: 1.95m (6ft 5in)	Radio: FuG Spr Ger 1
Height: 1.66m (5ft 5in)	Armament: 1/2 x 7.92mm (0.3in) MGs
Engine: Maybach HL42TRKM 6-cylinder	

36th Infantry Division (motorized)

The 36th Infantry Division was formed as a standard infantry division of the *Heer* at Kaiserslautern in the Pfalz region of western Germany on 1 October 1936.

THE DIVISION WAS LED by *Generalleutnant* Georg Lindemann, who would go on to command at corps, army, and army group level during World War II. The division was controlled by *Wehrkreis* XII, based nearby at Wiesbaden. The nucleus of the division was provided by *Infanterie-Ersatz-Bataillon* 87 (Infantry Replacement Battalion 87), which had been set up at Wiesbaden in October 1935.

The division had the standard pre-war structure for such formations, with three infantry regiments each of three battalions, an artillery regiment, a replacement battalion, a *Panzerjäger* (anti-tank) *Abteilung*, an *Aufklärungs* (reconnaissance) *Abteilung*, a *Nachrichten* (communications) *Abteilung* and a pioneer battalion.

The division was not involved in the attack on Poland. The *Wehrmacht* had committed most of its forces to the Polish campaign, gambling that the Western powers would not invade Germany. No more than a token covering force in the West was left to face an overwhelming French Army of 70 divisions and a small British Expeditionary Force. One of the formations in that covering force was the 36th Infantry Division, which had moved forwards into the Saarland.

War in the West

Although dangerously overexposed, Hitler had calculated correctly that the Allies would do nothing. Once the subjugation of Poland was completed in early October, Hitler was free to turn his attention to further campaigns in the West.

Over the winter of 1939/40, the 25th Infantry Division was part of the Army high command's

reserve. In May, it was assigned to Sixteenth Army in Luxembourg, which provided flank security to von Rundstedt's Army Group A as it made its surprise Panzer attack through the Ardennes. While Kleist's Panzers raced westwards towards the English Channel, the 36th Division was part of the force that tied down the French armies trapped in the bypassed Maginot Line. During the Battle of France, the division advanced slowly through and around the French defences, ending the campaign at Verdun.

After three months of occupation duties, the division was returned to Germany in September, where it was to be transformed into a motorized infantry division. In the process, it lost Infantry Regiment 70, since combat experience had shown that the three-regiment structure could be difficult to control. The division's horse-drawn units were transferred to the 126.*Infanterie-Division*.

In May 1941, the fully motorized and trained 36th Infantry Division (mot) was briefly assigned to

Commanders	
Generalleutnant Georg Lindemann *September 1939 – October 1940*	Generalmajor Rudolf Stegmann *August 1943 – January 1944*
Generalmajor Otto Ottenbacher *October 1940 – October 1941*	Oberst Horst Kadgien *January 1944*
Generalleutnant Hans Gollnick *October 1941 – August 1943*	Generalmajor Egon von Neindorff *January 1944*
Oberst Gottfried Frölich *August 1943*	Generalmajor Alexander Conrady *January 1944 – July 1944*

Divisional History	Formed
36.Infanterie-Division	1936
36.Infanterie-Division (mot)	1940
36 Infanterie-Division	1943
36.Grenadier-Division	1944
36.Volksgrenadier-Division	1944

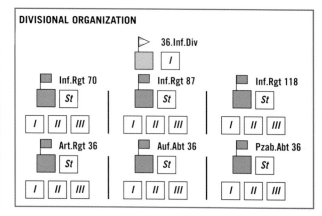

DIVISIONAL ORGANIZATION

36.Inf.Div — I

Inf.Rgt 70 — St — I II III

Inf.Rgt 87 — St — I II III

Inf.Rgt 118 — St — I II III

Art.Rgt 36 — St — I II III

Auf.Abt 36 — St — I II III

Pzab.Abt 36 — St — I II III

Guderian's *2.Panzergruppe* in preparation for Operation *Barbarossa*, the invasion of the USSR. However, it was transferred to XXXXI corps of *4.Panzergruppe* and Army Group North, where it took part in the encirclement of Leningrad.

In October 1941, the 36th Division moved south when the corps was transferred to Hermann Hoth's *3.Panzergruppe* with Army Group Centre, where the division was thrown into the attack on Moscow. By the beginning of December, it had reached Klin, northwest of the Soviet capital. Driven back by the Soviet counteroffensive, the division came to a halt in the Rzhev salient, where it was heavily engaged repelling a series of Soviet offensives between January and August 1942.

A long-planned withdrawal from the salient in March 1943 saw the division pulled back to Dorogobusz near Smolensk, where it was stood down for rest and refitting.

◢ **Invasion of France, 1940**

German motorized troops move past abandoned French transport on 14 June 1940.

▶ **Schwere Kraftrad 750-cc BMW R75 mit Seitenwagen**

Kradschützen-Bataillon 36

The 36th Motorcycle Battalion was formed from the 11th Machine Gun Battalion when the 36th Infantry Division was motorized in November 1940.

Specifications

Crew: 2	Engine: BMW 750cc petrol (26hp)
Weight: 1.65 tonnes (1.5 tons)	Speed: 92km/h (57mph)
Length: 2.4m (7 ft 10in)	Range: 340km (211 miles)
Width: 1.73m (5ft 8in)	Radio: None
Height: 1m (3ft 3in)	Armament: 1 x 7.92mm (0.3in) MG (if fitted)

▶ **Krupp Protz (Kfz 69)**

36.Infanterie-Division

Used by divisional light Flak detachments to tow 2cm (0.7in) Flak 36 guns.

Specifications

Crew: 2	Height: 1.96m (6ft 5in)
Weight: 2.45 tonnes (2.23 tons)	Engine: Krupp 3.3L 4-cylinder (60hp)
Length: 5.10m (16ft 8in)	Speed: 70km/h (43mph)
Width: 1.93m (6ft 4in)	Range: 450km (280 miles)

With Army Group Centre
1943–1944

Between March and June 1943, the 36th Infantry Division (mot) was out of the front line. However, while being refitted east of Smolensk, it underwent two transformations.

IN APRIL 1943, WHILE BEING REBUILT, it was ordered that the division should be upgraded to become a Panzergrenadier formation. However, in May the Army high command changed its plans and decided that the division should be demotorized, becoming a standard infantry division.

In August 1943, the 36th Infantry Division was assigned to Ninth Army and moved to the Orel sector, but it was almost immediately transferred to Ninth Army at Smolensk. It arrived just in time for the opening of the Soviet Operation *Suvorov*.

Staged almost simultaneously with the Battle of the Dnieper, the offensive lasted more than two months and was aimed at clearing the Germans from the Smolensk and Bryansk regions. Smolensk had been occupied by the Germans since 1941. Despite several Red Army breakthroughs, the overall advance was quite slow in the face of heavy German resistance.

It was not until October that the Germans were finally pushed back from the Smolensk region. By December, the 36th Infantry Division had taken up a position at Bobruisk.

Destruction of Army Group Centre

After the Smolensk offensive, the central part of the Soviet-German front stabilized until late June 1944, while the major fighting shifted to the south for the Dnieper Line and the territory of the Ukraine.

On 22 June 1944, the Soviets launched Operation *Bagration*, one of largest military operations in history. When the massive offensive got under way, the advancing Soviet units were able to bypass, encircle and destroy large German troop concentrations. Some 30,000 German troops were surrounded at Vitebsk on 25 June. Two days later, Bobruisk, on the Berezina River in Byelorussia (modern-day

ORGANIZATION

▷ Füs.Btl 36

☐ HQ

füs | füs | füs | scw

DIVISIONAL ORGANIZATION 1943

▷ 36.Inf.Div
☐ I

Inf.Rgt 87
☐ St
I | II | III

Inf.Rgt 118
☐ St
I | II | III

Div.Grp 268
☐ St
I | II | III

Füs.Btl 36
☐ St
I | II | III

Art.Rgt 36
☐ St
I | II | III

Pzjr.Abt 36
☐ St
I | II | III

ORGANIZATION

▷ Nach.Abt 36

☐ HQ

tel | rad | trs

▶ **Werkstatt Kraftwagen Lkw A-Typ Opel Blitz 4x4 3t (Kfz 305)**

36.Infanterie-Division (mot) / Versorgungsdienste

Opel were the largest producers of 4x4 trucks for the German armed forces, producing 25,000 vehicles at the Brandenburg/Havel plant in a wide variety of body styles.

Specifications

Crew: 1	Engine: Opel 6-cylinder petrol
Weight: 3.29 tonnes (3 tons)	(73.5hp)
Length: 6.02m (19ft 9in)	Speed: 80km/h (50mph)
Width: 2.27m (7ft 5in)	Range: 410km (255 miles)
Height: 2.18m (7ft 2in)	Radio: None

Belarus), was encircled. As many as 40,000 troops from the German Ninth Army found themselves caught in the steel pincer of attacking Soviet tank units. The pocket was quickly eliminated, and the 36th Infantry Division was one of the formations wiped out in the process.

Between 3 August and 15 September, the division was reformed as the 36th Grenadier Division. After

hasty training, it was sent to the Saarland, where it joined Army Group G's LXXXII Corps.

On 9 October 1944, the formation was again renamed, becoming the 36th Volksgrenadier Division. It remained in the Saar until driven back through Franconia into Bavaria. At the end of the war, survivors of the division surrendered to the US Army at Traunstein to the north of Berchtesgaden.

▶ Schwerer Einheits Protzkraftwagen Horch 40 (Kfz 69)

36.Artillerie-Regiment / Flak-Abteilung

Based on the Horch heavy car chassis, it was intended to replace the Krupp Protz as a light artillery tractor.

Specifications

Crew: 1	Engine: Horch 6-cylinder petrol (90hp)
Weight: 2.4 tonnes (2.2 tons)	Speed: 88km/h (55 mph)
Length: 4.44m (14 ft 7in)	Range: 400 km (250 miles)
Width: 1.68m (5ft 6in)	Radio: None usually fitted
Height: 1.73m (5ft 8in)	

▶ Mittlerer geländegängige Lkw Henschel 33D1

36.Infanterie-Division (mot) / 37.Infanterie-Regiment

Built between 1934 and 1943, the Henschel 33 was produced with both diesel engines (Henschel 33D) and petrol engines (Henschel 33G).

Specifications

Crew: 1	Engine: 10.7 litre (650ci),
Weight: 6.1 tonnes (6 tons)	six-cylinder petrol (100hp)
Length: 7.4m (24ft)	Speed: 60km/h (37mph)
Width: 2.25m (7ft 4in)	Payload: 3 tonnes (2.95 tons)
Height: 3.2m (10ft 6in)	or 18 troops

▶ Druckerei Kraftwagen (Kfz 72)

36.Infanterie-Division (mot) / Divisionsstab

To cope with the huge amount of paperwork generated by large military formations, most divisional headquarters had a printing detachment that printed maps and operational orders.

Specifications

Crew: 1 + maintenance	Engine: 6-cylinder petrol
section	(90bhp)
Weight: 9 tonnes (8.85 tons)	Speed: 45km/h (28mph)
Length: 7.4m (24ft 5in)	Range: not known
Width: 2.5m (8ft 2in)	Payload: printing equipment
Height: 3m (9ft 9in)	

60th Infantry Division (mot)

The 60th Infantry Division was established in Danzig on 15 October 1939. Unlike other German Army divisions, its troops were drawn from the Stormtroopers of the SA and the police.

T HE ORIGINS OF THE 60TH DIVISION lie with the *Feldherrnhalle* units that drew their manpower from the SA (*Sturmabteilung*) and traced their history back to the days of the 1923 Beer Hall Putsch in Munich. The *Feldherrnhalle* was the monument in the city where the attempted coup was crushed, and the units that bore the title were considered the elite formations of the SA.

The *SA-Standarte Feldherrnhalle* was formed after the death of Ernst Röhm during the Night of the Long Knives, when the SA's position as the major paramilitary formation of the Nazi Party was seized by the SS (*Schutzstaffel*). In March 1938, men from the *Standarte* were among the first to march into Austria during the *Anschluss*. In September 1938, the *Feldherrnhalle* was placed under the control of the *Wehrmacht*. Its cadre was transferred to the *Luftwaffe*, forming the *Luftlande-Regiment Feldherrnhalle*, a part of *7.Flieger-Division*. The remainder of the regiment was transferred to the *Heer*, forming the 120th Infantry Regiment of the 60th Infantry Division.

However, the bulk of the division came from *Gruppe Eberhardt*, a collection of SA units that had been engaged in the capture of Danzig during the invasion of Poland, together with two regiments drawn from the *Landespolizei Danzig*.

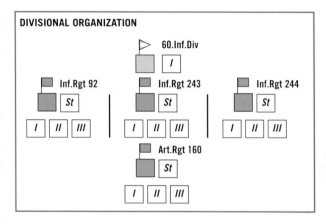

DIVISIONAL ORGANIZATION

INSIGNIA

The arms of the ancient Prussian city of Danzig (now known as Gdansk in Poland) incorporate two crosses in a red shield.

During World War II, the 60th Infantry Division used a simplified version of the Danzig Crosses as the formation's tactical symbol.

After the division was re-formed and renamed *Feldherrnhalle* in 1943, it adopted a new symbol using a variant of the runic Wolf's Hook symbol.

Commanders

Generalmajor Friedrich-Georg Eberhardt *September 1939 – May 1942*	Generalleutnant Otto Kohlermann *June 1943 – April 1944*
Generalmajor Otto Kohlermann *May 1942 – November 1942*	Generalmajor Friedrich-Carl von Steinkeller *April 1944 – July 1944*
Generalmajor Hans-Adolf von Arenstorff *November 1942 – February 1943*	Generalmajor Günther Pape *July 1944 – May 1945*

▼ **3.7-cm Panzerabwehrkanone 36 (Pak 36)**

92.Infanterie Regiment / Panzerjäger Zug (mot)

Each infantry regiment in the 60th Infantry Division had a Panzerjäger platoon equipped with 12 Pak 36 guns.

Divisional History	Formed
Gruppe Eberhardt	1939
60.Infanterie-Division	1939
60.Infanterie-Division (mot)	1940
60.Panzergrenadier-Division Feldherrnhalle	1944
Panzergrenadier-Division Feldherrnhalle	1944
Panzer-Division Feldherrnhalle 1	1944

Specifications

Crew: 3

Weight: 0.43 tonnes (0.39 tons)

Length: 1.67m (5ft 5.5in)

Calibre: 37mm (1.5in)

Muzzle Velocity: 762m/s (2500 fps)

Range: 600m (656 yards)

Ammunition: Armour-piercing

▶ **Infantry tank killers**

The Pionier, or combat engineer, battalion of a German division was responsible for mine-laying and mine-clearing, This pioneer is carrying a pair of Teller Mines, powerful enough to rip the tracks off an enemy tank.

▼ **Skoda Kommandokraftwagen Typ 952 (Kfz 21)**

60. Infanterie Division (mot) / Divisionsstab

The same chassis with a two-door body was designated Kfz 15 and was used in large numbers by divisional support services.

Specifications

Crew: 6 including staff	Engine: Steyr 3.5L 8-cylinder petrol (85hp)
Weight: 2.5 tonnes (2.28 tons)	Speed: 90km/h (55.9mph)
Length: 5.8m (19ft 0in)	Range: 400km (248.5 miles)
Width: 2.03m (6ft 8in)	Radio: None
Height: 2.32m (7ft 9in)	

✠ France and Yugoslavia

MAY 1940 – APRIL 1941

For the first months of its existence, the division was engaged in working up to operational readiness, but it also performed occupation duties in Poland.

IN MAY 1940, THE DIVISION had completed working-up, but it was too late to be deployed in the opening stages of the campaign in the West. The 60th Infantry Division was assigned to OKH reserve and was moved to St Ingbert near Saarbrücken on the French border. In June, the division attacked and broke through the Maginot Line. Later in June, it was transferred to Lorraine, where it was attached to XXIV Corps of First Army, part of Army Group C.

In July, the division was withdrawn to Gross-Born in Pomerania (now Wielkie Bory near Jastrowo, Poland), where it began the process of motorization. In the process, as with other divisions of the time, its infantry complement was reduced from three regiments to two, losing the 243rd Infantry Regiment. In November, the division was assigned to XVI Corps of Eighteenth Army in Poland, later switching to XXXX Corps of Twelfth Army.

ORGANIZATION
⚑ Pz.Abt 160
⬜ HQ
lt · lt · md · mnt

Balkan interlude

In January 1941, the division was moved to Romania with the rest of Twelfth Army. In April, the 60th Infantry Division (mot) took part in Operation *Marita*, the German invasion of the Balkans and Greece. The SA formation acquitted itself well in the fighting in Serbia, and at the end of the campaign was moved back into Romania to join Army Group South, which was making ready for Operation *Barbarossa*, the invasion of the Soviet Union.

▲ Schwere Kraftrad 750-cc BMW R75

60.Infanterie-Division (mot) / Divisionsstab / Kraftrad-Zug

The messenger detachment at divisional HQ operated at least 25 motorcycles.

▲ Leichte Personenkraftwagen (Kfz 2)

60.Infanterie-Division (mot) / Divisionsstab

The motor pool of the divisional headquarters usually had 15 cars, with an increasing proportion of Volkswagen Kübels as the war progressed.

Specifications

Crew: 1	Speed: 92km/h (57mph)
Weight: 1.65 tonnes (1.5 tons)	Range: 340km (211 miles)
Length: 2.4m (7 ft 10in)	Radio: None
Width: 1.73m (5ft 8in)	Armament: 1 x 7.92mm (0.3in) MG
Height: 1m (3ft 3in)	(on sidecar if fitted)
Engine: BMW 750cc petrol (26hp)	

Specifications

Crew: 1	Engine: Volkswagen 998cc petrol (24hp). Later
Weight: 0.64 tonnes (0.58 tons)	Volkswagen 1131cc petrol (25hp)
Length: 3.73m (12ft 3in)	Speed: 100km/h (62mph)
Width: 1.60m (5ft 3in)	Range: 600km (375 miles)
Height: 1.35m (4ft 5in)	Radio: None

▶ Mittlere Kraftfahrzeug (Kfz 15)

120.Infanterie-Regiment / I.Bataillon / Stab

The headquarters company of most divisional units had at least one Kfz 15.

Specifications

Crew: 1	Engine: Mercedes-Benz 6-cylinder petrol
Weight: 2.4 tonnes (2.2 tons)	(90hp)
Length: 4.44m (14 ft 7in)	Speed: 88km/h (55mph)
Width: 1.68m (5ft 6in)	Range: 400km (248 miles)
Height: 1.73m (5ft 8in)	Radio: None usually fitted

▶ Protzkraftwagen Auto-Union/Horch 1a (Kfz 69)

120.Infanterie Regiment / Infanterie-Geschütz-Kompanie

Designed to replace the Krupp Protz, the Kfz 69 was based on the standard heavy 4x4 car chassis. It had 50 per cent more power than the older designs, and in the Auto-Union/Horch model 1a variant also had four-wheel steering.

Specifications

Crew: Up to 6	Engine: Auto-Union/Horch V8 3.8L petrol
Weight: 3.6 tonnes (3.28 tons)	(81hp)
Length: 4.85m (15ft 11in)	Speed: 70km/h (43mph)
Width: 2.0m (6ft 7in)	Range: 400km (248 miles)
Height: 2.04m (6ft 8in)	Radio: None

▶ 160.Panzer-Abteilung, leichte Panzer-Kompanie

In 1941, the light panzer company attached to motorized divisions had five Panzer IIs and two Panzer IIIs in its HQ platoon, with three further Panzer III platoons.

Stab

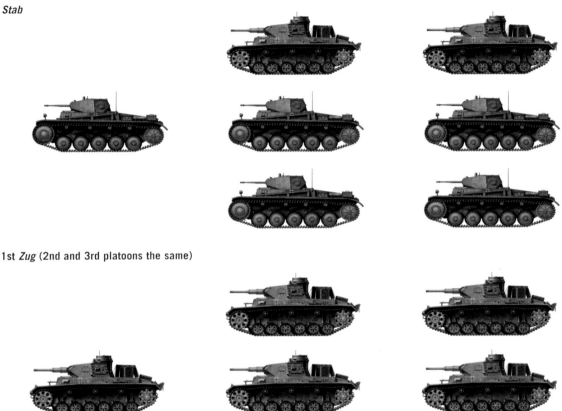

1st *Zug* (2nd and 3rd platoons the same)

☩ Southern Russia
1941–1942

Refitting after the campaign in the Balkans meant that the division was still not fully up to combat strength when Germany launched its invasion of the Soviet Union.

IN JUNE 1941, AT THE START of Operation *Barbarossa*, the division crossed the Soviet border and began the advance towards the Crimea and eventually Rostov-on-Don. Initially moving towards Zhitomir as part of the OKH reserve, it was brought into action in August when it was assigned to II Corps. During the *Blitzkrieg* campaign, the division proved to be highly effective in combat, advancing through Uman, across the Dnieper River and at Mariupol as a part of von Kleist's 1.*Panzergruppe*. By the end of the campaign, the division had taken part in the capture of Rostov-on-Don before the army group was ordered to abandon the city and form defensive lines for the winter. Over the winter of 1941–42, the division managed to hold its position despite terrible conditions and ceaseless Soviet

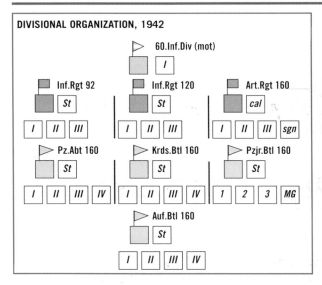

DIVISIONAL ORGANIZATION, 1942

60.Inf.Div (mot)

Inf.Rgt 92 — St | Inf.Rgt 120 — St | Art.Rgt 160 — cal
I | II | III || I | II | III || I | II | III | sgn

Pz.Abt 160 — St | Krds.Btl 160 — St | Pzjr.Btl 160 — St
I | II | III | IV || I | II | III | IV || 1 | 2 | 3 | MG

Auf.Btl 160 — St
I | II | III | IV

▲ *Fall Blau*
A Panzergrenadier platoon forms up in preparation for an assault on a Red Army strongpoint in Stalingrad, September 1942.

counterattacks. In March 1942, the division took part in the Battle of Kharkov, Field Marshal von Manstein's crunching victory that annihilated three Soviet armies.

Plan Blue

In April 1942, Hitler set out his objectives for the coming summer offensive, codenamed Operation Blue (*Fall Blau*). He set his revitalized armies, now numbering some 215 divisions, the task of destroying the last remaining enemy formations, and as far as possible, capturing the main sources of raw materials on which their war economy depended.

All available forces were to be concentrated on the southern sector. Their mission was firstly to annihilate the enemy on the Don. Then they were to swing north and take Stalingrad, followed by a combined assault to conquer the oil-producing areas of the Caucasus. Finally, they were to take the passes through the Caucasus Mountains, which provided access to the Middle East.

Hitler moved his HQ to Vinnitsa in the Ukraine to oversee the next stage of the campaign. Army Group South, renamed Army Group B, was to advance into the bend of the Don River then on to the Volga at Stalingrad. The second claw in a gigantic pincer movement would be Army Group A, a new formation consisting of First Panzer Army, Seventeenth Army and Third Romanian Army. This would link up with Army Group B west of the Volga, hopefully encircling more Russian troops. Once having removed a further host of Soviet forces from the fray, Army Group A would then move south and east into the Soviet oilfields.

▶ **Panzerkampfwagen IV Ausf E (SdKfz 161)**

160.Panzer-Abteilung / mittlerer Panzer-Kompanie

The nominal strength of a medium Panzer company in 1941 and 1942 was three platoons of four Panzer IVs. However, in June 1942 the 160th Panzer Battalion had only four Panzer IVs on its inventory.

Specifications

Crew: 5	Speed: 40km/h (24.9mph)
Weight: 25.9 tonnes (23.5 tons)	Range: 210km (130.5 miles)
Length: 5.92m (19ft 5in)	Radio: FuG5
Width: 2.84m (9ft 4in)	Armament: 1 x 75mm (3in) KwK 37
Height: 2.68m (8ft 9.5in)	L/24 gun; 2 x 7.92mm (0.3in) MG
Engine: Maybach HL120TRM	(one hull-mounted, one coaxial)

On 28 June, the great summer offensive got under way. Army Group B, under the recalled Field Marshal Fedor von Bock, attacked on a 150km (93-mile) front. The spearhead was General Hermann Hoth's Fourth Panzer Army. General Friedrich Paulus' Sixth Army extended the front a further 80km (50 miles) to the south. Two days later, Army Group A under Field Marshal Siegmund Wilhelm List burst over the Donets bend and drove southwards to Proletarskaya and the Caucasus.

In August, the 60th Infantry Division (mot) was transferred from First Panzer Army to Sixth Army, with which it would take part in the German drive towards the Volga and Stalingrad.

▸ Krankenkraftwagen Opel Blitz Typ A (Kfz 31)

160.Krankenkraftwagen-Kompanie / 1.Zug

The medical facilities assigned to the 60th Division included a medical company, a field hospital and an ambulance company.

Specifications

Crew: 1	Engine: Opel 6-cylinder petrol
Weight: 3.29 tonnes (3 tons)	(73.5hp)
Length: 6.02m (19ft 9in)	Speed: 80km/h (50mph)
Width: 2.27m (7ft 5in)	Range: 410km (255 miles)
Height: 2.18m (7ft 2in)	Radio: None

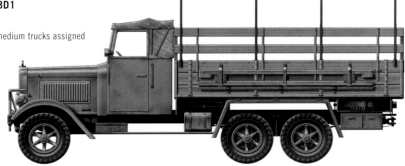

▸ Mittlerer geländegängige Lkw Henschel 33D1

Pionier-Versorgungscolonne

The division's combat engineer battalion had at least 10 medium trucks assigned to its motorized supply column.

Specifications

Crew: 1	Engine: 10.7 litre (650ci),
Weight: 6.1 tonnes (6 tons)	six-cylinder petrol (100hp)
Length: 7.4m (24ft)	Speed: 60km/h (37mph)
Width: 2.25m (7ft 4in)	Payload: 3 tonnes (2.95 tons)
Height: 3.2m (10ft 6in)	or 18 troops

Specifications

Crew: 2	Engine: Maybach NL38TR (100hp)
Weight: 5.9 tonnes (5.37 tons)	Speed: 40km/h (24.8 mph)
Length: 4.42m (14ft 6in)	Range: 170 km (105.6 miles)
Width: 2.06m (6ft 9.5 in)	Radio: FuG2
Height: 1.72m (5ft 7in)	Armament: Two 7.92mm MGs (turret mounted)

▲ Mittlerer Zugkraftwagen 8t / 8.8cm Flak 18

Heeres-Flak-Abteilung 282

The 60th Division took control of the 282nd Army Flak Battalion in 1941. It was renamed as the 4th Battalion of the 160th Artillery Regiment, and its heavy battery was equipped with four 8.8cm (3.5in) Flak 18 guns, which were towed by the 8-tonne (7.84-ton) SdKfz 7 medium half-track.

✠ Stalingrad

AUGUST 1942 – JANUARY 1943

The initial stages of the attack on Stalingrad promised a relatively easy victory for the German Army, but early advances soon bogged down in bitter fighting in the ruins of the city.

THE GERMAN SIXTH ARMY reached the banks of the Volga on 23 August. In spite of furious Soviet counterattacks, a defensive line was established upstream of Stalingrad. That night, Stalingrad was subjected to an air raid reminiscent of the heaviest London blitz. The bulk of the bombs dropped were incendiaries and the wooden buildings of the city burned in a spectacular holocaust. An assault on the city was now planned. But it was to prove an infinitely more difficult task, now that Stalingrad's defenders had had time to prepare their defences.

Initial German optimism that the city would be taken rapidly was quickly dashed. From the very first engagements in the increasingly bitter street fighting, it was clear to the Germans that the Soviets had recovered beyond anyone's expectations. By the middle of September, General von Richthofen, commander of *Luftflotte* IV, wrote in his diary: 'In the town itself progress is desperately slow. The Sixth Army will never finish the job at this rate.'

In early autumn, the fighting had concentrated in the rubble-strewn streets of downtown Stalingrad. Hitler had vowed not to allow another 'Verdun' to

Panzer-Abteilung 160	Strength
PzKpfw II	17
PzKpfw III (long barrel)	35
PzKpfw IV (long barrel)	4
PzBefwg (Pz III)	1

ORGANIZATION

■ Art.Rgt 160
cal

| *I* | *II* | *III* | *sgn* |

take place, referring to the most famous and costly trench warfare episode of World War I, but this is exactly what the Battle of Stalingrad became. Instead of fighting in trenches, Soviet soldiers and their German counterparts fought from behind shattered buildings, often no more than 15m (50ft) apart.

Wiped out

The 60th Infantry Division (mot) was in the thick of the fighting for the city. It was engaged in the northern sector of the battlefield, attacking south along the Volga towards the strongly fortified Soviet positions in the Stalingrad Tractor Factory, scene of some of the bitterest, most vicious fighting of the war.

When the Soviets launched Operation *Uranus* on 19 November, a massive encircling movement to the north and south of the city, Sixth Army was cut off. By 23 November, the encirclement was complete. Some 300,000 Axis soldiers were trapped inside Stalingrad. The 60th Division manned the defensive line at the north of the pocket, north of the railway station at Konnaja. By the end of December, the division was reporting that though it was capable of defensive operations, its mobility was limited.

The division bore the brunt of the attack by the Soviet Twenty-fourth and Sixty-sixth Armies, launched on 9 January 1943. Short of food, warm clothing and ammunition, there was little that the surviving members of the 60th could do in the face of overwhelming enemy force, and within days the division had been wiped out.

▲ StuG III
At Stalingrad, German forces commonly used StuGs to support infantry attacks against Soviet defensive positions. The StuGs were expected to destroy heavy emplacements and soften up Soviet forces before the German infantry engaged at close quarters.

Feldherrnhalle Division and Corps
1944–1945

The destruction of the 60th Infantry Division at Stalingrad was followed by orders for the division to be rebuilt, maintaining the formation's links with the Stormtroopers of the SA.

T HE REMNANTS OF THE DIVISION who had been on leave or convalescing were ordered to the south of France to begin re-forming the division, which was to be upgraded to a Panzergrenadier division and redesignated as the 60th Panzergrenadier Division *Feldherrnhalle*. There it was joined by the survivors of the 271st Infantry Regiment *Feldherrnhalle*, which had fought with distinction as part of the 93rd Infantry Division in France and on the Leningrad Front with Army Group North. The new division spent the rest of the year forming and training in southern France. In November, all the divisional units had their numbers removed and were granted the title *Feldherrnhalle*.

In December, the division was ordered back to the Eastern Front, to join 3.*Panzerarmee*, which was involved in heavy fighting near Vitebsk in Byelorussia. After executing a fighting withdrawal through Byelorussia, the division was transferred to the Narva Front, where it fought exceptionally.

Destroyed with Army Group Centre

In May, the division was ordered south to bolster the forces of Army Group Centre, engaged near Mogilev and Orscha. With the launch of the Soviet Operation *Bagration* in June 1944, the division was pushed back towards Minsk, where it was encircled. In late July,

after heavy resistance and several failed breakout attempts, the division was annihilated near the city.

The *Panzergrenadier-Division Feldherrnhalle* was only partially re-formed by September 1944, when it was ordered to the front in Hungary to strengthen *Armeegruppe Fretter-Pico*. In mid-October, the division was ordered to hold a major crossing point on the Tisza River. The division fought in cooperation with *schwere Panzer-Abteilung* 503 and was soon involved in the withdrawal towards Budapest. By now exhausted and dangerously understrength, the *Feldherrnhalle* units were pushed back into the city. On 21 December 1944, *schwere*

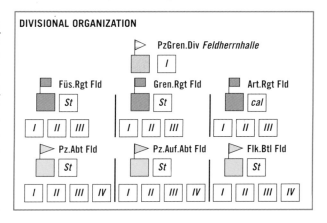

DIVISIONAL ORGANIZATION

▷ Leichte Feldhaubitze 18/2 auf fahrgestell PzKpfw II (Sf) Wespe (SdKfz 124)

Artillerie-Regiment Feldherrnhalle / I.Bataillon / 1.Batterie

The Wespe self-propelled howitzer suffered from a high silhouette and had insufficient protection for its crew. Nevertheless, it was popular with its operators, being an effective artillery piece with good mobility.

Specifications

Crew: 5	Speed: 40km/h (24.9mph)
Weight: 12.1 tonnes (11 tons)	Range: 220km (136.7 miles)
Length: 4.81m (15ft 10in)	Radio: FuG Spr 1
Width: 2.28m (7ft 6in)	Armament: 1 x LeFH 18M L/28 105mm
Height: 2.25m (7ft 4.5in)	(4.1in) howitzer
Engine: Maybach HL62TR	

Panzer-Abteilung 503 was renamed *schwere Panzer-Abteilung Feldherrnhalle* and on the 31st, the *Feldherrnhalle* units were encircled along with IX.*SS-Gebirgskorps*. The pocket collapsed and the divisions were destroyed on 12 February 1945.

Plans were now made for the creation of a Panzer Corps, along the lines of the *Panzerkorps Grossdeutschland*. The survivors of the encirclement, along with large numbers of new SA recruits, were formed into three new units. The remnants of the *Panzergrenadier-Division Feldherrnhalle* became *Panzer-Division Feldherrnhalle* 1. Although not a full-strength division, the formation was equipped with the latest equipment and was well trained. The 13.*Panzer-Division Feldherrnhalle*, meanwhile, became *Panzer-Division Feldherrnhalle* 2.

The corps was activated at the end of February, with most of the combat units being sent into action at the end of March 1945. The Panzer Corps executed a fighting withdrawal towards Vienna and then into southern Austria. By the beginning of May 1945, the shattered remnants of the corps broke up and attempted to reach the American lines, where they surrendered on 9 May 1945.

▶ **Panzerspähkompanie (SPW)**

In 1943 and 1944, the *Panzer-Aufklärungs-Abteilung* of the *Feldherrnhalle* Panzergrenadier Division had three main reconnaissance companies: an armoured car company, a light half-track reconnaissance company (seen here) and a heavy half-track reconnaissance company.

Stab

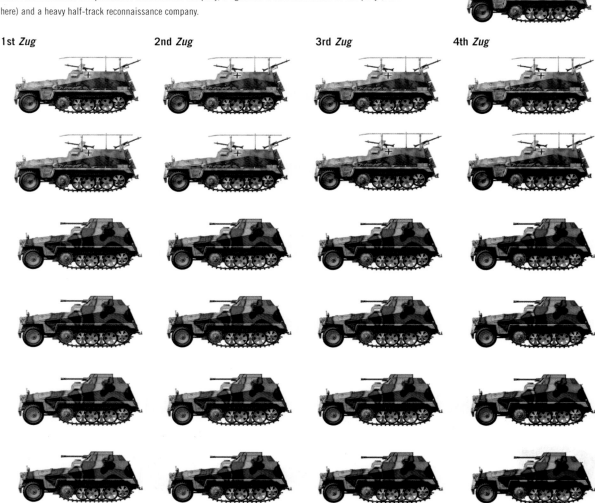

1st *Zug*　　2nd *Zug*　　3rd *Zug*　　4th *Zug*

Specifications

Crew: 5

Weight: 24 tonnes (21.5 tons)

Length: 6.28m (20ft 7in)

Width: 2.95m (9ft 9in)

Height: 2.50m (8ft 2in)

Engine: Maybach HL120TRM petrol (300hp)

Speed: 40km/h (24.9mph)

Range: 155km (96.3 miles)

Radio: FuG5

Armament: 1 x 50mm (2in) KwK 39 L/60 gun;
2 x 7.92mm (0.3in) MG (one coaxial,
one hull-mounted)

▲ Panzerkampfwagen II Ausf J (SdKfz 141/1)

160.Panzer-Abteilung

The 5cm (2in) gun of the Panzer III, while adequate against light armour, had little effect against the frontal armour of Soviet T-34 tanks.

Specifications

Crew: 4

Weight: 26.3 tonnes (23.9 tons)

Length: 6.77m (22ft 2in)

Width: 2.95m (9ft 8in)

Height: 2.16m (7ft 0in)

Engine: Maybach HL120TRM

Speed: 40km/h (24.9mph)

Range: 155km (96.3 miles)

Radio: FuG15 and FuG16

Armament: 1 x 75mm (3in) StuG L/48 cannon

▲ 7.5-cm Sturmgeschütz 40 Ausf G (SdKfz 142/1)

Panzer-Abteilung Feldherrnhalle

When formed in 1943, the *Feldherrnhalle* Panzer Battalion was equipped with three batteries of 14 StuGs.

◀ Schwere Panzerspähwagen 8-Rad (SdKfz 234/3)

Panzer-Aufklärungs-Abteilung Feldherrnhalle / schwere Zug

Feldherrnhalle was one of the first divisions to be equipped with the close-support variant of the new SdKfz 234.

Specifications

Crew: 4

Weight: 11.50 tonnes (10.47 tons)

Length: 6.0m (19ft 8in)

Width: 2.40m (7ft 10.5in)

Height: 2.21m (7ft 4in)

Engine: Tatra 103 12-cylinder (220hp)

Speed: 80km/h (49.7mph)

Range: 900km (559 miles)

Radio: FuG Spr Ger 'a'

Armament: 1 x 75mm (3in) KwK 51 L/24
cannon; 1 x 7.92 mm (0.3in) MG

Chapter 3

Panzergrenadier Divisions

In the summer of 1943, it was decided to upgrade the German Army's motorized infantry divisions by giving them extra armour and by converting their motorized infantry regiments into armoured infantry, or Panzergrenadier, units. Many of the new Panzergrenadier divisions operated with assault guns rather than tanks in their new Panzer battalions, and there were never enough armoured half-tracks to fully re-equip these formations. Nevertheless, those divisions which were converted became fighting formations of considerable power.

◀ **A long war**

By 1943, the war was turning against Germany. The easy triumphs of 1939, 1940 and 1941 were a long way in the past, and the Allies were growing more powerful. Yet the professionalism of the German Army remained high, and new weapons and unit organizations were being introduced to increase fighting power.

90th *Leichte Afrika* Division

The 90th Light Africa Division was the only German division formed entirely outside Europe, originally being created as a temporary formation in North Africa.

THE DEFEAT OF ITALY'S FORCES in North Africa over the winter of 1940/41 threatened Germany's 'Fortress Europe'. For his own security, Hitler felt that he had no option but to intervene on behalf of his ally. By the middle of February 1941, the first contingent of German support had reached Tripoli. It was not very large – in fact, it consisted of one general and two staff officers; but the general was a man called Rommel. As the commanding officer of the 'Ghost' Division in France, Major-General Erwin Rommel had won a reputation as a brilliant commander. His orders were to stabilize the situation. Rommel's force initially included only the Fifth Light Division. For the moment, he was simply expected to stiffen Italian resistance.

But Rommel would not wait. Within days, he was planning a full-scale counterattack. And with that began two years of cut-and-thrust battles with British and Commonwealth forces. The battlefield was to be the Libyan desert, an area aptly described as a tactician's paradise and a quartermaster's nightmare.

Afrika-Division
Rommel's initial attack drove the British back through Libya and had reached the Egyptian border by mid-April. By this time, there was an assortment of German units of varying sizes arriving in North Africa, and in August the *Afrika-Division zbV* was created to control them. The first major action by the new unit came in November 1941, during Rommel's unsuccessful attempt to capture the vital port of Tobruk. The Libyan port's Commonwealth garrison had been cut off by advancing German and Italian forces in April, but was still holding out.

Later that month, the division was engaged in the first major tank battle of the campaign, when Rommel responded to the launch of the British Operation *Crusader* on 18 November by launching a rapid counterattack at Sidi Rezegh, a vital airfield about 25km (15.5 miles) southeast of Tobruk. After stopping the Allied advance, Rommel struck for the Halfaya Pass on the Egyptian border. But the British stood firm, and Auchinleck, the commander-in-chief,

ordered a further attack westwards to cut off Rommel's forces. As a result, Rommel withdrew to Gazala. On 27 November 1941, the *Afrika-Division* received an official designation, becoming the 90.*Leichte Infanterie-Division.*

INSIGNIA

Originally an ad hoc formation, the 90th Light Division used a simple geometrical divisional symbol during its time in Africa.

Rebuilt as the 90th Panzergrenadier Division utilizing troops drawn from Sardinia, the new formation used a map of the island as its symbol.

Commanders

Generalmajor Max Sümmermann
September 1941 – December 1941

Generalleutnant Richard Veith
December 1941 – April 1942

General der Panzertruppen Ulrich Kleemann
April 1942 – July 1942

Generalleutnant Carl-Hans Lungershausen
July 1942 – August 1942

General der Panzertruppen Ulrich Kleemann
August 1942 – November 1942

Generalleutnant Theodor Graf von Sponeck
November 1942 – May 1943

Generalleutnant Carl-Hans Lungershausen
July 1943 – December 1943

Generalleutnant Ernst-Günther Baade
December 1943 – December 1944

General der Panzertruppen
Gerhard Graf von Schwerin *December 1944*

Generalmajor Heinrich Baron von Behr
December 1944 – April 1945

DIVISIONAL ORGANIZATION

90.Afrika.Div
I

Sch.Rgt 155 — St — I II III

Sch.Rgt 200 — St — I II III

Inf.Rgt 361 — cal — I II III

Pz.Abt 190 — St — I II III IV

Pzjr.Abt 190 — St — I II III IV

Pz.Auf.Abt 90 — St — I II III IV

Art.Rgt 190 — St — I II III

Divisional History	Formed
Divisions-Kommando zbV Afrika	1941
Afrika-Division zbV	1941
90.Leichte Afrika-Division	1941
90.Leichte Infanterie-Division	1942
90.Afrika-Division	1942
Division Sardinien	1943
90.Panzergrenadier-Division	1943

◄ **Captured transport**

A Canadian Ford truck captured in North Africa is put to use by German infantrymen. Note the swastika air identification flag on the nose.

▶ **Leichte Zugkraftwagen 3t (SdKfz 11)**

200.Schützen-Regiment / II.Bataillon

The SdKfz 11 was used to tow artillery pieces up to the size of the Pak 40, but in North Africa it was also used as a troop transport, being better suited than trucks to operations in the sands of the desert.

Specifications

Crew: 1 plus 8 troops

Weight: 7.1 tonnes (6.46 tons)

Length: 5.48m (18ft 0in)

Width: 1.82m (5ft 11.5in)

Height: 1.62m (5ft 4in)

Engine: 6-cylinder petrol (100hp)

Speed: 53km/h (32.9mph)

Range: 122km (75.8 miles)

Radio: None

◇ Libya to El Alamein

JANUARY–NOVEMBER 1942

Although the war in North Africa seemed to have turned against the *Afrika Korps*, Rommel realized that the British position had weakened after Operation *Crusader*.

Now it was the British who were operating at the end of long supply lines. On 21 January 1942, Rommel launched a new attack from his positions around El Agheila, driving the British 1st Armoured Division from its positions around Adjabiya. The British were again retreating with Rommel in pursuit.

Near Msus, Rommel swung his forces northeast, striking out through rough but undefended terrain to try to reach Benghazi and cut off the retreating Commonwealth forces. Though the Germans reached the coast on 28 January, the British managed to smash through the lead elements of the *Afrika*

Korps and continued their retreat eastwards. At this point, Rommel was forced to stop his advance while his troops were resupplied; the Germans and their Italian allies had captured valuable supplies in Benghazi, but German supply woes continued to affect Rommel's tactical and operational decisions. The British used the pause to retreat to prepared positions around Gazala.

In the spring of 1942, Rommel decided that the time was ripe for *Panzerarmee Afrika* to finally take Tobruk. Rommel pre-empted a possible British attack out of Gazala on 26 May 1942, by launching

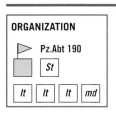

ORGANIZATION

Pz.Abt 190

St

lt | lt | lt | md

his own attack first. After a feint to the north, Axis mobile forces swung south around deep minefields and the tough French-held position at Bir Hacheim. After a clash near Bir el Gubi, Rommel pressed on, shrugging off a series of disorganized British assaults. On 13 June, the Axis forces inflicted heavy casualties on Commonwealth troops south of El Adam, before pushing the British further east past Sidi Rezegh. With only 70 tanks left, the British continued to retreat while Rommel turned back to smash through the defences of Tobruk. On 21 July, the division was again renamed, becoming the 90.*Afrika-Division*.

The early summer of 1942 had been a period of almost constant retreat for British and Commonwealth forces in North Africa, but from their powerful defensive line at El Alamein, the Eighth Army held off two powerful Axis attacks in June and August. Now, massively reinforced and with the Axis troops exhausted, it was time to strike back.

▲ **Assault on Tobruk**

German infantry await the command to attack in the protracted siege of Tobruk, November 1941.

▶ **Personenkraftwagen VW Kübel (Kfz 1)**

155.Schützen-Regiment / 1.Infanterie-Kompanie

Early Kübels had problems handling desert sands until the *Afrika Korps* took a leaf from the British book and fitted them with large low-pressure tyres.

Specifications	
Crew: 1	Engine: Volkswagen 998cc petrol (24hp). Later
Weight: 0.64 tonnes (0.58 tons)	Volkswagen 1131cc petrol (25hp)
Length: 3.73m (12 ft 3in)	Speed: 100km/h (62mph)
Width: 1.60m (5ft 3in)	Range: 600km (375 miles)
Height: 1.35m (4ft 5in)	Radio: None

▶ **7.62-cm FK36(r) auf SF Zugkraftwagen 5t (SdKfz 6)**

605.Panzerjäger-Abteilung

Nine captured Soviet 7.62cm (3in) guns were mounted on half-track chassis and sent to the independent 605.*Panzerjäger-Abteilung* in Africa. The unit was assigned to the 90th Light Division in March 1942.

Specifications	
Crew: 6	HL54TUKRM 6-cylinder
Weight: 1.16 tonnes	(115hp)
(1.06 tons)	Speed: 50km/h (31mph)
Length: 6.33m (20ft 9in)	Range: 317km (197 miles)
Width: 2.26m (7ft 5in)	Radio: None
Height: 2.98m (9ft 9in)	Armament: 1 x 76.2mm (3in)
Engine: Maybach	PaK(r) L/51 anti-tank gun

Safe behind strong defences, flanked to the north by the Mediterranean and to the south by the impassible sands of the Qattara Depression, the British could concentrate on building up forces for a major attack on the Axis army. Under new commander General Bernard Law Montgomery, the Eighth Army soon had a massive materiel superiority over Rommel's command.

By October 1942, the reinforced Commonwealth forces could deploy 250,000 men, 1200 tanks and over 750 aircraft against an Axis force of 80,000 men, 489 tanks and 675 aircraft. The imbalance was made greater by the fact that Rommel's men were tired and poorly supplied, and most of his hard-used equipment was close to breakdown.

El Alamein

On the night of 23/24 October, Montgomery launched Operation *Lightfoot*, the first phase of a meticulously planned, multi-stage offensive. By morning, the infantry had gained most of their objectives, but the armour had been delayed in the

night and were still under the guns of the German artillery. As a result, a grim battle was fought over the next eight days in the vast dust bowl between the sea and the Miteirya Ridge.

Meanwhile, Montgomery planned another massive strike – Operation *Supercharge*. Rommel had by now realized that he could not win such a set-piece battle and began planning his withdrawal. Unfortunately he received orders from the *Führer* to stand fast. By 2 November, he had only 35 operational tanks left and most of his divisions, including the 90th Africa Division, had suffered serious combat losses.

At 01.05 on the morning of 2 November, another massive artillery barrage signalled the start of Operation *Supercharge*. By dawn on 4 November, British reconnaissance patrols had passed south of Tel el Akkakir, only to find that the expected Axis defences were not there. To save his army, Rommel had disobeyed his *Führer*, and the entire Axis force was now withdrawing westwards. The battle was over. Now it was time for the pursuit.

▶ 2-cm Flak 38 (Sf) auf sgl Einh PKW

190.Leichte-Flak-Abteilung

A few standard Horch heavy 4x4 cars were converted to carry a 2cm (0.7in) Flak gun instead of towing it. The vehicle had a crew of seven, and could carry up to 800 rounds of 2cm (0.7in) ammunition.

Specifications

Crew: Up to 7	(81hp)
Weight: 3.6 tonnes (3.28 tons)	Speed: 70km/h (43mph)
Length: 4.85m (15ft 11in)	Range: 400km (248.5 miles)
Width: 2.0m (6ft 7in)	Radio: None
Height: 2.04m (6ft 8in)	Armament: 1 x 20mm (0.7in) Flak 38
Engine: Auto-Union/Horch V8 3.8L petrol	

▶ Bedford OYD 3-ton 4x2

90.Leichte-Afrika-Division

With the German forces always short of supplies and equipment, captured trucks were an important part of the German inventory in North Africa. The Bedford OYD was the standard British 3-ton truck, introduced in 1940.

Specifications

Crew: 1	Engine: Austin 6-cylinder petrol
Weight: 7.5 tonnes (6.83 tons)	(72hp)
Length: 6.7m (22ft 0in)	Speed: 80km/h (49.7mph)
Width: 2.3m (7ft 7in)	Range: 300km (186.3 miles)
Height: 3m (9ft 9in)	Radio: None

◇ Battle for Tunisia
NOVEMBER 1942 – MAY 1943

As *Panzerarmee Afrika* retreated before the advancing Eighth Army, Rommel must have believed that this was simply another phase in the backwards and forwards North African campaign.

BEFORE LONG, AS HE CAME CLOSER to his bases, he would be reinforced, while as the British supply lines grew longer his opponents would eventually be weak enough for him to counterattack. Any such thoughts must have been dashed on 8 November, when news came of massive Allied landings in Algeria, at the other end of North Africa.

The Germans that did manage to make it to Rommel's first makeshift defensive line at Fuka after the Battle of Alamein were worth little more than a battalion, and even when joined by the survivors of the 90th and 164th Divisions they constituted in battle-ready terms a brigade only. Hitler, who had for so long starved Rommel of troops when victory had seemed in his grasp, now in extremis poured in men and materials to bolster the Tunisian bridgehead.

Two-front campaign
The weather in North Africa was terrible that winter, and campaigning came to an abrupt halt. Both sides used the opportunity to build up their supplies – a race that could only be won by the Allies. By early 1943, the Axis was being squeezed between the Eighth Army driving north and the Anglo-American armies driving east. Rommel did manage to inflict a

defeat on the Americans at Kasserine, but he was defeated by Montgomery at Medenine. Constant Allied pressure meant that by May 1943, the remnants of the Axis forces had been compressed into a small enclave.

Once the Allied Operation *Vulcan* was launched on 6 May, the remnants of the once mighty *Afrika Korps* disintegrated. Across the north of Tunisia, Allied forces mopped up the last German resistance. When the dust had settled, more than 150,000 Axis troops had fallen into Allied hands, in a defeat of Stalingrad proportions. Among the units destroyed was the 90th Africa Division.

190.Artillerie-Regiment (mot), I.Bataillon	Strength
1.Batterie:	
10.5cm (4.1in) leFH 18	4
2.Batterie:	
10.5cm (4.1in) leFH 18	4
3.Batterie:	
10cm (3.9in) K17 guns	4

ORGANIZATION

Art.Rgt 190

St

I   II

The light sand-coloured vehicles used in Africa meant that the standard German *Balkankreuz* was difficult to see, so it was sometimes modified by painting the centre of the crosses white.

▶ **8.76-cm FK280(e) / Ordnance, QF, 25-pdr**

580.Aufklärungs-Abteilung (mot)

The 90th Light Division had a mix of captured and German equipment. The division's artillery regiment had at least two batteries of the excellent British 25-pdr gun-howitzer, and another battery served in the reconnaissance battalion.

Specifications
Crew: 5	Muzzle Velocity: 518m/s (1684fps)
Weight: 1.8 tonnes (1.46 tons)	Range: (HE) 13400m (12550 yards)
Length: 2.4m (7ft 6in)	Ammunition: Armour-piercing, high
Calibre: 87.6mm (3.45in)	explosive or smoke

▶ 15-cm sIG 33 auf Fahrgestell PzKpfw II

708.Schwere-sIG-Kompanie

Only 12 of these Panzer II-based infantry guns were built, and all served with the 90th Light Division. They first saw action at Gazala in the spring of 1942, and the last was destroyed in Tunisia in 1943.

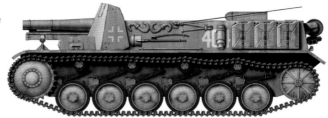

Specifications

Crew: 4	Engine: Maybach HL62TRM
Weight: 12.3 tonnes (11.2 tons)	Speed: 40km/h (24.9mph)
Length: 5.41m (17ft 8.5in)	Range: 160km (99.4 miles)
Width: 2.6m (8ft 6in)	Radio: FuG Spr 'f'
Height: 1.9m (6ft 2.5in)	Armament: 1 x 150mm (5.9in) sIG 33 gun

▶ Panzerbefehlswagen III Ausf K (SdKfz 101)

190.Panzer-Abteilung / Stab / Regimental Signals Officer

The 190th Panzer Battalion arrived in Africa in November 1942. When formed, the battalion was equipped with 7 Panzer IIs, 55 Panzer IIIs, 14 Panzer IVs and 2 Panzer III command tanks.

Specifications

Crew: 5	(300hp)
Weight: 25.4 tonnes (23 tons)	Speed: 40km/h (24.9mph)
Length: 6.41m (21ft 0in)	Range: 155km (96.3 miles)
Width: 2.95m (9ft 9in)	Radio: FuG5 plus FuG7 or FuG8
Height: 2.51m (8ft 2in)	Armament: 1 x 50mm (2in) KwK L/38
Engine: Maybach HL120TRM petrol	gun; 2 x 7.92mm (0.3in) MG

Rebuilt in Italy
1943

The 90th Africa Division had gained a reputation as a fighting unit in North Africa, so when it was destroyed the high command decided that it should be re-formed to continue the tradition.

THE DIVISION was reconstituted on Sardinia, Corsica and Elba from various service units that had not been sent to Africa, cadres and convalescents evacuated from Africa, together with replacements. Originally known as the *Division Sardinien*, it was renamed 90th Panzergrenadier Division in July 1943. During the summer, while building up to combat readiness, the division was transferred to Corsica and was then moved to northern Italy in late September 1943, where it continued to absorb replacements and train.

The division's Panzergrenadier regiments were only partially motorized, though the addition of a Panzer battalion gave the formation a considerable rise in fighting power.

In October 1943, the unit was once more re-formed, this time emerging as 90th Panzer-grenadier Division.

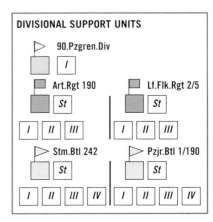

DIVISIONAL SUPPORT UNITS

90.Pzgren.Div
I

Art.Rgt 190 — St
Lf.Flk.Rgt 2/5 — St

I II III
I II III

Stm.Btl 242 — St
Pzjr.Btl 1/190 — St

I II III IV
I II III IV

DIVISIONAL ORGANIZATION, 1943

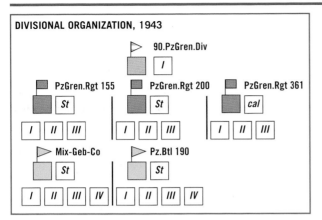

Panzer-Abteilung 190 (1943)	Strength
PzKpfw III	1
PzKpfw III (short-barrel 7.5cm/3in)	20
PzKpfw IV (long barrel)	37

▲ **Leichte Personenkraftwagen (Kfz 1)**

90.Leichte-Afrika-Division

Kübels were used for a variety of tasks in the desert – including acting as an improvised ambulance. Note the white stripe on the 'Jerrycan' above the rear mudguard. This indicated that it was to be used only for drinking water.

Specifications

Crew: 1

Weight: 0.64 tonnes (0.58 tons)

Length: 3.73m (12 ft 3in)

Width: 1.60m (5ft 3in)

Height: 1.35m (4ft 5in)

Engine: Volkswagen 998cc petrol (24hp). Later

    Volkswagen 1131cc petrol (25hp)

Speed: 100km/h (62mph)

Range: 600km (375 miles)

Radio: None

▶ **Mittlerer Landkraftwagen (Opel Blitz 3.6-36S)**

90.Leichte-Afrika-Division

It took some time for the Germans to realize that twin rear tyres, so useful for heavy loads and added traction on normal roads, were a handicap in desert sand. German trucks in the desert were eventually fitted with single rear tyres.

Specifications

Crew: 1

Weight: 3.29 tonnes (3 tons)

Length: 6.02m (19ft 9in)

Width: 2.27m (7ft 5in)

Height: 2.18m (7ft 2in)

Engine: Opel 6-cylinder petrol

    (73.5hp)

Speed: 80km/h (50mph)

Range: 410km (255 miles)

Radio: None

▶ **Panzerkampfwagen IV Ausf E (SdKfz 101)**

190.Panzer-Abteilung

The 190th Panzer Battalion was assigned to the division in March 1942 but did not actually arrive in Africa until November of that year. At that time, the medium Panzer company had 14 Panzer IVs.

Specifications

Crew: 5

Weight: 23.2 tonnes (21 tons)

Length: 5.92m (19ft 5in)

Width: 2.84m (9ft 4in)

Height: 2.68m (8ft 9.5in)

Engine: Maybach HL120TRM

Speed: 42km/h (26mph)

Range: 200km (124.3 miles)

Radio: FuG5

Armament: 1 x 75mm (3in) KwK 37

    L/24 gun; 2 x 7.92mm (0.3in) MG

    (one hull-mounted, one coaxial)

▶ **Panzerjäger 38(t) für Pak 36(r) Marder III**

90.Panzerjäger-Abteilung / 1.Kompanie

Over 60 tank-destroyers fitted with Soviet 76mm (3in) guns were sent to North Africa between July and November 1942. The 90th Division's Panzerjäger battalion had three companies, but the battalion HQ was still in Italy when Tunisia fell.

Specifications

Crew: 4	Speed: 42km/h (26mph)
Weight: 11.76 tonnes (10.67 tons)	Range: 185km (115 miles)
Length: 5.85m (19ft 2in)	Radio: FuG Spr 'd'
Width: 2.16m (7ft 0in)	Armament: 1 x 76.2mm (3in) Pak 36(r) anti-
Height: 2.5m (8ft 2in)	tank gun; 1 x 7.92mm (0.3in) MG
Engine: Praga EPA or EPA/2	

Retreat through Italy
NOVEMBER 1943 – APRIL 1945

Taking place in the small Adriatic port of Ortona, the battle against the 1st Canadian Division saw some of the deadliest close-quarter combat engagements of the entire war.

THE MAIN GERMAN defenders were paratroopers of the 1st Fallschirmjäger Division, supported by elements of the the newly arrived 90th Division. Using the common German tactic of immediate counterattack against any Canadian advance, the Panzergrenadiers took extremely heavy losses, particularly from Allied artillery.

After the Ortona battles, the division would need to be rebuilt for a third time. Withdrawn into reserve, it was deployed piecemeal along the front in response to the Allied offensives at Cassino and Anzio. It served as a rearguard while the balance of the German forces in the south of Italy fell back to the Winter Line. While fighting in the Po Valley in April 1945, the 90th was destroyed. The unit's remnants surrendered to the Americans with the capitulation of the remainder of the German forces in Italy.

DIVISIONAL ORGANIZATION

90 Pzgren.Div

I

Gren.Rgt 200 | Gren.Rgt 361

St | St

I | II | III | I | II | III

▶ **Leichte Feldhaubitze 18/2 auf Fahrgestell PzKpfw II (Sf) Wespe (SdKfz 124)**

190.Artillerie-Regiment / III.Bataillon / 1.Batterie

When the division was re-formed as the 90th Panzergrenadier Division, the artillery regiment's self-propelled 3rd Battalion had two batteries of *Wespe* light howitzers and a third equipped with six of the heavy *Hummel* 15cm (5.9in) weapons.

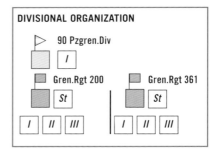

Specifications

Crew: 5	Speed: 40km/h (24.9mph)
Weight: 12.1 tonnes (11 tons)	Range: 220km (136.7 miles)
Length: 4.81m (15ft 10in)	Radio: FuG Spr 1
Width: 2.28m (7ft 6in)	Armament: 1 x LeFH 18M L/28 105mm (4.1in)
Height: 2.25m (7ft 4.5in)	howitzer
Engine: Maybach HL62TR	

▶ **Leichtes Kraftwagen Fiat 618MC**

90.Panzergrenadier-Division

From its earliest days, the 90th Division made extensive use of foreign vehicles,
and in Italy it pressed a number of different types into service. The Fiat 618 was a
light 4x2 truck with a 1.25-tonne (1.2-ton) payload.

Specifications

Crew: 1	Engine: 4-cylinder petrol (43bhp)
Weight: 3.5 tonnes (3.4 tons)	Speed: 65km/h (40mph)
Length: 4.7m (15ft 5in)	Range: not known
Width: 1.94m (6ft 4in)	Payload: 1.25 tonnes (1.2 tons)
Height: 2.5m (8ft 2in)	

▶ **Sturmgeschütz M42 mit 75/18 850(i)**

247.Sturmgeschütz-Kompanie

Nearly 300 of these Italian assault guns were confiscated from the Italian Army in
September 1943. They were issued to a total of 12 German divisions in Italy and
the Balkans in 1943 and 1944.

Specifications

Crew: 3	Engine: SPA 15-TM-41 V-8
Weight: 12 tonnes (11.4 tons)	petrol engine
Length: 5.04m (16ft 6in)	Speed: 38km/h (24 mph)
Width: 2.23m (7ft 4in)	Range: 230km (145 miles)
Height: 1.85m (6ft 1in)	Radio: n/a

▼ **5.Luftwaffe-Flak-Regiment, 2.Abteilung, Schwere Flak-Batterie**

In December 1943, a *Luftwaffe* Flak battalion with three heavy batteries was assigned to the division. Below is the composition of a heavy battery.

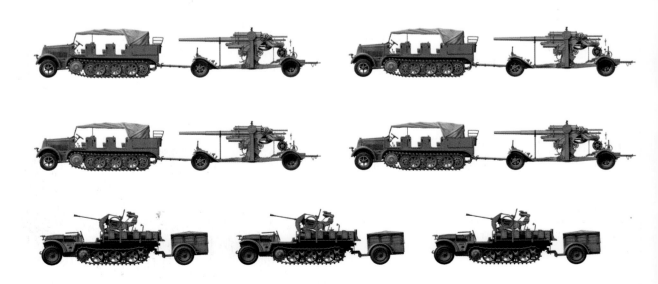

155th Infantry Division (motorized)

A number of military formations that started out with a non-combat replacement or training role found themselves in action in the later stages of the war.

ESTABLISHED IN PRAGUE ON 26 August 1939 with the title *Kommandeur der Ersatztruppen V* (Commander of Replacement Troops), this division was a reserve and replacement unit gathering troops from *volksdeutsch* (ethnic German) citizens of the Protectorate of Bohemia and Moravia, the former Czechoslovakia. On 9 November that year, the replacement unit was given a proper military structure and became known as *Division Nr. 155*. On 23 August 1941, the division was transferred from Prague to *Wehrkreis* V in Stuttgart, where it became one of the military district's replacement and training units.

Divisional parts

The division's main constituent units included *Infanterie-Ersatz-Regiment 5, Infanterie-Ersatz-Regiment 25, Infanterie-Ersatz-Regiment 35,*

Divisional History	Formed
Kommandeur der Ersatztruppen V	1939
Division Nr. 155	1939
Division Nr. 155 (mot)	1942
Panzer-Division Nr. 155	1943
155.Reserve-Panzer-Division	1943
Absorbed by 9.Panzer-Division	1944

▼ **Training and replacement**

The 155th Division spent most of its life as a training and replacement unit for infantry, motorized infantry and Panzer divisions. Here, soldiers carry out repairs on an Opel-type truck.

Commanders

Generalleutnant Otto Tscherning
August 1939 – April 1942

Generalmajor Franz Landgraf
May–August 1942

Generalmajor Max Fremerey
October 1942 – August 1943

Generalmajor Kurt von Jesser
August–September 1943

Generalleutnant Franz Landgraf
September 1943

Generalleutnant Max Fremerey
October 1943 – April 1944

DIVISIONAL ORGANIZATION

Div Nr. 155 — I

Inf.Er.Rgt 5 — St — I | II | III

Inf.Er.Rgt 25 — St — I | II | III

Inf.Er.Rgt 35 — cal — I | II | III

MG.Er.Btl 4 — St — I | II | III | IV

Kav.Er.Abt 18 — St — I | II | III | IV

Pzjr.Er.Abt 5 — St — I | II | III | IV

Art.Er.Rgt 25 — St — I | II | III

147

Maschinegewehr-Ersatz-Bataillon 4, Artillerie-Ersatz-Regiment 25, Kavallerie-Ersatz-Abteilung 18, Panzerjäger-Ersatz-Abteilung 5, Nachrichten-Ersatz-Abteilung 5, Pionier-Ersatz-Bataillon 5, and *Fahr-Ersatz-Abteilung 5.*

On 10 May 1942, the division staff was moved to Ludwigsburg, where it would become a replacement unit for motorized troops. It was redesignated as the *Division Nr. 155 (mot).* On 5 April 1943, it was again redesignated, becoming an armoured training division known as *Panzer-Division Nr. 155.* This became a reserve Panzer formation around Rennes and Nimes in France, before its elements were absorbed by the 9th Panzer Division, which had been transferred to France after suffering heavy losses on the Eastern Front.

Field training division

On 2 November 1944, a new 155th Division was established by Army Group C in Italy. Known as the *155.(Feldausbildung) Division* (155th Field Training Division), it was set up around the shattered remnants of the *20.Luftwaffen-Sturm-Division.* This had originally been the 20th *Luftwaffe* Field Division, a truck-mounted unit that was based in Denmark and which had been transferred as an assault division to Italy and had been destroyed on the Adriatic coast in October 1944. Divisional numbers were made up by drafting in members of the *Reichs Arbeits Dienst* (RAD, or *Reich* Labour Service).

In early 1945, the unit was thrown into combat as the 155th Infantry Division. It consisted of three grenadier regiments, a fusilier battalion, an artillery battalion, a communications battalion and a logistics regiment. Initially based in Florence, it retreated to the Po Valley, where it surrendered to the Americans.

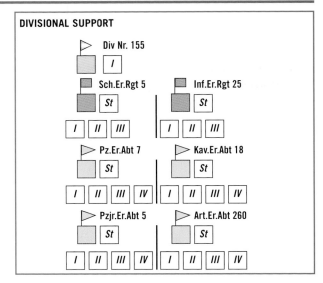

DIVISIONAL SUPPORT

▷ Div Nr. 155 / I

Sch.Er.Rgt 5 / St / I II III
Inf.Er.Rgt 25 / St / I II III

▷ Pz.Er.Abt 7 / St / I II III IV
▷ Kav.Er.Abt 18 / St / I II III IV

▷ Pzjr.Er.Abt 5 / St / I II III IV
▷ Art.Er.Abt 260 / St / I II III IV

▲ **3.7-cm Panzerabwehrkanone (Pak 36)**

Division Nr. 155 (mot) / 5.Panzerjäger-Ersatz-Abteiling

As a non-combat formation, the 155th Division was a long way down the supply chain and had a high proportion of obsolete equipment like the 3.7cm (1.5in) Pak 36 anti-tank gun.

Specifications

Crew: 3	Range: 600m (656yards)
Weight: 0.43 tonnes (0.39 tons)	Ammunition: Armour-piercing
Length: 1.67m (5ft 5.5in)	
Calibre: 37mm (1.5in)	
Muzzle Velocity: 762m/s (2500fps)	

▷ **Protz Kw Krupp L2H143 (Kfz 69)**

Division Nr. 155 (mot)

By 1943, the Krupp L2H143 had been superseded by Mercedes, Horch, Skoda and Steyr heavy 4x4 cars, although it was never completely replaced, especially in second line, training and replacement divisions.

Specifications

Crew: 2	Engine: Krupp 3.3L 4-cylinder (60hp)
Weight: 2.45 tonnes (2.23 tons)	Speed: 70km/h (43mph)
Length: 5.10m (16ft 8in)	Range: 450km (280m)
Width: 1.93m (6ft 4in)	Radio: None
Height: 1.96m (6ft 5in)	

▶ **Leichte Personenkraftwagen VW Kübel (Kfz 1)**

1227.Grenadier-Regiment

In the last two months of the war, the 155th Division fought as a standard infantry formation, although it was lightly equipped with motor transport. Among the few vehicles available in any numbers was the ubiquitous VW Kübel.

Specifications

Crew: 1	Engine: Volkswagen 998cc petrol (24hp). Later
Weight: 0.64 tonnes (0.58 tons)	Volkswagen 1131cc petrol (25hp)
Length: 3.73m (12 ft 3in)	Speed: 100km/h (62mph)
Width: 1.60m (5ft 3in)	Range: 600km (375 miles)
Height: 1.35m (4ft 5in)	Radio: None

164th *Leichte Afrika* Division

Sent to Africa to reinforce Rommel's *Deutsches Afrika Korps*, the 164th Light Africa Division suffered heavily at El Alamein, and lost all of its vehicles defending the Mareth Line in 1943.

THE ORIGINAL 164TH Infantry Division was set up on 27 November 1939 at *Truppenübungsplatz* Königsbrück near Dresden. Its function was to act as a replacement formation for units involved in the invasion of Poland.

To Africa

In January 1940, the division was brought up to full strength with the addition of three *Feldersatz-Bataillone* (replacement battalions). In January 1942, the division was placed on active service, transferring to the Mediterranean to become *Festungs-Division Kreta* (Fortress Division Crete). In July 1942, the division was ordered to North Africa, where it would become the 164.*Leichte Afrika-Division*; it began transferring to Tunisia, leaving the occupation of Crete to a unit known as *Festungs-Brigade Kreta*.

When the 164th Light Africa Division arrived in Africa, it was sent to the front to relieve *90.Leichte Afrika-Division*. It first saw action against Australian troops near El Alamein, and its first major engagement came with the massive Eighth Army offensive in November 1942. It suffered heavy losses during the retreat and its surviving units were distributed among the Panzer divisions. At that moment, Rommel's force consisted of just 4000 men, 11 tanks, 24 of the feared '88s', 25 other anti-tank guns and 40 assorted artillery pieces.

The 164th Division was stationed in Tripoli for refitting until December 1942, when it was sent to Buerat to build defence installations. The German position looked fairly promising at the end of 1942,

Commanders

Generalleutnant Konrad Haase *December 1939*	Oberst Siegfried Westphal *December 1942*
Generalleutnant Josef Flottmann *January 1940 – August 1942*	Generalmajor Kurt Freiherr von Liebenstein *January 1943*
Oberst Carl-Hans Lungershausen *August 1942*	Oberst Becker *January 1943*
Oberst Hermann Hans Hecker *August 1942*	Generalmajor Fritz Krause *February 1943*
Oberst Carl-Hans Lungershausen *September–December 1942*	Generalmajor Kurt Freiherr von Liebenstein *March–May 1943*

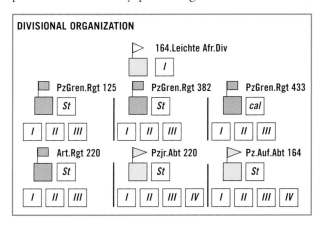

DIVISIONAL ORGANIZATION

at any rate in comparison to the dire predictions made two months previously at the beginning of Operation *Torch*. But the delicate balance on the battlefield at the beginning of 1943 was tipped in the Allies' favour by their success in overcoming supply difficulties, which also reflected the waning power of the *Luftwaffe*.

Attack at Medenine

Rommel's last offensive in Africa came when he attacked the Eighth Army at Medenine. He walked into a trap set by Montgomery. The British general had concentrated 2nd New Zealand Division's two infantry brigades and two armoured brigades on a 38km (24-mile) front at right angles to Rommel's expected line of attack. He had 810 medium artillery pieces and anti-tank guns, including some of the excellent new 17-pdrs.

The killing ground in front of the British positions was a graveyard of German tanks – tanks that *Panzerarmee Afrika* would be hard-put to replace and which would be sorely missed by the Germans in the coming weeks of the campaign.

In the first two hours, 50 out of 141 Panzers that moved onto the battlefield had been knocked out. Some of these were new and immensely powerful Tigers. Firing a series of concentrated salvoes at the slightest sign of enemy movement within range, the British artillery forced Rommel to break off his attack with the loss of 52 tanks and 640 dead and wounded. The British lost one Sherman and 130 men.

Two days later, Rommel left Africa for good, although his absence was concealed to prevent a collapse of morale. Hans-Jürgen von Arnim now took over as commander-in-chief.

The Mareth Line

The *Afrika Korps* had launched its final offensive. It was now the turn of Montgomery to finish the job. Ever cautious, however, he took great pains before embarking on Operation *Pugilist*, the attack on the

The Palm and Swastika, originally a vehicle insignia for the 15th and 21st Panzer Divisions, was later used in a number of variants by most German units attached to the *Deutsches Afrika Korps*.

▶ **Leichte Zugkraftwagen 3t (SdKfz 11)**
220.Artillerie-Regiment / 1.Batterie
Over 25,000 examples of the 3-tonne (2.9-ton) SdKfz 11 were built between 1937 and 1945. It became the prime-mover for the 10.5cm (4.1in) light field howitzer.

Specifications

Crew: 1 plus 8 troops	Engine: 6-cylinder petrol (100hp)
Weight: 7.1 tonnes (6.46 tons)	Speed: 53km/h (32.9mph)
Length: 5.48m (18ft 0in)	Range: 122km (75.8 miles)
Width: 1.82m (5ft 11.5in)	Radio: None
Height: 1.62m (5ft 4in)	

▶ **m. gl. Einheits Pkw (4x4) Horch Typ EFm (Kfz 15)**
125.Panzergrenadier-Regiment Afrika / Stab-Kompanie
Externally, all Auto-Union/Horch heavy cars looked alike irrespective of actual chassis model, their designation depending on the kind of body they carried. The Kfz 15 body was one of the most numerous in any division.

Specifications

Crew: 1	Engine: Horch 6-cylinder petrol (90hp)
Weight: 2.4 tonnes (2.2 tons)	Speed: 88km/h (55mph)
Length: 4.44m (14 ft 7in)	Range: 400km (250 miles)
Width: 1.68m (5ft 6in)	Radio: None usually fitted
Height: 1.73m (5ft 8in)	

German defensive network known as the Mareth Line. On the 5 April, Montgomery launched a night attack on the Mareth Line with two infantry divisions. Elements of the 4th Indian Division overran German positions in the hills, the tactics of the North-West Frontier proving a match even for German veterans.

A ferocious infantry battle took place on the plain before the Germans were driven back, but despite the Allies' overwhelming advantage in armour the Germans still managed to break away as a still effective fighting force. The 164th Division was not part of that force. When Montgomery attacked the Mareth Line, the division was attached to the Italian XXI Corps and in the attack it had two battalions of troops killed or captured, and lost all of its transport; the survivors had to retreat northwards on foot.

Army Group Africa still theoretically had 16 divisions, but the nine German divisions numbered only 60,000 men with 100 tanks. It was obvious that the end had come. The final Allied assault came on 6 May 1943, and the remnants of the 164th Division surrendered on the 13th.

Divisional History	Formed
164.Infanterie-Division	1939
Festungs-Division Kreta	1942
164.Leichte Afrika-Division	1942

▲ **Retreat in Tunisia**
German infantry rereat across open desert in Tunisia following Montgomery's offensive, May 1943.

▶ **Fahrgestell Bren(e)**
220.Aufklärungs-Abteilung
Large numbers of Bren Gun carriers captured at Dunkirk were pressed into German service in a wide variety of roles. This reconnaissance example was field-modified in the desert to carry a 2cm (0.7in) gun.

Specifications

Crew: 2	Engine: Ford V8 petrol (85hp)
Weight: 4.1 tonnes (3.75 tons)	Speed: 48km/h (29.8mph)
Length: 3.65m (12ft 0in)	Range: 250km (156 miles)
Width: 2.11m (6ft 4in)	Radio: Various
Height: 1.57m (5ft 2in)	Armament: 1 x 20mm (0.7in) KwK cannon

▶ **Truck, 15-cwt, Morris Commercial CS8**
164.Leichte Afrika-Division
This was an early wartime British infantry truck captured at Dunkirk. Note the large low-pressure tyres, which gave better traction in deep sand than normal tyres, and the prominent air-recognition flag.

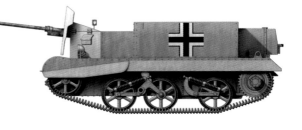

Specifications

Crew: 1	Engine: four-cylinder, 3.5 litre (213ci)
Weight: 0.99 tonnes (0.9 tons)	petrol engine
Length: 4.80m (15ft 9in)	Speed: 75km/h (47mph)
Width: 1.80m (5ft 11in)	Range: 225km (136 miles)
Height: 1.85m (6ft 1in)	Radio: None

179th Infantry Division (motorized)

The German Army had a comprehensive training and replacement system inherited from the *Reichswehr*. *Division Nr.* 179 was used in these roles from its base at Weimar.

THE DIVISION WAS established on 5 January 1940 in Weimar, as a unit answering to the Replacement Troops Commander (*Kommandeur der Ersatztruppen*) of *Wehrkreis* IX. A *Wehrkreis* was a German military district, established as far back as 1919 under the Weimar Republic.

The main functions of the *Wehrkreise* included recruitment (and later conscription) as well as providing basic training to prepare the new recruits for posting to a frontline unit. It was also the main organizational element used to mobilize divisions, providing formation training before they went into combat. Another major function of the military district was to provide combat formations with fully trained replacement personnel.

Although Hitler's seizure of power in 1933 heralded a major change in military organization, with the *Wehrmacht* replacing the *Reichswehr*, the *Wehrkreis* system was retained. Initially the *Wehrkreise* worked directly under the *Oberkommando des Heeres* (OKH, or Army High Command), but in 1938 the Home Army (also known as the Replacement Army – *Ersatzheer*) was created to oversee and coordinate

▲ **River crossing**
German troops practise a river crossing using an improvised combination of floats and platforms. Note the camouflage foliage attached to the sides.

Commanders	
Generalleutnant Herbert Stimmel *(10 Jan 1940 – 11 Apr 1940)*	Generalleutnant Walter von Boltenstern *(20 Jan 1942 – 27 Apr 1942)*
Gen.Lt Max von Hartlieb gennant Walsporn *(11 Apr 1940 – 20 Jan 1942)*	Generalleutnant Walter von Boltenstern *(30 July 1943 – 10 May 1944)*

Divisional History	Formed
Division Nr. 179	1940
Division Nr. 179 (mot)	1942
179.Reserve-Panzer-Division	1943
Absorbed by 116.Panzer-Division	1944

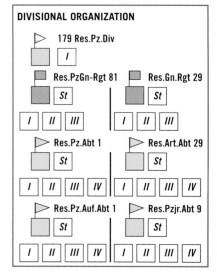

DIVISIONAL ORGANIZATION

Wehrkreise operations, though little of their functions changed until late 1942.

During the huge expansion of the German armed forces, seven original *Wehrkreise* had been expanded to 19 by 1943. Although they lost some of their training functions, they remained responsible for refitting depleted divisions until as late as 1944.

The German Army was mobilized in *Welle*, or 'waves', of divisions and this continued throughout the war. This was carried out by the *Wehrkreise* under supervision of the Replacement Army. This system continued until the end of the conflict. From 1934 to 1945, there were at least 38 *Welle*.

Wehrkreis IX was in central Germany and included Kassel, Frankfurt-am-Main and Weimar. *Division Nr.* 179 was one of a small group of what were known as numbered divisions. These were divisions in name only, with a divisional staff but with few permanently assigned combat units or weapons. Their non-standard status was apparent from their non-standard designations: the division was called *Division Nr. 179* instead of 179.*Infanterie-Division*, for example.

On 27 April 1942, the division completed motorization, becoming *Division Nr. 179 (mot)*. It took responsibility for the training and provision of replacement motorized troops for combat formations. On 5 April 1943, it was assigned to armoured training, becoming *Panzer-Division Nr. 179*. In July, it was again re-formed, becoming the 179th Reserve Panzer Division. It was sent to France to provide replacement units for the occupation forces but was disbanded in May 1944 and its units were absorbed by the 116th Panzer Division.

▶ Mittlerer Zugkraftwagen 8t (SdKfz 7)

Division Nr. 179 (mot)

Most often seen as the tractor for the 8.8cm (3.5in) Flak gun, the SdKfz 7 was able to carry up to 12 men or a considerable quantity of cargo. The vehicle could tow loads of up to 8 tonnes (7.84 tons).

Specifications

Crew: 2	cylinder (140hp)
Length: 6.85m (20ft 3in)	Weight: 1.16 tonnes (1.06 tons)
Width: 2.40m (7ft 10.5in)	Speed: 50km/h (31mph)
Height: 2.62m (8ft 7.1in)	Range: 250km (156 miles)
Engine: 1 Maybach HL 62 6-	Radio: None

▶ Mercedes-Benz G5/W152

Unknown formation

Developed as a cross-country personnel carrier, the G5 was rejected by the *Wehrmacht* as too complex and expensive. However, some of the 320 built were used as communications vehicles or command cars.

Specifications

Crew: 1	Engine:Mercedes-Benz six-cylinder OHV
Weight: 1.6 tons (3580lb)	petrol engine
Length: 4.52m (14ft 10in)	Range: 480km (300 miles)
Width: 1.70m (5ft 7in)	Speed: 75km/hr (46mph)
Height: 1.80m (5ft 11in)	Radio: none

▶ Opel Blitz 3.6-36S

Panzer-Division Nr. 179

Two-wheel-drive trucks were less than effective in combat areas, but they were used in lieu of anything more suitable. Similar vehicles were built by Borgward, Büssing-NAG, Citroen, Fiat, Henschel, Krupp and many more manufacturers.

Specifications

Crew: 1	Engine: Opel 6-cylinder petrol
Weight: 3.29 tonnes (3 tons)	Speed: 80km/h (50mph)
Length: 6.02m (19ft 9in)	Range: 410km (255 miles)
Width: 2.27m (7ft 5in)	Radio: None
Height: 2.18m (7ft 2in)	

233rd Panzergrenadier Division

Like the 179th Division, *Division Nr. 233 (mot)* was formed as a training and replacement unit, but from the start it was intended to support motorized units.

FORMED AT FRANKFURT AN DER ODER on 15 May 1942, *Division Nr. 233 (mot)* was one of the training units assigned to *Wehrkreis* III. One of the most important military districts, *Wehrkreis* III was headquartered in Berlin, and included the Prussian territories of Altmark, Neumark and Brandenburg.

The 233rd Division was tasked with the supervision and support of *schnelle*, or motorized, troop training in *Wehrkreis* III, and when many of the German Army's motorized infantry divisions were upgraded as Panzergrenadier divisions, the 233rd also took responsibility for training replacement armoured troops and units for these formations. On 7 July 1942, the division became the 233rd Panzergrenadier Division.

The division included a replacement battalion for Panzer units, as well as battalions training

Divisional History	Formed
Division Nr. 233 (mot)	1942
233.Panzergrenadier-Division	1942
233.Panzer-Division	1943
233.Reserve-Panzer-Division	1943
Panzer-Division *Clausewitz*	1945

Commanders

Generalleutnant Heinrich Wosch
April 1943 – April 1945

Generalleutnant Max Fremerey
April 1945

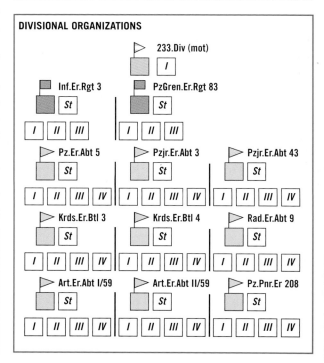

DIVISIONAL ORGANIZATIONS

▶ **Panzerkampfwagen IV Ausf F (SdKfz 101)**

233.Panzer-Division / 55.Panzer-Abteilung

At the end of the war, the 55th Panzer Battalion had a mix of obsolete Panzer IIIs and Panzer IVs on strength, including two short-barrelled Panzer IVs. It also had four Flak Panzers with 3.7cm (1.5in) guns.

Specifications

Crew: 5	Speed: 40km/h (24.9mph)
Weight: 25.9 tonnes (23.5 tons)	Range: 210km (130.5 miles)
Length: 5.92m (19ft 5in)	Radio: FuG5
Width: 2.84m (9ft 4in)	Armament: 1 x 75mm (3in) KwK 37
Height: 2.68m (8ft 9.5in)	L/24 gun; 2 x 7.92mm (0.3in) MG
Engine: Maybach HL120TRM	(one hull-mounted, one coaxial)

Panzergrenadiers, motorized infantry, Panzerjägers, motorcycle reconnaissance units, artillery batteries, armoured engineers, and even cavalrymen (though this quickly became a bicycle training unit).

Upgraded

After less than a year, the formation was upgraded and became the 233rd Panzer Division, taking its new name on 5 April 1943. The *Ersatz* bicycle battalion became a reconnaissance training unit.

In August 1943, the division became 233.*Reserve-Panzer-Division*, and was sent to Denmark, where it would remain until the end of the war. In May 1944, the division provided replacements for the 6th, 19th and 25th Panzer Divisions.

The 233rd Reserve Panzer Division was redesignated the 233rd Panzer Division on 21 February 1945. At this time, the division's main fighting strength was provided by three Panzergrenadier regiments and the 55th Panzer Battalion. By April 1945, the division's tank strength included only 20 Panzer IIIs, five Panzer IVs (two of which were early models with short 7.5cm/3in guns) and four FlakPanzers armed with 3.7cm (1.5in) guns.

Wehrmacht's last Panzer division

Under its nickname of the *Holstein* Division, the 233rd provided the staff and some of the strength for

▲ **SdKfz 251**

The 233rd Division did not acquire armoured half-tracks until the end of the war, when it formed the nucleus of *Panzer-Division Clausewitz*.

the *Clausewitz* Panzer Division, the last created by the *Wehrmacht* in World War II. Formed on 6 April 1945, the *Clausewitz* Division assembled on the Elbe at Lauenburg, with additional units coming from survivors of *Panzer-Brigade* 106, the *Feldherrnhalle* Division and the *Grossdeutschland* Division.

The division was destroyed by the US 5th Armored Division on 21 April 1945 at Fallersleben, remnants of the formation surrendering at Prinitz on the Elbe.

▲ **Jagdpanther (SdKfz 173)**

Panzer-Abteilung Putlos

Another unit absorbed into the newly formed *Clausewitz* Division was *Kampfgruppe Putlos*, formed from the tank school at Putlos, near Lübeck. It had a mix of Panzer IVs, Panthers and Tigers.

Specifications	
Crew: 5	Speed: 46km/h (28.6mph)
Weight: 50.7 tonnes (46 tons)	Range: 160km (99.4 miles)
Length: 9.9m (32ft 5in)	Radio: FuG5 plus FuG2
Width: 3.42m (11ft 2in)	Armament: 1 x 88mm (3.5in) PaK 43/4 L/71
Height: 2.72m (8ft 11in)	gun; 1 x 7.92mm (0.3in) MG (hull-mounted)
Engine: Maybach HL230P30	

▶ **Mittlere Schützenpanzerwagen (SdKfz 251/1)**

Panzer-Regiment Clausewitz / II.Panzergrenadier Bataillon

Transferred from the *Feldherrnhalle* Panzer Regiment when the *Clausewitz* Division was formed in April 1945, the 2nd Battalion did not have tanks. It was an armoured infantry unit equipped with half-tracks.

Specifications

Crew: 2 plus 12 troops	Engine: Maybach HL42TUKRM
Weight: 9.9 tonnes (9 tons)	Speed: 53km/h (33mph)
Length: 5.98m (19ft 7in)	Range: 300km (186 miles)
Width: 2.1m (6ft 11in)	Radio: FuG Spr Ger 1
Height: 1.75m (5ft 8in) or 2.16m	Armament: 1/2 7.62mm
(7ft) including MG shield if fitted	(0.3in) MG

345th Infantry Division (mot)

Like *Division Nr.* 179, the 345th Infantry Division was formed in central Germany under the control of *Wehrkreis* IX headquartered at Kassel.

IT WAS ONE OF THE 'KRIEMHILDE' divisions, formed at very short notice from the *Ersatzheer*, or Replacement Army, to free up combat divisions for Operation *Gisela*. This was a planned occupation of the Atlantic coasts of Spain and Portugal in the event of an Allied landing on the Iberian Peninsula. Operation *Gisela* never took place, so the division was earmarked for the Eastern Front.

Established on 24 November 1942 at the *Truppenübungsplatz* (TrpÜbPl) Wildflecken, a troop training area on the border of Bavaria and Hesse, the division had a short life. In January 1943, instead of being sent East, the 345th Division was sent to the

◀ **Italy, November 1944**

Trained for operations in Russia, the 345th Infantry Division (mot) spent its operational career as the 29th Panzergrenadier Division in Italy. Here, a grenadier keeps watch for advancing Allied forces on the Gothic Line, late in 1944.

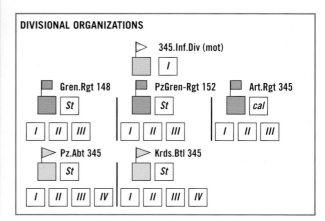

DIVISIONAL ORGANIZATIONS

345.Inf.Div (mot)

Gren.Rgt 148 — PzGren-Rgt 152 — Art.Rgt 345

Pz.Abt 345 — Krds.Btl 345

South of France, attached to Army Group D. On 1 March, it was absorbed into the 29th Infantry Division, being re-created in France after the original division was destroyed at Stalingrad. On 23 June 1943, the division became the 29th Panzergrenadier Division, and in July it was sent to Sicily. It would remain on the Italian Front until the end of the war.

Commanders

Generalleutnant Karl Böttcher
November 1942 – March 1943

Divisional History	Formed
345.Infanterie-Division (mot)	
Absorbed by 29.Panzergrenadier-Division	1943

▶ L.Lkw (o) 1t Opel Blitz 2.0-12

345.Infanterie-Division (mot) / Versorgungsdienste

The (o) in the vehicle's designation indicated that it was a '*handelsbuch*', or commercially available, design. A huge variety of such light trucks equipped reserve formations in Germany.

Specifications

Crew: 1	Engine: Opel 1920cc 6-cylinder
Weight: 3.29 tonnes (3 tons)	petrol (36hp)
Length: 6.02m (19ft 9in)	Speed: 80km/h (50mph)
Width: 2.27m (7ft 5in)	Range: 410km (255 miles)
Height: 2.18m (7ft 2in)	Radio: None

▶ Leichte Spähpanzerwagen (SdKfz 222)

345.Kradschützen-Bataillon

As formed, the 345th Division's reconnaissance unit was the 345th Motorcycle Battalion. Motorcycle battalions had one light armoured car company equipped with SdKfz 222 armoured cars and 223 radio cars.

Specifications

Crew: 3	Speed: 85km/h (52.8mph)
Weight: 5.3 tonnes (4.8 tons)	Range: 300km (186 miles)
Length: 4.8m (15ft 8in)	Radio: FuG Spr Ger 'a'
Width: 1.95m (6ft 5in)	Armament: 1 x 20mm (0.7in) KwK 30 L/55
Height: 2.00m (6ft 7in)	cannon; 1 x 7.92mm (0.3in) MG (coaxial)
Engine: Horch 3.5L or 3.8L petrol	

▶ 15-cm sIG 33 Sf (SdKfz 138/1)

152.Grenadier-Regiment (mot) / schwere Infanteriegeschütz-Kompanie

The 152nd Grenadier Regiment was converted into a Panzergrenadier regiment when the 345th Division was used to re-form the 29th Division in March 1943. It later became the 71st Panzergrenadier Regiment.

Specifications

Crew: 5	Speed: 35km/h (21.7mph)
Weight: 12.7 tonnes (11.5 tons)	Range: 185km (115 miles)
Length: 4.61m (15ft 1in)	Radio: FuG16
Width: 2.16m (7ft 0in)	Armament: 1 x 150mm (5.9in)
Height: 2.40 (7ft 10.5in)	sIG 33 gun
Engine: Praga EPA/2	

386th Infantry Division (mot)

The division was established on 1 April 1940 in the *Generalgouvernement* (German-occupied Poland) under the control of the *Oberbefehlshaber Ost*, or *Oberost*.

THE 386TH DIVISION WAS PART OF the 9. *Welle* (ninth wave) of the German Army's mobilization, ordered in February and March of 1940 to create a number of divisions for static or garrison duties. The divisions were of little military use, and orders for their disbandment were issued in July 1940.

In August 1940, the units of the 386th Division were used to form *Landesschützen-Bataillone* 343 to 349 in *Wehrkreis* III. *Landesschützen*, or local defence, battalions were composed of two to six companies, which were employed on guard duties at vital installations and as support for the military administration in occupied territories.

On 25 November 1942, a new 386th Division was established as part of the 'Kriemhilde' mobilization. The 386.*Infanterie-Division (mot)* was controlled by

Commanders

Generalmajor Kurt von Jesser
December 1942 – March 1943

Divisional History	Formed
386.Infanterie-Division	1940
Disbanded: used to form Landesschützen-Bataillone 343 to 349	1940
Re-formed as 386.Infanterie-Division (mot)	1942
Absorbed by 3.Panzergrenadier-Division	1943

Wehrkreis III in Prussia and was based at Frankfurt an der Oder.

After formation, in January 1943, the division was relocated to the South of France, where it was intended to be used as an occupation unit and to provide a reserve resource for frontline divisions. On 1 March 1943, the division was ordered to be disbanded and absorbed by the 3rd Infantry Division (mot), which had been destroyed at Stalingrad. While being assembled, the division became the 3rd Panzergrenadier Division. This was sent to Italy in June 1943 and fought at Salerno, Cassino, and Anzio.

The division saw action against the Americans, fighting to the southeast of Paris before retreating to the Saar. It was refitted in Germany in November 1944 before fighting in the Ardennes. It was destroyed in the Ruhr pocket in April 1945.

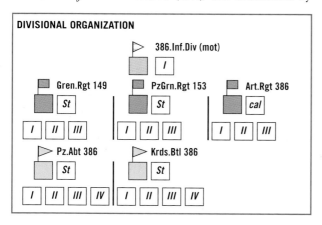

DIVISIONAL ORGANIZATION

▷ 386.Inf.Div (mot)
386. Gren.Rgt 149 · PzGrn.Rgt 153 · Art.Rgt 386
Pz.Abt 386 · Krds.Btl 386

▶ **Leichte Einheits Pkw Stöwer 40 (Kfz 2)**

386.Kradschützen-Bataillon / Stab / Nachrichten-Zug

Many of the Kfz 2 light cars in service were used as radio cars. Three-door variants were designated Kfz 2/40. The Stöwer company was an old-established engineering and vehicle-building concern based in Stettin.

Specifications

Crew: 1

Weight: 1.81 tonnes (1.65 tons)

Length: 3.58m (11ft 9in)

Width: 1.57m (5ft 2in)

Height: 1.78 (5ft 10in)

Engine: Stöwer AW2 or R180W petrol (50hp)

Speed: 100km/h (62.5mph)

Range: 500km (311 miles)

Radio: Various

▶ **Opel Blitz 3.6-36S**

153.Panzergrenadier-Regiment (later 29.Infanterie-Regiment)

When the 386th Infantry Division (mot) was redesignated as the 3rd Infantry Division (mot), its component units were also renamed. The 153rd Panzergrenadier Regiment briefly became the 29th Infantry Regiment before reverting to a Panzergrenadier unit.

Specifications

Crew: 1	Engine: Opel 6-cylinder petrol
Weight: 3.29 tonnes (3 tons)	(73.5hp)
Length: 6.02m (19ft 9in)	Speed: 80km/h (50mph)
Width: 2.27m (7ft 5in)	Range: 410km (255 miles)
Height: 2.18m (7ft 2in)	Radio: None

▶ **Leichte Personenkraftwagen VW Kübel (Kfz 1)**

386.Kradschützen Bataillon / Stab

The division's reconnaissance unit was the 386th Motorcycle Battalion, though by the time of its formation at the end of 1942 the VW Kübel was starting to replace sidecar combinations in such units.

Specifications

Crew: 1	Engine: Volkswagen 1131cc petrol (25hp)
Weight: 0.64 tonnes (0.58 tons)	Speed: 100km/h (62mph)
Length: 3.73m (12 ft 3in)	Range: 600km (375 miles)
Width: 1.60m (5ft 3in)	Radio: None
Height: 1.35m (4ft 5in)	

Brandenburg Panzergrenadier Division

Formed relatively late in the war, the *Brandenburg* Panzergrenadier Division was an elite fighting unit that had evolved out of the German Army's special operations forces.

THE ORIGINS OF THE *BRANDENBURG* Division were in the Brandenburgers, the German Army's commandos. Units of Brandenburgers operated on all fronts from the invasions of Poland, Denmark and Norway, through the Battle of France to Operation *Barbarossa*. Brandenburgers fought in Finland, Greece and took part in the invasion of Crete. They operated in the Balkans, and conducted special operations in India, Afghanistan, the Middle East and South Africa. They also trained for Operation *Seelöwe* and for Operation *Felix*, the planned seizure of Gibraltar. Early in the war, they acted as advance units, sent to capture strategic bridges, tunnels and rail yards in Poland and the Netherlands ahead of the advancing regular troops.

The unit was the brainchild of *Hauptmann* Theodor von Hippel who, after having his idea rejected by the traditionalist *Reichswehr*, approached Admiral Wilhelm Canaris, commander of the German military intelligence service, the *Abwehr*.

Commanders

Generalmajor Alexander von Pfuhlstein
February 1943 – September 1944

Generalleutnant Fritz Kühlwein
September 1944

Generalmajor Hermann Schulte Heuthaus
October 1944 – April 1945

Regiment Brandenburg evolved out of the *Abwehr*'s 2nd Department, and was used as a commando unit during the first years of the war. Initially the unit consisted mainly of former German expatriates fluent in other languages. Until 1944, it came under the direct control of the OKH, rather than serving as a unit of the regular army.

Volksdeutsche origins

The original formation, designated *Bataillon Ebbinghaus*, was formed mostly from *Volksdeutsche* (ethnic Germans), who were fluent in Polish. Although the unit was disbanded after the Polish campaign, Admiral Canaris gave Hippel the go-ahead to create an *Abwehr* unit along the lines of the *Ebbinghaus* Battalion.

Basing the new formation on many of the former *Ebbinghaus* members, Hippel formed the *Lehr und Bau Kompanie zbV* 800 (or Training and Construction Company No 800) on 25 October 1939.

Every recruit to the company had to be fluent in one foreign language at the very least, and many members could speak several. Knowing every habit and mannerism in their geographical area of operations would enable the men to blend in and operate as effective saboteurs.

The influx of new recruits meant that on 15 December 1939, the Training and Construction Company No 800 was expanded and redesignated as the *Bataillon Brandenburg* (Brandenburg Battalion). The members of the battalion came to be known as Brandenburgers.

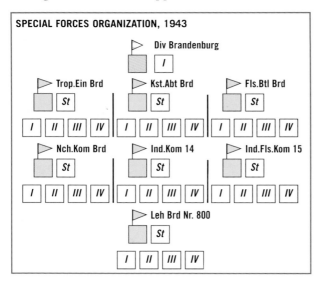

SPECIAL FORCES ORGANIZATION, 1943

DIVISIONAL ORGANIZATION, 1943

Divisional History	Formed
Bataillon Ebbinghaus	1939
Lehr und Bau Kompanie zbV 800 (Von Hippel Battalion)	1939
Bataillon Brandenburg	1939
Regiment Brandenburg	1940
Division Brandenburg	1943
Infanterie-Division Brandenburg (mot)	1944
Panzergrenadier-Division Brandenburg	1944

▶ **Mittlerer Zugkraftwagen 3t (SdKfz 11)**

Artillerie Regiment Brandenburg / I Bataillon / 1.Batterie

When the Brandenburg Division assumed a conventional infantry role, its artillery regiment had one self-propelled batallion and two towed battalions. The SdKfz 11 was the main prime mover for the 10.5cm (4.13in) light field howitzer.

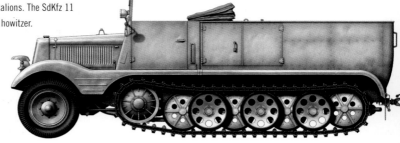

Specifications

Crew: 1 plus 8 troops
Weight: 7.1 tonnes (6.46 tons)
Length: 5.48m (18ft 0in)
Width: 1.82m (5ft 11.5in)
Height: 1.62m (5ft 4in)

Engine: 6-cylinder petrol
(100hp)
Speed: 53km/h (32.9mph)
Range: 122km (75.8 miles)
Radio: None

▸ **Opel Blitz 3.6-36S**

1.Jaeger Regiment (mot) Brandenburg / II Bataillon

For much of 1943, the bulk of the Brandenburg Division was used as motorized infantry on anti-partisan duties in the Balkans, although individual sub-units were still being used for special operations on the Eastern Front.

Specifications

Crew: 1	Engine: Opel 6-cylinder petrol
Weight: 3.29 tonnes (3 tons)	(73.5hp)
Length: 6.02m (19ft 9in)	Speed: 80km/h (50mph)
Width: 2.27m (7ft 5in)	Range: 410km (255 miles)
Height: 2.18m (7ft 2in)	Radio: None

▸ **Mittlerer Nachrichtenkraftwagen (Kfz 15/1)**

1.Jäger-Regiment Brandenburg (mot)

When the *Brandenburg* Division was formed, its infantry battalions were incorporated into motorized Jäger, or light infantry, regiments. Later, at the end of 1944, they were to be redesignated as Panzerjäger regiments.

Specifications

Crew: 1	Engine: Skoda 3.1L petrol (80-85hp)
Weight: 2.4 tonnes (2.2 tons)	Speed: 100km/h (62mph)
Length: 4.8m (15 ft 9in)	Range: 400km (250 miles)
Width: 1.80m (5ft 9in)	Radio: None
Height: 1.72m (5ft 3in)	

Special Operations Division
1943

The *Brandenburg* Battalion grew as more and more demands were made upon its members, and in 1940 the battalion was expanded in size to become a regiment.

OVER THE NEXT TWO YEARS, the Brandenburgers saw action in North Africa and Russia. In the desert, they raided behind enemy lines in British uniforms. During Operation *Barbarossa*, they acted as pathfinders, seizing road and rail crossings. They conducted small-scale amphibious raids in the Black Sea and the Baltic, and mounted long-range reconnaissance patrols.

In February 1943, the Brandenburgers were pulled out of the line and moved back to Germany.

▸ **Balkans fighters**
Brandenburgers saw a considerable number of small-unit actions in the Balkans and in the Greek islands, fighting Partisans and Allied units.

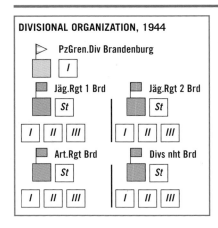

DIVISIONAL ORGANIZATION, 1944

PzGren.Div Brandenburg

I

Jäg.Rgt 1 Brd — St — I II III

Jäg.Rgt 2 Brd — St — I II III

Art.Rgt Brd — St — I II III

Divs nht Brd — St — I II III

The regiment was once again expanded and was designated as the *Division Brandenburg* commanded by *Generalmajor* Alexander von Pfuhlstein.

There were four regiments. One returned to the Eastern Front, where it was used as a 'fire brigade'. One battalion was sent back to Africa to harass the Allies in the Mediterranean. The remainder were sent to the Balkans on anti-Partisan duties. Between January and April 1943, as the Brandenburgers expanded to their full divisional size, specialized sub-units were formed, including artillery, tank, anti-tank and combat engineering outfits, as well as sub-units for U-boat operations and air defence. Men were transferred from the *Afrika Korps* and *Kriegsmarine*, and the unit also incorporated Muslims from Yugoslavia and volunteers from India.

Battle for Kos

One of the most successful of all Brandenburger operations came in the autumn of 1943. Following the ousting of Benito Mussolini, the Italian Government began negotiations with the Allies, and the Germans occupied Italy. Brandenburger units from the Balkans were sent to Italy, where they helped to disarm the Italian armed forces and secured key points vital to the German war effort.

One of those key points was the island of Kos, in the Dodecanese Islands. Kos had been secured by British troops in September 1943, and a large garrison of allied Italian troops was also present. The island had a vital airstrip, and had to be recaptured.

Along with *Luftwaffe* Fallschirmjäger, men of the *Küstenjäger-Abteilung* and the *Fallschirm-Kompanie* of the *Brandenburg* Division took part in the operation. Under the command of *Leutnant* Langbein, they landed at night on the south coast, and quickly seized the beach defences, controlled by Italian troops. The unit then advanced to the main town on the island, encountering no resistance. After investigating several caves, the unit discovered a supply of wine, and indulged themselves. Although they were not drunk, Langbein realized that the alcohol had made his men tired and dulled their alertness. He secured a stock of Pervitin, a stimulant, and administered it to his men. Mixed with the alcohol, the effect of the stimulant was enhanced. When the British and Italians attacked later in the evening, the Brandenburgers fought with a ferocity that enabled them to repel their attackers and capture the Allied positions. They then linked up with the Fallschirmjäger, securing the island.

Panzer-Regiment *Brandenburg* December 1944	Strength
HQ Company:	
3.7cm (1.5in) Flak AA guns	3
1st Battalion:	
PzKpfw V Panther	68
2cm (0.7in) Flakvierling self-propelled AA guns	3
2nd Battalion:	
PzKpfw IV	68
2cm (0.7in) Flakvierling self-propelled AA guns	3

▶ **Leichte Schützenpanzerwagen (SdKfz 250/9)**

Aufklärungs-Abteilung Brandenburg

The conversion of the Brandenburgers from their special operations role into a more conventional fighting formation in 1944 saw the division re-equipped with a full range of reconnaissance assets.

Specifications

Crew: 3

Weight: 6.9 tonnes (6.3 tons)

Length: 4.56m (14ft 11.5in)

Width: 1.95m (6ft 5in)

Height: 2.16m (7ft 1in)

Engine: Maybach HL42TRKM 6-cylinder

(100hp)

Speed: 60km/h (37mph)

Range: 320km (199 miles)

Radio: FuG Spr Ger 'f'

Armament: 1 x 20mm (0.7in) KwK 30/38 L/55 cannon; 1 x 7.92mm (0.3in) MG (coaxial)

▶ **2-cm Flakvierling 38 auf Zugkraftwagen 8t (SdKfz 7/1)**

Panzer-Regiment Brandenburg / I.Abteilung / Flak-Kompanie

Each of the *Brandenburg* Panzer Regiment's two battalions had a self-propelled
armoured Flak company equipped with three quadruple 2cm (0.7in) Flak guns. The
Flakvierling had a high rate of fire and was
effective against low-flying aircraft. However,
its range was limited, and later in the war
a single 3.7cm (1.5in) Flak gun was preferred.

Specifications

Crew: 7	6-cylinder (140hp)
Weight: 1.16 tonnes	Speed: 50km/h (31mph)
(1.06 tons)	Range: 250km (156 miles)
Length: 6.55m (21ft 6in)	Radio: None
Width: 2.40m (7ft 10.5in)	Armament: Quad 20mm
Height: 3.20m (10ft 6in)	(0.7in) Flak 38
Engine: Maybach HL62TUK	

Specifications

Crew: 4 or 5	Speed: 50km/h (31 mph)
Weight: 8 tonnes (7.28 tons)	Range: 300 km (186 miles)
Length: 5.98m (19ft 7in)	Radio: None
Width: 2.1m (6ft 11in)	Armament: One 20mm KwK 38
Height: 2.25m (7ft 4.5 in)	L/55 cannon plus one 7.92mm
Engine: Maybach HL42TUKRM 6-	MG (coaxial)
cylinder petrol (100hp)	

▲ **Mittlere Schützenpanzerwagen Ausf D (SdKfz 251/23)**

Panzer-Aufklärungs-Abteilung Brandenburg

First listed as operational in December 1944, the SdKfz 251/23 was a reconnaissance variant. It carried the same 2cm (0.7in) turret as the SdKfz 234/1 armoured car
and the SdKfz 250/9 light armoured half-track. Early in 1945, three of the *Brandenburg* Reconnaissance Battalion's four companies were mounted in half-tracks.

▶ **15-cm schwere Panzerhaubitze auf Geschützwagen III/IV Sf (SdKfz 165)**

Artillerie-Regiment Brandenburg / I.Bataillon / 3.Batterie

The 3rd Battery of the *Brandenburg* Artillery Regiment's 1st Battalion was equipped
with Hummel 15cm (5.9in) self-propelled howitzers.

Specifications

Crew: 6	Speed: 42km/h (26mph)
Weight: 26.5 tonnes (24 tons)	Range: 215km (133.6 miles)
Length: 7.17m (23ft 6in)	Radio: FuG Spr 1
Width: 2.97m (9ft 8in)	Armament: 1 x 150mm (5.9in)
Height: 2.81m (9ft 2in)	sFH 18/1 L/30; 1 x 7.92mm
Engine: Maybach HL120TRM	(0.3in) MG
(265hp)	

Panzergrenadiers
1944–1945

The *Abwehr* had never been trusted by the Nazis, and the outcome of a power struggle in Germany's intelligence services saw a change in the role of the *Brandenburg* Division.

SINCE THE BEGINNING of the Nazi era, Admiral Canaris and the *Abwehr* had been watched with suspicion by Himmler's SS intelligence service, the *Sicherheitsdienst*, or SD. The power struggle came to a head in July 1944, when several high-ranking *Abwehr* officials, including Canaris himself, were implicated in the July Plot to kill Hitler and were arrested, tried and executed. Control of the *Brandenburg* Division was passed to the SD, but in September 1944 it was decided that army special operations units were no longer necessary. The *Brandenburg* Division became *Infanterie-Division Brandenburg (mot)*, was equipped as a motorized infantry division and transferred to the Eastern Front. Nearly 2000 men managed to transfer to SS-*Standartenführer* Otto Skorzeny's SS-*Jagdverbande* and continued as special forces till the end of the war.

Frontline combat

For the rest of the division, the return to conventional operations damaged morale, but despite this, the Brandenburgers were still considered elite fighting troops, and so the division was assigned to the *Grossdeutschland* Panzer Corps alongside the *Grossdeutschland* Division (which had trained alongside the original *Brandenburg* Regiment in 1940 and 1941). The *Brandenburg* Division fought hard on

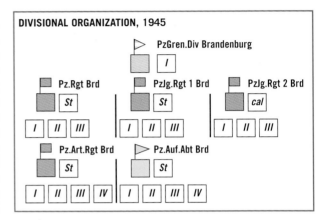

DIVISIONAL ORGANIZATION, 1945

the Eastern Front, being involved in the fighting retreat through the Baltic States and into East Prussia.

Late in 1944, the division was equipped with a Panzer regiment and redesignated *Panzergrenadier-Division Brandenburg*. The Brandenburgers were involved in heavy fighting near Memel until their withdrawal, along with the *Grossdeutschland* Division, via ferry to Pillau.

The division was all but annihilated during the heavy fighting near Pillau, and while some survivors surrendered to the British in Schleswig-Holstein in May, many Brandenburgers, highly skilled in evading detection, simply disappeared.

▶ **Schwere Panzerspähwagen Pak 40 (SdKfz 234/4)**

Aufklärungs-Abteilung Brandenburg

Only 90 SdKfz 234/4s armed with the 7.5cm (3n) Pak 40 anti-tank gun were completed by the end of the war. The *Brandenburg* Division was issued with at least three examples in January 1945.

Specifications		
Crew: 4	Speed: 80km/h (50mph)	
Weight: 11.50 tonnes (10.47 tons)	Range: 900km (559 miles)	
Length: 6.0m (19ft 8in)	Radio: FuG Spr Ger 'a'	
Width: 2.40m (7ft 10.5in)	Armament: 1 x 75mm (3in) PaK 40	
Height: 2.21m (7ft 4in)	L/46 cannon; 1 x 7.92 mm (0.3in)	
Engine: Tatra 103 12-cylinder (220hp)	MG	

Specifications

Crew: 5

Weight: 47.4 tonnes (43 tons)

Length: 8.86m (29ft 0in)

Width: 3.4m (11ft 2in)

Height: 2.95m (9ft 8in)

Engine: Maybach HL230P30

Speed: 46km/h (28.6mph)

Range: 200km (124.4 miles)

Radio: FuG5

Armament: 1 x 75mm (3in) KwK 42 L/70; 2 x
7.92mm (0.3in) MG (one hull-mounted,
one coaxial)

▲ Panzerkampfwagen I Ausf B (SdKfz 101)
Panzer-Regiment Brandenburg / I.Abteilung

The *Brandenburg* Division's Panzer Regiment was formed late in 1944. The 1st Battalion was equipped with PzKpfw V Panthers, while the 2nd Battalion was equipped with Panzer IVs.

▼ Panzer-Kompanie
Panzer-Regiment Brandenburg / I.Abteilung / 1.Kompanie

Upgraded to Panzergrenadier division in late 1944, the *Brandenburg* Division received a Panzer battalion and a reconnaissance battalion soon afterwards. By December 1944, a second Panzer battalion had completed the *Brandenburg* Panzer Regiment. Each battalion comprised four companies each of 17 Panzers.

Hermann Göring Division

The roots of the various *Göring* divisions can be traced back to the first days of the Third *Reich*, when Hermann Göring, as Prussian Interior Minister, took control of the Prussian police.

GÖRING SET UP A SPECIAL police unit known as the *Polizeiabteilung zbV Wecke* (Special Police Battalion *Wecke*). Working in conjunction with Göring's other creation, the *Gestapo*, it gained a brutal reputation as an enforcer of Nazi policy.

In 1934, Göring was forced to hand over all police powers to Heinrich Himmler and the SS, but he retained control of his police regiment, renamed the *Landespolizeigruppe General Göring*. With the SS, it was heavily involved in the suppression of Ernst Röhm's SA during the Night of the Long Knives.

The unit was transferred to the *Luftwaffe* in 1935. It provided the personnel for the first Fallschirmjäger in 1938. By this time, the *Regiment General Göring* had evolved into a personal bodyguard for Göring, and it was also tasked with providing Flak protection for Hitler's headquarters.

Occupation and combat

The regiment was one of the first units across the border during the *Anschluss* with Austria in 1938, and took part in the occupation of the Sudetenland. It was kept in Berlin during the invasion of Poland, but elements of the regiment took part in the invasion of the Low Countries. Later, during the Battle of France, the regiment was broken up into several small *Kampfgruppen* and these were attached to the Panzer divisions spearheading the advance. Its heavy Flak units were particularly effective.

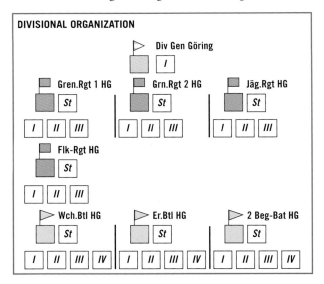

DIVISIONAL ORGANIZATION

Div Gen Göring
I

Gren.Rgt 1 HG — St — I II III
Grn.Rgt 2 HG — St — I II III
Jäg.Rgt HG — St — I II III

Flk-Rgt HG — St — I II III

Wch.Btl HG — St — I II III IV
Er.Btl HG — St — I II III IV
2 Beg-Bat HG — St — I II III IV

Divisional History	Formed
Landespolizeigruppe General Göring	1934
Regiment General Göring	1935
Regiment (mot) Hermann Göring	1941
Brigade Hermann Göring	1942
Division Hermann Göring	1942
Panzer-Division Hermann Göring	1943
Fallschirm-Panzer-Division 1. Hermann Göring	1944
Fallschirm-Panzergrenadier-Division 2. Hermann Göring	1944
Fallschirm-Panzerkorps Hermann Göring	1944

Commanders

Major Walther von Axthelm
August 1936 – May 1940

Oberst Paul Contath
June 1940 – July 1942

Generalmajor Paul Conrath
July 1942 – April 1944

Generalmajor Wilhelm Schmalz
April–September 1944

Generalmajor Horst von Necker
October 1944 – February 1945

Generalmajor Max Lemke
February–May 1945

INSIGNIA

The Göring Division's association with paratroopers is evident in its divisional symbol, which incorporates the diving eagle insignia of the Fallschirmjäger.

The basic *Fallschirm-Panzerkorps Hermann Göring* symbol was a diamond. This is the vehicle insignia of the corps staff.

Other units in the corps used the diamond with different interior designs. This is the symbol of the HQ company of Fallschirm-Pz.Art.Rgt 2 HG.

The flag of the *Hermann Göring* Panzer Corps carried the *Luftwaffe* Eagle on the pink *Waffenfarbe* of the *Panzertruppen*.

▶ **Panzerkampfwagen III Ausf J (SdKfz 141/1)**

Panzer-Regiment HG / II.Abteilung / 6.Kompanie / 3.Zug

When the *Hermann Göring* Brigade became the *Hermann Göring* Division in November 1942, it was brought up to Panzer division strength with the addition of the *Panzer-Regiment Hermann Göring*. However, this had only just started arriving in Tunisia when the division was destroyed in May 1943.

Specifications

Crew: 5	Speed: 40km/h (24.9mph)
Weight: 24 tonnes (21.5 tons)	Range: 155km (96.3 miles)
Length: 6.28m (20ft 7in)	Radio: FuG5
Width: 2.95m (9ft 9in)	Armament: 1 x 50mm (2in) KwK 39
Height: 2.50m (8ft 2in)	L/60 gun; 2 x 7.92mm (0.3in) MG
Engine: Maybach HL120TRM petrol	(one coaxial, one hull-mounted)
(300hp)	

▶ **Sturmgeschütz 7.5-cm Kanone Ausf C/D (SdKfz 101)**

Artillerie-Regiment Hermann Göring / V.StuG-Abteilung

Added to the division late in 1942, the Assault Gun Battalion was not ready for service until after the fall of Tunisia. By July 1943, it had been attached to the *Hermann Göring* Special Purpose Panzergrenadier Regiment in Sicily.

Specifications

Crew: 4	Speed: 40km/h (24.9mph)
Weight: 19.6 tonnes (17.9 tons)	Range: 160km (99.4 miles)
Length: 5.38m (17ft 8in)	Radio: FuG15 or FuG16
Width: 2.92m (9ft 7in)	Armament: 1 x 75mm (3in)
Height: 1.95m (6ft 5in)	StuK 37 L/24 gun
Engine: Maybach HL120TR (300hp)	

 # North Africa and Italy
1942–1943

After brief periods on the Channel coast and providing anti-aircraft protection to German positions in Paris, the regiment returned to its ceremonial duties in Berlin late in 1940.

EARLY IN 1941, the regiment was fully motorized. Since Hermann Göring had been promoted to the unique rank of *Reichsmarschall*, its name was changed from *Regiment General Göring* to the *Regiment (mot) Hermann Göring*. It was assigned to Army Group South for the invasion of Russia, but was briefly diverted to provide Flak protection for the Romanian oilfields during the invasion of the Balkans.

During Operation *Barbarossa*, the regiment was attached to the 11th Panzer Division and saw action at Radziechow, Kiev and Bryansk. Once again, the regiment's 8.8cm (3.5in) Flak guns proved their worth as tank-killers. At the end of 1941, the regiment returned to Germany to refit, leaving a single *Schützen*, or motorized infantry, battalion at the front until April 1942.

In July 1942, the regiment began enlargement to brigade size, and was redesignated as the *Brigade Hermann Göring*. In October 1942, while it was still being assembled and trained, it was decided to

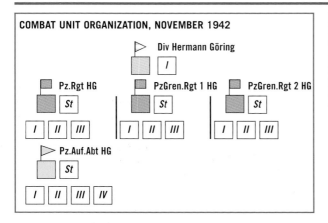

COMBAT UNIT ORGANIZATION, NOVEMBER 1942

Div Hermann Göring — I

- Pz.Rgt HG — St — I / II / III
- PzGren.Rgt 1 HG — St — I / II / III
- PzGren.Rgt 2 HG — St — I / II / III
- Pz.Auf.Abt HG — St — I / II / III / IV

Fallschirm-Panzer-Regiment HG September 1944	Strength
PzKpfw IV	88
PzKpfw V Panther	88
SdKfz 7/1 Flakvierling	6
SdKfz 7/2 3.7cm (1.5in) Flak	3

Fallschirm-Panzer-Regiment Hermann Göring June 1944	Strength
PzKpfw IV	64
Jagdpanzer IV	31
Flakpanzer 38	8

▲ **Leichte Personenkraftwagen VW Kübel (Kfz 1)**
Panzer-Aufklärungs-Abteilung HG / 2.Kompanie (VW)
Known as the Kübel, or 'Bucket', the Kfz 1 had two front seats and one rear seat.

Specifications

Crew: 1	Engine: Volkswagen 998cc petrol (24hp). Later
Weight: 0.64 tonnes (0.58 tons)	Volkswagen 1131cc petrol (25hp)
Length: 3.73m (12 ft 3in)	Speed: 100km/h (62mph)
Width: 1.60m (5ft 3in)	Range: 600km (375 miles)
Height: 1.35m (4ft 5in)	Radio: None

further upgrade the status of the formation to that of a division. The division would be organized along the lines of a German Army Panzer division.

Hermann Göring Division

To provide an experienced nucleus for his new showpiece formation, Göring arranged for veteran *Heer* Panzer crewmen to be transferred to his division, while inexperienced *Luftwaffe* personnel went the other way to the Army Panzer divisions for on-the-job training. All tanks and other equipment (apart from Flak guns) were supplied by the Army.

The motorized infantry component of the division was brought up to strength with the addition of 5000 *Luftwaffe* volunteers and the transfer of

5.*Fallschirmjäger-Regiment*, itself the result of combining the remnants of three parachute units that had fought on Crete and on the Eastern Front.

The German position in North Africa took a considerable turn for the worse while the division was in formation. In October 1942, the defeat at El Alamein forced Rommel's forces into full retreat

The standard summer *Balkenkreuz* in 1943 was a simple white outline as on the SdKfz 251 below. To increase visibility on light sand-coloured vehicles, black was often added as seen here.

▶ **Mittlerer Schützenpanzerwagen Ausf B (SdKfz 251/1)**
Panzergrenadier-Brigade zbV Hermann Göring / I.Panzergrenadier-Bataillon SKW
When the *Hermann Göring* Division was reformed in Sicily in 1943, it incorporated a non-standard Panzergrenadier regiment with one half-track battalion, one motorized battalion and one Sturmgeschütz battalion.

Specifications

Crew: 2 plus 12 troops	Engine: Maybach HL42TUKRM
Weight: 9.9 tonnes (9 tons)	Speed: 53km/h (33mph)
Length: 5.98m (19ft 7in)	Range: 300km (186 miles)
Width: 2.1m (6ft 11in)	Radio: FuG Spr Ger 1
Height: 1.75m (5ft 8 in) or 2.16m	Armament: 1/2 7.62mm (0.3in) MG
(7ft) including MG shield if fitted	

westwards across Libya, and Operation *Torch* – the massive Allied landings in Morocco and Algeria in November 1942 – threatened the rear of the German and Italian armies in Tunisia.

The incomplete *Hermann Göring* Division was ordered to move to Italy to finish its training near Naples, ready to be deployed to Africa. The 1st and 3rd Fallschirmjäger Regiments were the first to see

action in Tunisia, attached to 10th Panzer Division. Early in 1943, the transfer of the rest of the division's combat-ready units began. The majority had landed by March and went into action as *Kampfgruppe Schmidt*, after its commander, *Generalmajor* Schmidt. By 1 May, the estimated strength of the division in Africa was 11,000 officers and men, most of whom surrendered to Allied forces on 12 May.

▶ **Panzerkampfwagen IV Ausf G (SdKfz 161/1)**

Panzer-Regiment Hermann Göring / I.Battalion / 3.Kompanie

The first examples of the PzKpfw IV Ausf G were fitted with the KwK40 L/43 7.5cm (3in) gun. Only five HG Panzer IVs reached Tunisia before the final defeat in North Africa.

Specifications

Crew: 5	Speed: 40km/h (24.9mph)
Weight: 25.9 tonnes (23.5 tons)	Range: 210km (130.5 miles)
Length: 6.62m (21ft 8in)	Radio: FuG5
Width: 2.88m (9ft 5in)	Armament: 1 x 75mm (3in) KwK
Height: 2.69m (8ft 10in)	40/43; 2 x 7.92mm (0.3in) MG
Engine: Maybach HL120TRM	(one hull-mounted, one coaxial)

▶ **Panzerkampfwagen IV Ausf H (SdKfz 161/2)**

Panzer-Regiment Hermann Göring / II.Battalion / 4.Kompanie

Fitted with a long L/48 gun, the Panzer IV Ausf H had improved transmission and more armour.

Specifications

Crew: 5	Speed: 38km/h (23.6mph)
Weight: 27.6 tonnes (25 tons)	Range: 210km (130.5 miles)
Length: 7.02m (23ft 0in)	Radio: FuG5
Width: 2.88m (9ft 5in)	Armament: 1 x 75mm (3in) KwK
Height: 2.68m (8ft 10in)	40/43; 2 x 7.92mm (0.3in) MG
Engine: Maybach HL120TRM	(one hull-mounted, one coaxial)

◇ Panzer Division and Corps
1943–1945

After the destruction of the bulk of the *Hermann Göring* Division in Tunisia, it was almost immediately ordered to be re-formed around the remnants of the division still in training.

IN THE SUMMER OF 1943, these troops from all over Germany were transferred to Naples in Italy (with the exception of the I. and III. *Abteilungen*, who were based in Holland, and the IV. *Abteilung*, who were

based in Velten near Berlin), where they were fully trained and equipped. Once trained and equipped, they were flown to Sicily along with the 15th Panzergrenadier Division to counter the expected

---

FIGHTING UNIT ORGANIZATION

▷ St der Korps   ▷ Fls.Pz.Div 1 HG   ▷ Fls.PzGren.Div 2 HG

   ☐ *St*   ☐ *St*   ☐ *St*

Allied invasion. Fierce German resistance when the Allies landed meant that it took them longer than expected, but eventually the Axis troops were forced off the island. During Operation *Lehrgang*, the German evacuation of Sicily, the *Hermann Göring* Division formed part of the rearguard, being one of the last units to leave Sicily for the mainland.

With the overthrow of Mussolini, the new Italian Government signed an armistice with the Allies. The German reaction was to disarm all Italian forces in the area they controlled. When the Allies landed at Salerno, near Naples, on 9 September, the division, being stationed in the area, was immediately thrown into the fight. The division then executed a fighting withdrawal towards the Volturno-Termoli Line. After holding the line for as long as possible, the division fell back to the Gustav Line. Elements of the division caused a scandal when they transported priceless treasures from the monastery at Monte Cassino. Given Hermann Göring's predilection for collecting looted artworks, suspicion was aroused, but they were in fact acting with the full cooperation of the abbey's monks to save the treasures.

Re-formed again

The division was rushed to Anzio after the Allied landings in early 1944, and it continued to fight at Cisterna, on the Rapido River and at Minturno, where it was finally pulled out of the line for rest and refit, becoming the *Fallschirm-Panzer-Division 1. Hermann Göring* in the process. After a fighting withdrawal past Rome, the division was pulled out of

Specifications

Crew: 1 plus 8 troops	Engine: 6-cylinder petrol (100hp)
Weight: 7.1 tonnes (6.46 tons)	Speed: 53km/h (32.9mph)
Length: 5.48m (18ft 0in)	Range: 122km (75.8 miles)
Width: 1.82m (5ft 11.5in)	Radio: None
Height: 1.62m (5ft 4in)	

▽ **Zugkraftwagen 3t SdKfz 11 / 7.5-cm Pak 40**

Fallschirm-Panzergrenadier-Regiment HG / I.Bataillon / Panzerjäger-Zug

Each of the four Panzergrenadier battalions in the *Hermann Göring* Division had an anti-tank platoon of three towed 7.5cm (3in) Pak 40 anti-tank guns. By September 1944, these had been detached into separate Panzerjäger companies.

▶ **Schwere Lkw Mercedes-Benz L4500A / 3.7-cm Flak 43**

Panzer-Flak-Regiment HG / III.Battalion / 5.Batterie SF

In 1943 and 1944, the *Luftwaffe* received large numbers of self-propelled Flak guns mounted on lightly armoured Mercedes-Benz and Büssing-NAG 4.5-tonne (4.4-ton) four-wheel-drive trucks.

Specifications

Crew: 7 (3.7cm) or 10	Height: approx 4.3m (14ft) to
(2cm Flakvierling)	top of gunshield
Weight: 5.7 tonnes (5.6tons)	Engine: Daimler-Benz 6-
Length: 7.86m (26ft)	cylinder 7.2-litre diesel
Width: 2.35m (7ft 7in)	(112 bhp)

Italy in July and sent east to Poland. The division arrived on the Vistula Front in mid-September and immediately joined the action between Modlin and Warsaw alongside the 5th SS Panzer Division *Wiking*.

▲ **Panzerkampfwagen II Ausf L Luchs (SdKfz 123)**
I.Fallschirm-Panzer-Aufklärungs-Abteilung HG / 1.Kompanie

The armoured car company of the *Hermann Göring* Panzer Division was one of the few to be equipped with the Luchs. This was a completely redesigned development of the Panzer II with new suspension, thicker armour and a more powerful engine. Only 100 were built before manufacture was cancelled in January 1944.

Specifications

Crew: 4	Speed: 60km/h (37.3mph)
Weight: 14.3 tonnes (13 tons)	Range: 290km (180.2 miles)
Length: 4.63m (15ft 2in)	Radio: FuG12 plus FuG Spr 'a'
Width: 2.48m (8ft 1in)	Armament: 1 x 20mm (0.7in) EW 141 cannon;
Height: 2.21m (7ft 4in)	1 x 7.92mm (0.3in) MG (coaxial)
Engine: Maybach HL66P	

In a period of heavy fighting, the two elite German divisions destroyed the Red Army's III Tank Corps.

Hermann Göring Panzer Corps

On 1 October 1944, the division was ordered to be expanded further into a *Panzerkorps* with the addition of a new Panzergrenadier division: *Fallschirm-Panzergrenadier-Division* 2. The new corps was sent to East Prussia in an attempt to halt the Soviet offensive that had isolated Army Group North in the Kurland pocket. After heavy fighting, the Soviet assault came to an end in late November, and the *Hermann Göring* Panzer Corps began to dig in.

The Soviet offensive early in 1945 trapped the corps in the Heiligenbeiler pocket with the Fourth Army. In February, elements of the *Panzergrenadier-Division Grossdeutschland* were attached to the corps, which was evacuated by sea to Swinemünde in Pomerania. While defending the Oder-Niesse Line, the *Brandenburg* Division was attached to the corps.

In April, the remnants of the *Panzerkorps Hermann Göring* were sent to Silesia, and in heavy fighting they slowly pushed back into Saxony. The surviving units began breakout attempts to the west, but the formation was encircled by the Red Army and although small groups made it through to the Western Allies, the majority of the corps surrendered to the Soviets on 8 May 1945.

Specifications

Crew: 5	Speed: 46km/h (28.6mph)
Weight: 50.2 tonnes (45.5 tons)	Range: 200km (124.3 miles)
Length: 8.86m (29ft 0in)	Radio: FuG5
Width: 3.4m (11ft 2in)	Armament: 1 x 75mm (3in) KwK42 L/70;
Height: 2.98m (9ft 10in)	2 x 7.92mm (0.3in) MG (one hull-mounted,
Engine: Maybach HL230P30	one coaxial)

▲ **Panzerkampfwagen V Ausf A (SdKfz 171)**
Fallschirm-Panzer-Regiment HG / I.Abteilung / 1.Kompanie

The 1st Battalion of the *Hermann Göring* Panzer Regiment began to re-equip with the Panzerkampfwagen V Panther late in 1943, and all four of the battalion's companies were fully equipped by early 1944, when the division fought at Anzio.

22nd 'Luftlande' Division

Unique amongst German regular divisions, the 22nd Division was trained for air assault in support of airborne operations, but spent most of the war as an infantry or motorized unit.

THE FORMATION WAS ESTABLISHED as a standard infantry unit and was given the designation of 22.*Infanterie-Division* at Bremen in 1935. As part of the standing army before the outbreak of war, it was brought from a peacetime footing to full combat strength with the *Wehrmacht*'s 1.*Welle* (first wave) of mobilization in August 1939. One infantry regiment, 16.*Infanterie-Regiment*, took part in the fighting in Poland along the Bzura River; the rest of the division was garrisoned on the *Westwall* to guard against a pre-emptive French attack.

In October 1939, after the end of the Polish campaign, the 22nd Division was withdrawn from active service and sent to the *Truppenübungsplatz* (troop training area) at Sennelager, where it was to undergo preparation for a special role. It emerged retrained and redesignated as 22.*Luftlande-Infanterie-Division* (22nd Air Landing Infantry Division), and it was the only formation of its type in the *Wehrmacht*. The division was intended for rapid tactical deployment in transport aircraft or gliders to quickly reinforce enemy airbases captured by the *Luftwaffe*'s Fallschirmjäger.

The division was flown into Holland in the early hours of 10 May in the van of the attack on the Low Countries following the airborne assault of 7.*Flieger-Division*. The division's 47th Infantry Regiment and the 65th Infantry Regiment were flown to three landing zones north of Rotterdam in the Hague region, while the 16th Infantry Regiment landed nearer Rotterdam. At each location a combination of factors, including heavy Dutch resistance, poor coordination and unsuitable landing zones, led to very heavy losses.

Withdrawn for quick reinforcement and refitting, the division was ready for action early in June in time for the Battle of France. It took part in the advance into France as an ordinary infantry formation, fighting at Dinant, and Rocroi and Saint Quentin.

Fighting in Russia

The 22.*Luftlande-Infanterie-Division* took part next in the invasion of the Soviet Union as a part of Field Marshal von Rundstedt's Army Group South, fighting in southern Russia and the Ukraine with the Eleventh Army. Attacking out of Romania, again as an ordinary infantry division, it crossed the Pruth River, advanced to the Dniester River and fought its way through the Stalin Line.

Moving on to cross the Bug and Dnieper Rivers, the division eventually took part in the the Crimea campaign, where it was involved in the fierce and bloody fighting for Sevastopol. The division led the assault against the heavily defended fortress city in its sector and stormed numerous Soviet positions, notably taking the Stalin and Volga factories.

Commanders

Generalmajor Hans Graf von Sponeck *1938 – October 1941*	Generalmajor Heinrich Kreipe *February–April 1944*
Generalmajor Ludwig Wolff *October 1941 – July 1942*	Generalleutnant Helmut Friebe *May 1944 – April 1945*
Generalleutnant Friedrich-Wilhelm Müller *August 1942 – February 1944*	Generalleutnant Gerhard Kühne *April–May 1945*

COMBAT UNIT ORGANIZATION, 1940

Divisional History	Formed
22.Infanterie-Division	1935
22.Luftlande-Infanterie-Division	1939
22.Luftlande-Division (mot trop)	1943
22. Infanterie-Division	1943
22.Volksgrenadier-Division	1945

◀ Holland, 1940

German infantry advance warily through a small town following the invasion of Holland in May 1940.

▲ 15-cm schwere Infanterie Geschütz sIG 33

47.Infanterie-Regiment / Infanteriegeschütz-Kompanie

The infantry gun company in each of the airlanding division's infantry regiments fielded two 15cm (5.9in) sIG 33s and six light 7.5cm (3in) IGs.

Specifications

Crew: 5
Weight: 1.75 tonnes (1.6 tons)
Length: 1.64m (64.57in)
Calibre: 149.1mm (5.9in)
Muzzle Velocity: 241m/s (783fps)
Range: 5504m (6000 yards)
Ammunition: High explosive or smoke

▶ Mittlerer geländegängige Lkw Henschel 33D1

47.Infanterie-Regiment

Established as a standard infantry division in 1935, the 22nd Division marched into battle, supported by trucks and horse-drawn vehicles of the divisional transport columns.

Specifications

Crew: 1
Weight: 6.1 tonnes (6 tons)
Length: 7.4m (24ft)
Width: 2.25m (7ft 4in)
Height: 3.2m (10ft 6in)
Engine: 10.7 litre (650ci), six-cylinder petrol (100hp)
Speed: 60km/h (37mph)
Payload: 3 tonnes (2.95 tons) or 18 troops

▶ Car, heavy utility, Ford WOA2

Grenadier Regiment 47 / Kampfgruppe Buhse

While the division was being converted to a light motorized unit in Crete, the 47th Grenadier Regiment was detached and sent to Africa, where it was partially equipped with captured Allied vehicles.

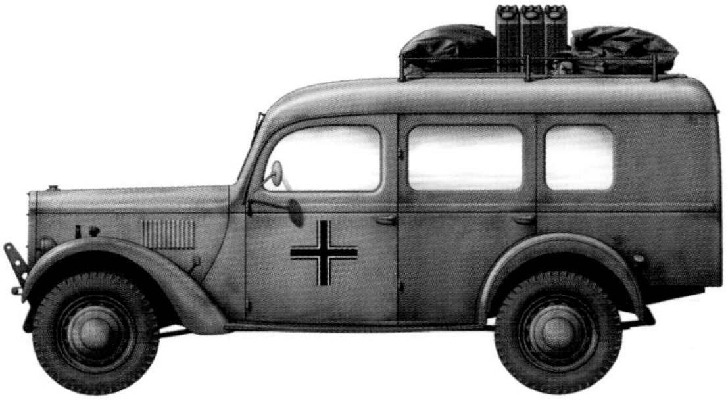

Specifications

Crew: 1
Weight: 1.61 tonnes (1.47 tons)
Length: 4.39m (14ft 5in)
Width: 2.48m (6ft 1in)
Height: 1.78m (5ft 10in)
Engine: Ford 3.6L V8 petrol (85hp)
Speed: Not Known
Range: Not Known
Radio: None

Crete and the Balkans
1942–1945

After 1940, the 22nd Air Landing Infantry Division was never again used in its intended role. It spent the rest of the war in Crete, the Aegean and the Balkans.

THOUGH PLANNED FOR USE in its air-landing role for the invasion of Crete, the 22nd's involvement in the Crimean battles meant that it was replaced by another division at the last minute. In July 1942, after the end of the fighting in the Crimea, the division was transferred to Crete, where it performed security and occupation duties around Rethymnon

and Heraklion until 1944. On arrival on Crete, the formation was converted into a light motorized division, and was given the designation *22.Luftlande-Division (mot trop)*, or 22nd Air Landing Motorized Tropical Division.

During its period in Crete, the 22nd Division provided a pool of highly trained personnel available for use on special operations. Some units were detached for service in North Africa, where they were destroyed in the German defeat in Tunisia in March 1943. The division provided the main assault force in a number of amphibious operations in the Aegean in 1943 and 1944, most notably against the islands of Kos, Kalymnos, Leros and Samos. The unit is well known for its role in the occupation of Leros against British and Italian resistance in November 1943.

On 26 April 1944, the divisional commander, *Generalmajor* Heinrich Kreipe, was abducted by a British Special Operations Executive team led by Major Patrick Leigh Fermor. Kreipe's car was ambushed on the way from Knossos to the divisional headquarters at Ano Arkhanais and he was taken over the mountains to the south coast, where the general and his captors were picked up by a British vessel on 14 May and transported to Egypt.

Retreat to the Balkans

Even as the German position in the eastern Mediterranean worsened through the first half of 1944, the 22nd Division was re-equipped before being transferred from Crete and the Aegean to Greece in August. It spent the rest of the war in anti-Partisan operations in southeastern Europe.

The division was renamed the *22.Volksgrenadier-Division* in March 1945. At that time, the division was part of the general withdrawal of German forces in the Balkans, who were making a fighting retreat northwards towards Austria. The division had reached northwestern Yugoslavia by the end of the war in May, when surviving units surrendered to Yugoslav forces.

COMBAT UNIT ORGANIZATION

22.Inf.Div (LL) / I

Gren.Rgt 16 — St — I II III
Gren.Rgt 47 — St — I II III
Gren.Rgt 65 — St — I II III

Aufkl.Abt 122 — St — I II III IV

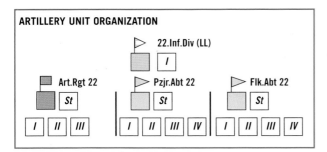

ARTILLERY UNIT ORGANIZATION

22.Inf.Div (LL) / I

Art.Rgt 22 — St — I II III
Pzjr.Abt 22 — St — I II III IV
Flk.Abt 22 — St — I II III IV

SUPPORT UNITS ORGANIZATION

22.Inf.Div (LL) / I

Sig.Btl 22 — St — I II III IV
Pnr.Btl 22 — St — I II III IV
Fld.Btl 22 — St — I II III IV

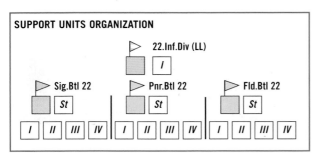

▶ 22.Panzerjäger-Abteilung

The 22nd Division moved from Russia to Crete in July 1942. Reorganized as an 'Air landing motorized tropical' formation, the 22nd Division had two Grenadier regiments, a Panzerjäger battalion, a reconnaissance battalion, an artillery regiment, a Flak battalion and the usual divisional support services. The Panzerjäger battalion consisted of three companies. The 1st Company was motorized with nine towed Pak 40s. The 2nd and 3rd Companies had self-propelled equipment, fielding Panzerjäger IIs which mounted captured Soviet 7.62cm (3in) guns.

1.Panzerjäger-Kompanie (mot)

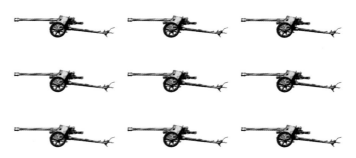

2.Panzerjäger-Kompanie (Sf)

3.Panzerjäger-Kompanie (Sf)

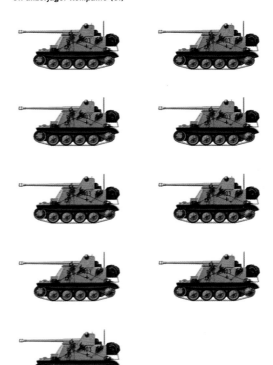

▶ Fiat 618MC

47.Grenadier-Regiment

During its period in the Balkans, the division utilized confiscated Italian vehicles.

Specifications

Crew: 1	Engine: 4-cylinder petrol (43bhp)
Weight: 3.5 tonnes (3.4 tons)	Speed: 65 km/h (41mph)
Length: 4.7m (15ft 5in)	Range: not known
Width: 1.94m (6ft 4in)	Payload: 1.25 tonnes (1.2 tons)
Height: 2.5m (8ft 3in)	

▶ **Zugkraftwagen 1t für 2-cm Flak 38 (SdKfz 10/5)**

22.Flak-Abteilung

The 22nd Division was fully re-equipped in the summer of 1944. The divisional Flak battalion operated two self-propelled batteries armed with 2cm (0.7in) Flak 38s, together with a third motorized battery with towed guns.

Specifications

Crew: 7	6-cylinder (100hp)
Weight: 5.5 tonnes (5 tons)	Speed: 65km/h (40mph)
Length: 4.75m (15ft 7in)	Range: 300km (186 miles)
Width: 2.15m (7ft 1in)	Radio: None
Height: 3.20m (10ft 6in)	Armament: Twin 20mm (0.7in)
Engine: Maybach HL42TRKM	Flak 38 L/112.5

▶ **m. gl. Lkw A-Typ Opel Blitz Allrad für 2-cm Flak 38**

22.Flak-Abteilung

To deal with the increased Allied air threat, German units mounted 2cm (0.7in) Flak 30 and 38 guns onto standard load-carrying vehicles like the Opel Blitz.

Specifications

Crew: 1	(73.5hp)
Weight: 3.29 tonnes (3 tons)	Speed: 80km/h (50mph)
Length: 6.02m (19ft 9in)	Range: 410km (255 miles)
Width: 2.27m (7ft 5in)	Radio: None
Height: 2.18m (7ft 2in)	Armament: Twin 20mm (0.7in)
Engine: Opel 6-cylinder petrol	Flak 38 cannon

Luftwaffe Fallschirmjäger divisions

The German *Luftwaffe* was the first military organization to use paratroopers in combat, but for most of the war the Fallschirmjäger were used as light or motorized infantry.

INITIALLY USED TO GREAT EFFECT but at considerable cost during the invasion of the Low Countries in May 1940, the *Luftwaffe*'s parachute force, *7.Flieger-Division*, saw its large-scale combat debut in the invasion of Crete in May 1942. The operation was successful, but the high casualties among the

3rd Fallschirmjäger Division Commanders

Generalmajor Walter Barenthin	Generalleutnant Richard Schimpf
September 1943 – February 1944	*January 1945 – March 1945*
Generalleutnant Richard Schimpf	Oberst Helmut Hoffmann
February 1944 – August 1944	*March 1945*
General der Fallschirmtruppen Eugen Meindl	Oberst Karl-Heinz Becker
August 1944	*March 1945 – April 1945*
Generalmajor Walter Wadehn	
August 1944 – January 1945	

Fallschirmjäger convinced Hitler that such mass airdrops were no longer feasible. From then onwards, the paratroops were used as highly trained and effective light infantry, an all-volunteer force that could quickly be moved to threatened parts of the front line. However, their light equipment scales meant they could not sustain prolonged operations without incurring heavy casualties. When the high command used them as line infantry at Leningrad and in Normandy, they suffered terrible losses.

In 1943, the *Luftwaffe* Fallschirmjäger units were reorganized and used as the core of a new series of elite *Luftwaffe* infantry divisions, numbered in a series beginning with *7.Flieger-Division*, which was redesignated as the 1st Fallschirmjäger Division.

4th Fallschirmjäger Division Commanders
Generalleutnant Heinrich Trettner
October 1943 – May 1945

During the Battle of Monte Cassino, the 1st Fallschirmjäger Division operated as ordinary infantry. When the Allies bombed the monastery at Cassino, they created an excellent fortress of rubble. This enabled the Fallschirmjäger to resist repeated Allied assaults and heavy bombardment. They were nicknamed 'Green Devils' for their ferocious fighting skills, though they were finally forced out of the position when the Cassino defences were bypassed by French colonial troops.

Several of these Fallschirmjäger formations were organized and equipped as motorized infantry divisions, and continued to play a 'fire brigade' role at the front. They were often deployed within *Kampfgruppen*, detached from their divisions or stiffening ad hoc collections of available troops. In accord with standard German practice, these were called by their commander's name, such as Group *Erdmann* in France and the *Ramcke* Parachute Brigade in North Africa.

Fallschirmjäger Divisions that were mostly or fully motorized included the 3rd, which fought in

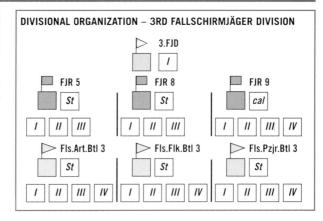

Normandy, the Saar, in the Battle of the Bulge and in the Ruhr pocket; the 4th, which served at Anzio and in the retreat through Italy; the 6th, which was destroyed in Normandy and was then re-formed in Holland and operated there; and the 9th, which was formed at Stettin at the end of 1944 and which saw brutal combat on the Oder Front.

▼ **4th Fallschirmjäger Division, Anzio**
Here operating with the heavy Tigers of *schwere Panzer-Abteilung 508*, the 4th Fallschirmjäger Division was attached to the I.*Fallschirmjäger-Korps*, which held the right flank of the Fourteenth Army's line on the coast to the north of Anzio.

Parachute Corps and Armies
1944–1945

Starting from the foundation of a single airborne division, Germany's Fallschirmjäger force was to grow into an entire parachute army in the last two years of the war.

AFTER MID-1944, THE FALLSCHIRMJÄGER were no longer trained as paratroops, but retained the Fallschirmjäger title to indicate their elite status. Near the end of the war, the series of new Fallschirmjäger divisions extended to over a dozen, with an inevitable reduction in quality in the later units. The 9th Division was the last such formation to be raised during World War II; it was destroyed during the Battle of Berlin in April 1945. These Fallschirmjäger divisions should not be confused with the *Luftwaffe* Field Divisions – *Feld-Divisionen (Lw)* – a poorly organized series of infantry units that were created from excess air force personnel from 1942.

Early in 1944, Göring's ambitions to raise his own private army were realized with the establishment of the 1st Parachute Army (1.*Fallschirm-Armee*), based on the command structure of the old XI.*Fliegerkorps*. This formation had been created in 1940 to control 7.*Flieger-Division* and 22.*Luftlande.Division* for the campaign in the Low Countries. In 1941, the corps controlled the units taking part in the landings on Crete, and then was involved in the training for and development of airborne warfare as well as planning for a projected airborne attack on Malta.

Parachute Army in operation

Formed at Nancy in France between May 1943 and January 1944, the 1st Parachute Army became operational in June 1944 under *Generaloberst* Kurt Student. However, Göring's ambitions were dashed when his force was absorbed by the German Army.

```
ORGANIZATION
                    ┌──┐  16.FJR
                    └──┘
                 ┌─────┐
                 │     │ ┌────┐
                 └─────┘ │ St │
                         └────┘
 ┌───┬───┬───┬───┬───┬─────┬────┬─────┐
 │Sig│Bic│ 1 │ 2 │ 3 │ Mrt │ Pz │ Pio │
 └───┴───┴───┴───┴───┴─────┴────┴─────┘
```

▶ **Kleines Kettenrad (SdKfz 2)**

Fallschirmjäger-Brigade Ramcke

The Kettenrad was designed in part as an artillery tractor for Fallschirmjäger.

Specifications	
Crew: 3	Engine: Opel Olympia 38 petrol (36hp)
Weight: 1.2 tonnes (1.1 tons)	Speed: 80km/h (49.7mph)
Length: 2.74m (9ft)	Range: 100km (62 miles)
Width: 1m (3ft 3in)	Radio: None
Height: 1.01m (3ft 4in)	

▶ **Schwere 750-cc Kraftrad Zundapp KS 750**

Fallschirmjäger-Brigade Ramcke

Identified as *Luftwaffe* vehicles by their 'WL' plates, bikes like these Zundapp 750cc machines were used by the *Ramcke* Parachute Brigade in Africa.

Specifications	
Crew: 2	Engine: 750cc petrol (26hp)
Weight: 0.40 tonnes (0.36 tons)	Speed: 95km/h (59mph)
Length: 2.38m (7ft 10in)	Range: 330km (205 miles)
Width: 1.65m (5ft 5in) (with sidecar)	Radio: None
Height: 1.01m (3ft 4in)	Armament: 1 x 7.92mm (0.3in) MG (if fitted)

6th Fallschirmjäger Division Commanders

Generalleutnant Rüdiger von Heyking
May 1944 – September 1944

Generalleutnant Hermann Plocher
October 1944 – May 1945

Oberst Harry Herrmann
September 1944 – October 1944

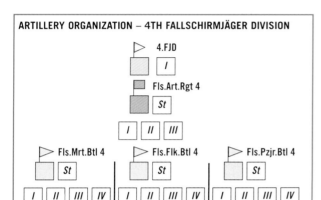

ARTILLERY ORGANIZATION – 4TH FALLSCHIRMJÄGER DIVISION

Following the German retreat from France, the 1st Parachute Army was assigned to the defensive lines in Belgium and eastern Holland. It controlled Panzer and heavy artillery units directly, as well as II. *Fallschirm-Korps* and several *Heer* corps.

The 1st Parachute Army was involved in fighting off Operation *Market Garden* in September 1944. In December 1944, it was part of Army Group H and in the last month of the war it came directly under the control of the *Oberbefehlshaber* Nordwest. The 1st Parachute Army remained in Holland until early 1945, when it was sent across the Rhine to assist in the defence of the river's east bank. The 1. *Fallschirm-Armee* surrendered in the area around Oldenburg in April 1945.

Initially, it was intended that the parachute army should consist of two corps – I. and II. *Fallschirm-Korps* – which would include five of the newly formed parachute divisions. In the event, control by the Army meant that the two corps were never purely paratroop organizations. Indeed, most of the Fallschirmjäger divisions were attached to other armies or corps. I. *Fallschirm-Korps* was sent to Italy early in 1944, where it controlled, to begin with, only the 4th Fallschirmjäger Division along with other regular army divisions, although in 1945, the 1st Fallschirmjäger Division was also placed under the corps' control. And in September 1944 the 1st Parachute Army contained only one Fallschirmjäger division, serving alongside six *Heer* infantry divisions.

Initially, 1. *Fallschirm-Armee* was used as a training command attached to *Heeresgruppe* D in France. When the Allies landed in Normandy, the Fallschirmjäger divisions were assigned to other commands, while the 1st Parachute Army staff came under the direct control of the *Oberkommando der Wehrmacht* (OKW), the German high command. The 1st Parachute Army mounted its first combat operations early in September 1944.

▶ Fallschirmjäger in the Ardennes

Although they still wore their distinctive jumpsuits and helmets, few of the Fallschirmjäger involved in the Battle of the Bulge were parachute-trained. Most were used as elite motorized infantry.

SdKfz definitions

Sonderkraftfahrzeug, abbreviated as SdKfz, means 'Special Purpose Motor Vehicle'. The term was applied to vehicles designed and built specifically for military service, rather than those adapted from non-military sources. Variants of a design were indicated by an oblique stroke and a number added to the original SdKfz designation. Major design changes were usually given a new SdKfz number.

Number	Vehicle	Description
SdKfz 2	kleines Kettenkraftrad	Motorcycle half-track tractor
SdKfz 3	Gleisketten Lkw 2t (Maultier)	2-tonne half-track lorry
SdKfz 4	schwere Gleisketten Lkw 4.5t (Maultier)	4.5-tonne half-track lorry
SdKfz 6	mittlerer Zugkraftwagen 5t	5-tonne half-track tractor
SdKfz 7	mittlerer Zugkraftwagen 8t	8-tonne half-track tractor
SdKfz 8	schwere Zugkraftwagen 12t	12-tonne half-track tractor
SdKfz 9	schwere Zugkraftwagen 18t	18-tonne half-track tractor
SdKfz 10	leichte Zugkraftwagen 1t	1-tonne half-track tractor
SdKfz 11	leichte Zugkraftwagen 3t	3-tonne half-track tractor
SdKfz 101	Panzerkampfwagen I Ausf A, B	Panzer I
SdKfz 111	Munitionsschlepper auf PzKpf I	Ammunition carrier
SdKfz 121	Panzerkampfwagen II Ausf a, A, B, C, D, E, F	Panzer II
SdKfz 122	Panzerkampfwagen II (Flamm)	Panzer II flamethrower
SdKfz 123	Panzerkampfwagen II Ausf L Luchs	Panzer II Model L Lynx
SdKfz 124	leFH 18/2 auf Fahrgestell PzKpfw II (Sf) Wespe	Self-propelled howitzer Wespe
SdKfz 131	7.5-cm Pak 40/2 auf Fahrgestell PzKpfw II (Sf)	Self-propelled anti-tank gun
SdKfz 132	7.62-cm Pak (r) auf Fahrgestell PzKpfw II (Sf)	Self-propelled anti-tank gun (Russian)
SdKfz 135	7.5-cm Pak 40/1 auf Lorraineschlepper (f) Marder I	Self-propelled anti-tank gun on Lorraine chassis
SdKfz 135/1	15-cm sFH 13 auf Lorraineschlepper (f)	Howitzer on Lorraine chassis
SdKfz 138	7.5-cm Pak 40/3 auf PzJäg 38(t)	Self-propelled anti-tank gun on Czech Pz 38 chassis
SdKfz 138/1	15-cm sIG 33 auf Geschützwagen 38(t)	Heavy infantry gun on Czech Pz 38 chassis
SdKfz 138/2	Jagdpanzer 38 Hetzer	Light tank-destroyer
SdKfz 138/2	Flammpanzer 38	Flamethrowing tank
SdKfz 138/2	Bergepanzer 38	Recovery tank
SdKfz 138/2	15-cm sIG 33/2 auf Jagdpanzer 38	Self-propelled heavy infantry gun
SdKfz 139	Panzerselbfahrlafette II für 7.62-cm Pak 36 (r) Marder III	Anti-tank gun (Russian) on Czech Pz 38 chassis
SdKfz 140	Flakpanzer 38(t) auf Selbstfahrlafette 38(t) (2-cm)	Self-propelled anti-aircraft gun
SdKfz 140/1	Aufklärungspanzer 38(t) 7.5-cm	Self-propelled heavy infantry gun on Hetzer chassis
SdKfz 141	Panzerkampfwagen III Ausf A, B, C, D, E, F, G, H	Panzer III
SdKfz 141/1	Panzerkampfwagen III Ausf J, L, M	Panzer III
SdKfz 141/2	Panzerkampfwagen III N	Panzer III
SdKfz 141/3	Panzerkampfwagen III (Flamm)	Panzer III flamethrower
SdKfz 142	gep. SF für StuG 7.5-cm Ausf A, B, C, D, E (StuG III 7.5 L/24)	Sturmgeschütz assault gun
SdKfz 142/1	gep. SF für StuG 7.5-cm 40 Ausf F, F/8, G	Sturmgeschütz assault gun
SdKfz 142/2	gep. SF für 10.5-cm StuH 42 (StuH 42)	Sturmhaubitze assault howitzer
SdKfz 143	Artillerie-Panzerbeobachtungswagen (PzBeobWg III)	Artillery observation tank
SdKfz 161	Panzerkampfwagen IV Ausf A, B, C, D, E, F	Panzer IV
SdKfz 161/1	Panzerkampfwagen IV Ausf F2, G	Panzer IV
SdKfz 161/2	Panzerkampfwagen IV Ausf H, J	Panzer IV
SdKfz 161/3	3.7-cm Flak auf Pz IV (Möbelwagen)	Anti-aircraft tank

Number	Vehicle	Description
SdKfz 162	StuG nA mit 7.5-cm Pak L/48 (Jagdpanzer IV)	Heavy tank-destroyer
SdKfz 162/1	Panzer IV/70(v) (Jagdpanzer IV lang)	Heavy tank-destroyer
SdKfz 164	8.8-cm Pak 43/1 L/71 auf Pz III und IV (Nashorn, früher Hornisse)	Self-propelled anti-tank gun
SdKfz 165	15-cm schwere Panzerhaubitze 18/1 auf Pz III/IV (Sf) (Hummel)	Self-propelled heavy field howitzer
SdKfz 166	StuH 43 L/12 auf Pz IV (Sf) Sturmpanzer (Brummbär)	Self-propelled armoured heavy infantry gun
SdKfz 167	StuG IV L/48	Heavy assault gun
SdKfz 171	Panzerkampfwagen V Ausf D, A, G Panther	Panzer V Panther
SdKfz 172	StuG für 8.8-cm StuK 43 auf Panther I – Jagdpanther	Original designation for Jagdpanther heavy tank-destroyer
SdKfz 173	8.8-cm Pak 43/3 L/71 auf Panzerjäger Panther (Jagdpanther)	Jagdpanther heavy tank-destroyer
SdKfz 179	Bergepanzerwagen Panther	Armoured recovery vehicle
SdKfz 181	Panzerkampfwagen VI Ausf E (Tiger I)	Panzer VI Tiger heavy tank
SdKfz 182	Panzerkampfwagen VI Ausf B (Tiger II, Königstiger)	Panzer VI Tiger II or King Tiger heavy tank
SdKfz 184	Pz Jäger Tiger(P) Ferdinand für 8.8-cm Pak 43/2 (Elefant)	Heavy tank-destroyer
SdKfz 185	Jagdtiger für 8.8-cm Pak 43 L/71	Heavy tank-destroyer
SdKfz 186	Jagdtiger für 12.8-cm Pak 44 L/55	Heavy tank-destroyer
SdKfz 221	leichter Panzerspähwagen (MG)	MG-armed light armoured car
SdKfz 222	leichter Panzerspähwagen (2-cm)	Cannon-armed light armoured car
SdKfz 223	leichter Panzerspähwagen (Fu)	Light armoured radio car
SdKfz 231	schwerer Panzerspähwagen 6-Rad	Heavy 6x4 armoured car
SdKfz 231	schwerer Panzerspähwagen 8-Rad	Heavy 8x8 armoured car
SdKfz 232	schwerer Panzerspähwagen 6-Rad (Fu)	Heavy 6x4 armoured radio car
SdKfz 232	schwerer Panzerspähwagen 8-Rad (Fu)	Heavy 8x8 armoured radio car
SdKfz 233	schwerer Panzerspähwagen 7.5-cm KwK 37 L/24	7.5cm (3in) heavy 8x8 armoured car
SdKfz 234/1	schwerer Panzerspähwagen (2-cm)	2cm (0.7in) heavy 8x8 armoured car
SdKfz 234/2	schwerer Panzerspähwagen Puma (5-cm) KwK39/1 L/60	5cm (2in) Puma heavy 8x8 armoured car
SdKfz 234/3	schwerer Panzerspähwagen (7.5-cm) KwK51 L/24	7.5cm (3in) heavy 8x8 armoured car
SdKfz 234/4	schwerer Panzerspähwagen (7.5-cm) Pak40 L/46	7.5cm (3in) heavy 8x8 tank-destroyer armoured car
SdKfz 247	geländegangiger gepanzerter Personenkraftwagen	Heavy armoured staff car
SdKfz 250	leichter Schützenpanzerwagen	Light armoured half-track personnel carrier
SdKfz 250/I-I	leichter Schützenpanzerwagen (Fu)	Light armoured radio half-track
SdKfz 250/2	leichter Fernsprechwagen	Light armoured telephone and wire-carrying half-track
SdKfz 250/3	leichter Funkpanzerwagen	Light armoured radio half-track
SdKfz 250/4	Luftschütz Panzerwagen (2 MG34)	Light armoured anti-aircraft half-track
SdKfz 250/5-I	leichter Beobachtungspanzerwagen	Light armoured observation half-track
SdKfz 250/5-II	leichter Aufklärungspanzerwagen	Light armoured reconnaissance half-track
SdKfz 250/6	leichter Munitionspanzerwagen Ausf A, B	Light armoured ammunition-carrier half-track
SdKfz 250/7	leichter Schützenpanzerwagen (schwerer Granatwerfer)	Light armoured mortar-carrying half-track
SdKfz 250/7	leichter Schützenpanzerwagen (Munitionsfahrzeug)	Light armoured mortar ammunition half-track
SdKfz 250/8	leichter Kanonenpanzerwagen mit 7.5-cm KwK37	Light armoured fire-support half-track
SdKfz 250/9	leichter Schützenpanzerwagen (2-cm)	Light armoured reconnaissance half-track
SdKfz 250/10	leichter Schützenpanzerwagen (3.7-cm Pak)	Light armoured platoon-leader half-track with 3.7cm (1.5in) anti-tank gun
SdKfz 250/11	leichter Schützenpanzerwagen (sPzB41)	Light armoured platoon-leader half-track with 2.8cm (1.1in) Panzerbuchse anti-tank gun
SdKfz 250/12	leichter Messtrupp-panzerwagen	Light armoured artillery calibration half-track
SdKfz 251	mittlerer Schützenpanzerwagen	Medium armoured half-track personnel carrier
SdKfz 251/I-II	mittlerer Schützenpanzerwagen (Fu)	Medium armoured radio half-track
SdKfz 251/2	mittlerer Schützenpanzerwagen (Granatwerfer)	Medium armoured mortar-carrying half-track

Number	Vehicle	Description
SdKfz 251/3	mittlerer Funkpanzerwagen	Medium armoured radio half-track
SdKfz 251/3-IV	mittlerer Funkpanzerwagen (Kommandowagen)	Medium armoured command half-track
SdKfz 251/4	mittlerer Schützenpanzerwagen mit Munition und Zubehör für leIG18	Medium armoured half-track prime-mover for 7.5cm (3in) light infantry gun
SdKfz 251/5	mittlerer Pionierpanzerwagen	Medium armoured combat engineer half-track
SdKfz 251/6	mittlerer Kommandopanzerwagen	Medium armoured command half-track
SdKfz 251/7	mittlerer Pionierpanzerwagen	Medium armoured combat engineer half-track
SdKfz 251/8	mittlerer Krankenpanzerwagen	Medium armoured ambulance half-track
SdKfz 251/9	mittlerer Schützenpanzerwagen (7.5-cm KwK 37)	Medium armoured self-propelled gun half-track
SdKfz 251/10	mittlerer Schützenpanzerwagen (3.7-cm Pak)	Medium armoured platoon-leader half-track with 3.7cm (1.5in) anti-tank gun
SdKfz 251/11	mittlerer Funksprechpanzerwagen	Medium armoured telephone cable half-track
SdKfz 251/12	mittlerer Messtrupp- und Gerätepanzerwagen	Medium armoured artillery calibration section half-track
SdKfz 251/13	mittlerer Schallaufnahmepanzerwagen	Medium armoured sound-recording half-track
SdKfz 251/14	mittlerer Schallauswertungspanzerwagen	Medium armoured sound-ranging half-track
SdKfz 251/15	mittlerer Lichtauswertepanzerwagen	Medium armoured flash-ranging half-track
SdKfz 251/16	mittlerer Flammpanzerwagen	Medium armoured flamethrower half-track
SdKfz 251/17	mittlerer Schützenpanzerwagen mit 2-cm FlaK 38	Medium armoured anti-aircraft half-track
SdKfz 251/18	mittlerer Beobachtungspanzerwagen	Medium armoured observation half-track
SdKfz 251/19	mittlerer Fernsprechbetriebspanzerwagen	Medium armoured telephone operations half-track
SdKfz 251/20	mittlerer Schützenpanzerwagen mit Infrarotscheinwerfer (Uhu)	Medium armoured infra-red projector half-track
SdKfz 251/21	mittlerer Schützenpanzerwagen mit Fla MG Drilling (1.5 oder 2-cm)	Medium armoured self-propelled triple anti-aircraft gun half-track
SdKfz 251/22	7.5-cm Pak 40 L/46 auf mittlerer Schützenpanzerwagen	Medium armoured tank-destroyer half-track
SdKfz 251/23	2-cm Hängelafette 38 auf mittlerer Schützenpanzerwagen	Medium armoured reconnaissance half-track
SdKfz 252	leichter gepanzerter Munitionskraftwagen	Light armoured munitions carrier half-track
SdKfz 253	leichter gepanzerter Beobachtungskraftwagen	Light armoured observation half-track
SdKfz 254	mittlerer gepanzerter Beobachtungskraftwagen	Medium armoured observation half-track
SdKfz 260	kleiner Panzerfunkwagen (4-Rad)	Light armoured radio car
SdKfz 261	kleiner Panzerfunkwagen (4-Rad)	Light armoured radio car
SdKfz 263	schwerer Panzerfunkwagen (6-Rad)	Heavy 6x4 armoured radio car
SdKfz 263	schwerer Panzerfunkwagen (8-Rad)	Heavy 8x8 armoured radio car
SdKfz 265	kleiner Panzerbefehlswagen (Pz I)	Light command tank (Panzer I)
SdKfz 266	Panzerbefehlswagen Ausf E, H, 5-cm KwK L/42, Ausf K	Medium command tank (Panzer III)
SdKfz 267	Panzerbefehlswagen Ausf D (Pz III)	Medium command tank (Panzer III)
SdKfz 267	Panzerbefehlswagen Panther	Command tank (Panther)
SdKfz 267	Panzerbefehlswagen Tiger I	Command tank (Tiger)
SdKfz 268	grosse Panzerbefehlswagen	Large command tank (Panzer III, Panther or Tiger)
SdKfz 280	gepanzerter Munitionsschlepper	Armoured munitions carrier
SdKfz 300	Minenräumwagen Ausf I und II	Mine-clearing vehicle
SdKfz 301	schwerer Ladungsträger Ausf A, B and C	Heavy remote-controlled demolition vehicle
SdKfz 302	leichter Ladungsträger Ausf A (Goliath)	Light remote-controlled demolition vehicle
SdKfz 303	leichter Ladungsträger Ausf B (Goliath)	Light remote-controlled demolition vehicle
SdKfz 304	mittlerer Ladungsträger (Springer)	Medium remote-controlled demolition vehicle

Kfz definitions

Kraftfahrzeug, or Kfz, stands for 'powered vehicle'. Kfz numbers were applied to soft-skin military vehicles according to their roles – either as personnel carriers (PKW) or load carriers (LKW).

Number	Vehicle	Description
Kfz 1	leichte Personenkraftwagen	Light personnel vehicle (3 or 4 seats)
Kfz 2	le.Nachrichten-Kw	Light communications vehicle
Kfz 2/1	le.Fernsprech-Kw	Light telephone vehicle
Kfz 2/2	le.Funk-Kw	Light radio vehicle
Kfz 2/40	le.Instandsetzungs-Kw	Light communications repair vehicle (2-seat with storage)
Kfz 3	le.Messtrupp-Kw	Light calibration vehicle
Kfz 4	le.Truppen-Luftschütze-Kw	Light anti-aircraft vehicle (twin machine gun)
Kfz 5	mittlerer.Kessel-Kw	Medium tanker
Kfz 11	m.Pkw	Medium personnel vehicle
Kfz 12	m.Pkw mit Zughaken	Medium personnel vehicle with towing hook
Kfz 13	m.gepanzert Pkw	Medium armoured car (MG)
Kfz 14	m.gepanzert Pkw (Funk)	Medium armoured radio car
Kfz 15	m.Pkw	Medium personnel vehicle
Kfz 15	m.Fernschreibe-Kw	Medium telex vehicle
Kfz 15/1	m.Nachrichten-Kw	Medium communications vehicle
Kfz 15/1	m.Fernsprech-Kw	Medium telephone vehicle
Kfz 15/2	m.Funk-Kw	Medium radio vehicle
Kfz 15/4	m.Funk-Kw	Medium radio vehicle
Kfz 15/5	m.Funk-Kw	Medium radio vehicle
Kfz 15/6	m.Funk-Kw	Medium radio vehicle
Kfz 15/7	m.Funk-Kw	Medium radio vehicle
Kfz 16	m.Mess-stelle-Kw	Medium calibration station vehicle
Kfz 16	m.Mess-trupp-Kw	Medium calibration section vehicle
Kfz 17	kleines Verstärker-Kw	Small amplifier van
Kfz 17	kl.Kabelmess-Kw	Small wire calibration van
Kfz 17	kl.Fernsprechbetriebs-Kw	Small telephone operations van
Kfz 17/1	kl.Funktrupp-Kw	Small radio section van
Kfz 17/2	kl.Fernsprechtrupp-Kw	Small telephone section van
Kfz 17/3	kl.Funk-Kw	Small radio van
Kfz 18	schwere Pkw	heavy personnel vehicle
Kfz 18	Gefechts-Pkw	heavy personnel vehicle with storage and towing hook
Kfz 19	Fernsprechbetriebs-Kw	Telephone exchange van
Kfz 19	Fernsprech-Kw	Telephone van
Kfz 19	Funk-Kw	Radio van
Kfz 21	s.Pkw (Kommandeurwagen)	Heavy field staff car
Kfz 23	Fernsprech-Kw	Telephone equipment van
Kfz 24	Verstärker-Kw	Amplifier van
Kfz 31	Sanitätswagen (Sanka) or Krankenkraftwagen (KrKw)	Ambulance
Kfz 42	Sammler-Kw	Generator van (also accumulator or battery van)
Kfz 42	Sammlerwerkstatt-Kw	Generator repair van
Kfz 42	Nachrichten-Kw	Communications repair van
Kfz 42	Werkstatt-Kw	Workshop van
Kfz 43	Flakauswert-Kw	Anti-aircraft test and evaluation van
Kfz 44	Sauer und Stickstoff-Erzeugungs-Kw	Oxygen and nitrogen generator van
Kfz 51	Werkstatt-Kw	medium/large workshop van
Kfz 61	grosse Nachrichten-Kw	Large communications van
Kfz 61	gr.Schlüssel-Kw	Large code/cipher van
Kfz 61	gr.Funk-Kw	Large radio van
Kfz 61	gr.Funkbetriebs-Kw	Large radio operations van

Number	Vehicle	Description
Kfz 61	gr.Fernsprechbetriebs-Kw	Large telephone operations van
Kfz 61	gr.Fernschreib-Kw	Large telex van
Kfz 61	gr.Verstärker-Kw	Large amplifier van
Kfz 61	gr.Peil-Kw	Large sound-ranging van
Kfz 61	gr.Mess-trupp-Kw	Large calibration section van
Kfz 61/1	gr.Funk-Kw	Large radio van
Kfz 62	gr.Nachrichten-Kw	Large communications van
Kfz 62	gr.Fernsprechbetriebs-Kw	Large telephone operations van
Kfz 62	gr.Funk-Kw	Large radio van
Kfz 62	gr.Wetter-Kw	Large weather van
Kfz 62	gr.Druckerei-Kw	Large printing van
Kfz 62	gr.Schallaufnahme-Kw	Large sound-recording van
Kfz 62	gr.Schallauswertungs-Kw	Large sound evaluation van
Kfz 62	gr.Vermessungs-Geräte-Kw	Large calibration evaluation van
Kfz 62	gr.Licht-Auswertunds-Kw	Large flash evaluation van
Kfz 62	gr.Stabs-Auswertungs-Kw	Large command evaluation van
Kfz 63	gr.Nachrichten-Kw	Large communications van
Kfz 63	gr.Mess-Stellen und Gerät-Kw	Large calibration station and equipment van
Kfz 63	gr.Vermessungs-Gerät-Kw	Large calibration equipment van
Kfz 63	gr.Lichtmess-Stellen-Kw	Large flash-ranging station van
Kfz 63	gr.Lichtmess-Gerät-Kw	Large flash-ranging equipment van
Kfz 63	gr.Schallmess-Stellen-Kw	Large sound-ranging station van
Kfz 63	gr.Schallmess-Gerät-Kw	Large sound-ranging equipment van
Kfz 63	gr.Vorwarner-Kw	Large early-warning equipment van
Kfz 64	gr.Vermessungs-Gerät-Kw	Large calibration equipment van
Kfz 68	Funkmast-Kw	Radio antenna van
Kfz 68	Fernsprech-Kw	Telephone van
Kfz 68/1	Funkmast-Kw	Radio antenna van
Kfz 69	Protz-Kw	Light artillery tractor
Kfz 70	Mannschaft-Kw	Personnel vehicle
Kfz 71	Truppen-Luftschütze-Kw	Anti-aircraft gun carrier
Kfz 71	s.Truppenluftschütze-Kw	Heavy anti-aircraft gun carrier
Kfz 72	Fernsprechbetriebs-Kw	Telephone operations van
Kfz 72	Fernsprechvermittlungs-Kw	Telephone exchange van
Kfz 72	Fernschreib-Kw	Telex van
Kfz 72	Fernschreibvermittlungs-Kw	Telex exchange van
Kfz 72	Verstärker-Kw	Amplifier van
Kfz 72	Funk-Kw	Radio van
Kfz 72	Funkbetriebs-Kw	Radio operations van
Kfz 72	Funkhorch-Kw	Radio intercept van
Kfz 72	Befehls-Kw	Medium command vehicle
Kfz 72	Druckerei-Kw	Printing van
Kfz 72	m.Wetter-Kw	Medium weather van
Kfz 72/1	Fernschreib-Kw	Telex van
Kfz 74	Flakmesstrupp-Kw	Anti-aircraft calibration section van
Kfz 76	Beobachtungs-Kw	Observation vehicle
Kfz 77	Feldkabel-Kw	Cable carrier
Kfz 77	Fernsprech-Kw	Telephone vehicle
Kfz 77	Fernsprechbau-Kw	Telephone manufacture vehicle
Kfz 79	Werkstatt-Kw	Workshop van
Kfz 81	le.Flak-Kw	Light Flak prime-mover
Kfz 83	le.Scheinwerfer-Kw	Light searchlight prime-mover
Kfz 92	Mannschaft-Entgiftlungs-Kw	Personnel decontamination van
Kfz 93	Bekleidungs-Entgiftungs-Kw	Clothing decontamination van
Kfz 94	Wasser-Kw (Kessel)	Hot water shower van for decontamination
Kfz 95	Kammer-Kw	Stores van
Kfz 100	Drehkran	Revolving crane (3- to 5-tonne)

Motorized symbols

In official German military organizational charts and maps of World War II, standard symbols were used to indicate the size, mission and mobility of a unit or formation. Any German soldier looking at such a symbol was expected to know the type of unit indicated. Slightly simplified forms of the organisational symbol were used as vehicle identification in addition to the divisional markings carried by all fighting vehicles and softskin transports.

Size, Function and Mobility

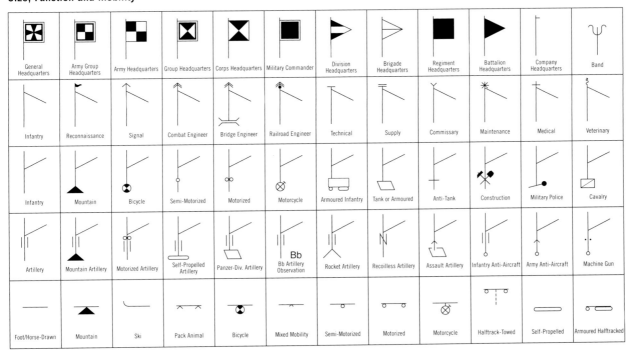

Panzertruppen Inspectorate Units

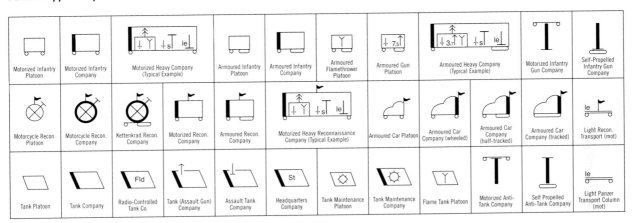

Index

Page numbers in *italics* refer to illustrations and photographs.